Bulldozer Revolutions

Bulldozer Revolutions

A RURAL HISTORY OF
THE METROPOLITAN SOUTH

Andrew C. Baker

The University of Georgia Press

Athens

Portions of chapter 2 originally published as "From Rural South to Metropolitan Sunbelt: Creating a Cowboy Identity in the Shadow of Houston," *Southwestern Historical Quarterly* 118, no. 1 (2014): 1–22. Copyright © 2014 Texas State Historical Association. Reprinted by permission. Portions of chapter 3 originally published as "Metropolitan Growth along the Nation's River: Power, Waste and Environmental Politics in a Northern Virginia County, 1943–1971," *Journal of Urban History* 42, no. 1 (2016): 1–17. Copyright © 2016 Andrew C. Baker. Reprinted by permission of SAGE Publications. DOI: 10.1177/0096144215601054, juh.sagepub.com.

Paperback edition, 2022
© 2018 by the University of Georgia Press
Athens, Georgia 30602
www.ugapress.org
All rights reserved
Set in 10.5/13.5 Adobe Garamond Pro Regular by
Graphic Composition, Inc., Bogart, Georgia

Most University of Georgia Press titles are
available from popular e-book vendors.

Printed digitally

The Library of Congress has cataloged the hardcover edition of this book as follows:

NAMES: Baker, Andrew C., author.
TITLE: Bulldozer revolutions : a rural history of the metropolitan South / Andrew C. Baker.
DESCRIPTION: Athens : The University of Georgia Press, 2018. |
    Includes bibliographical references (pages 183–228) and index.
IDENTIFIERS: LCCN 2018008693 (print) | ISBN 9780820354149 (hardcover: alk. paper) |
    ISBN 9780820354156 (ebook)
SUBJECTS: LCSH: Metropolitan areas—Southern States. | Human ecology—
    Southern States. | Sociology, Rural—Southern States. | Urban-rural migration—
    Southern States—Case studies. | Southern States—Rural conditions. |
    Montgomery County (Tex.) | Loudoun County (Va.)
CLASSIFICATION: LCC HT334.S68 B35 2018 (print) |
    DDC 307.76/40975—dc23
LC record available at https://lccn.loc.gov/2018008693

Paperback ISBN 978-0-8203-6364-6

CONTENTS

ILLUSTRATIONS

ABBREVIATIONS

AGR   Attorney General Records, Texas State Library, Austin

ASSSC   Albert and Shirley Small Special Collections Library, University of Virginia, Charlottesville

C&O   Chesapeake and Ohio

CC   *Conroe Courier / Conroe Daily Courier*

CCM   Montgomery County Commissioner Minutes, Montgomery County Annex, Conroe, Tex.

CCR   Montgomery County Commissioner Records, East Montgomery County Annex, Conroe, Tex.

CH   *Chronicle of the Horse*

ETJ   extraterritorial jurisdiction

FEMA   Federal Emergency Management Administration

GSLT   General and Special Laws of Texas

HC   *Houston Chronicle*

HGAC   Houston-Galveston Area Council

HMRC   Houston Metropolitan Research Center, Houston, Tex.

HP   *Houston Post*

ICPRB   Interstate Commission on the Potomac River Basin

JCWMP   Joint Committee on Washington Metropolitan Problems

JP   justice of the peace

KLB   Keep Loudoun Beautiful

KLBC   Keep Loudoun Beautiful Collection, Thomas Balch Library, Leesburg, Va.

LCOHP   Loudoun County Oral History Project, Thomas Balch Library, Leesburg, Va.

LFOHC   Loudoun Farm Oral History Collection, Loudoun Heritage Farm Museum, Sterling, Va.

LTM   *Loudoun Times-Mirror*

LUT   land-use taxation

MGD   million gallons per day

MUD   municipal utility district

NIMBY   not in my backyard

NSLM   National Sporting Library and Museum, Middleburg, Va.

NYT	*New York Times*
ORN	Oak Ridge North Municipal Records, Oak Ridge North, Tex.
PEC	Piedmont Environmental Council
PEPCO	Potomac Electric Power Company
PPM	parts per million
PSLC	Preservation Society of Loudoun County
SJRA	San Jacinto River Authority
SJRAR	San Jacinto River Authority Records, Lake Conroe, Tex.
SJSCD	San Jacinto Soil Conservation District
SWCD	soil and water conservation district
TAES	Texas Agricultural Experiment Station
TBL	Thomas Balch Library, Leesburg, Va.
TBLOHP	Thomas Balch Library Oral History Project, Thomas Balch Library, Leesburg, Va.
TBWE	Texas Board of Water Engineers
TGF	*Texas Game and Fish*
TRA	Trinity River Authority
TWQB	Texas Water Quality Board
USDA	United States Department of Agriculture
WFLHC	Waterford Foundation Local History Collection, Waterford, Va.
WMCOG	Washington Metropolitan Council of Governments
WMRT	Wallace, McHarg, Roberts and Todd
WP	*Washington Post*
WV	*Woodlands Villager*

FOREWORD

In 1958 the residents of Houston, Texas, faced a decision: Were they willing to drink from the water that Dallas residents had flushed down their toilets? At least that was how local businessman W. B. Weisinger basically framed it. Houston had grown so dramatically in the previous two decades that the city's wells had proven insufficient to keep the hot southern metropolis with a stable water supply during any period of drought. As local agencies considered a variety of solutions to slake the growing metropolis's thirst, political and environmental battle lines developed. For Weisinger, the solution was for Houstonians to get their water not from a river system that passed first through Dallas— hence the toilet remark—but from a series of reservoirs along Weisinger's native San Jacinto River watershed. Like those from a long line of rural southern boosters before him, his interest was more than giving city residents access to clean water. In addition to sitting on the powerful board of the San Jacinto River Authority, Weisinger was, as Andrew Baker tells us, "a Lion, a Mason, a Shriner, a Methodist, a board member of the local bank, a trustee of the Real Estate Development Fund of the Montgomery County Industrial Foundation, and owner of the local TV and radio stations." Weisinger saw a future not only in a new water supply for Houston but also in suburban reservoirs and lakes that could be used as recreation for Houstonians looking for escape from the city's heat and hustle. His connections added up to real power when it came to planning for the growing metropolis's water future. The result was Lake Conroe, not only a water supply for Houston, but a wonderland for recreation— and pricey waterfront real estate—just as Weisinger had imagined.

Historians have often framed environmental and urban histories of metropolitan growth, like those of Houston, as narratives of urban imperialism. A city moves outward for land and resources, annexing former farms for tract housing and sucking natural resources back into the metropole. Scholars have described these moments of expansion as if those in power in the city center were choosing from a menu of rural resources: a little fresh water here, a hole to put trash in there, and golf courses along a ridge for dessert. Like suburbanization itself, the classic historical narrative keeps the metropolis at its center and the hinterlands as merely faceless space for the taking.

This book changes that. As Andrew Baker explains, rural communities were far from ancillary actors in the drama of urban expansion during the rise of the Sunbelt. Indeed, *Bulldozer Revolutions* argues not only that the rural fringe is central to the story of suburban expansion but also that understanding that process means thinking about the role that the environment played in shaping the long-term transformation of the communities that existed in that fringe. Centered outside two cities, Washington, D.C., and Houston, the book offers intertwined case studies for how people and governments used environmental resources to both court and spurn metro development, all the while crafting and harnessing incomplete cultural portrayals of each rural place. What these hinterland areas offered was more than simply drinking water and bass fishing. Historians, Baker tells us, have been wrong to think of the postwar southern countryside as a site "of historical memory rather than historical drama." In the case of Montgomery County, Texas, locals had a rural tradition to offer, a cattle-ranching culture that had kernels of legitimacy around which much artifice was built to attract beleaguered urbanites. Likewise, Loudon County, Virginia, offered a "horsey" veneer that could not be found closer to D.C. So it was the combination of cultivated space and history that together, Baker argues, "sanctified the landscape."

But the story of the metropolitan fringe does not end once former urbanites literally bought in to the dreams of suburban bliss sold by developers. Baker reminds us that while plenty of historians have described the white middle-class exodus to the metropolitan fringe, they have said less about what it meant to carve out a life there. Most scholars have described the process of movement from the urban core as a reflection of the failure of democracy in city centers and have little sympathy for the plight of suburbanites once they move into their homes in former farm fields. In turn, environmental historians have followed the suburban story farther but only to trace surging environmentalism born of septic tank fields and bulldozer exhaust. For Baker's new residents of the metropolitan fringe, environmentalism was a more complicated idea. In Montgomery County, Texas, locals first embraced the "good ol' boy" system of government: low taxes, few services, patronage based on a system of personal ties. But eventually the pressure of new developments and population produced not only environmental crises but also calls for environmental regulations, calls that tested the structure and philosophy of the microgovernment of the county. In Loudon County, Virginia, Baker finds environmentalists already thinking about protection of their local resources even before the invasion of D.C. commuters. In fact, a pervasive rural protectionist strain rose up to spurn the transformations brought by suburbanization and to protect countryside aesthetics, which included the natural environment at its heart. The result was a hybrid environmentalism unlike what historians have described elsewhere, one that put together unlikely allies. In both places, the history Baker uncovers diverges from what historians have told us before about the environmentalism of suburbs.

In reality, what drives this explanation of life on the southern metropolitan fringe is a host of characters who influenced development, regulation, and expansion, including a former heavyweight boxer turned county clerk, countless small-town bureaucrats and developers, and historic preservationists. One of this book's greatest contributions, then, is Baker's use of rural voices to tell the story. His casting of urban expansion from the outside in allows these mostly forgotten historical actors to drive the plot. With these people and in these particular moments, as areas that are neither suburban nor rural become part of a metroplex, a lost history of nature, politics, and culture can be resurrected. Indeed, the "fringe" never lasted long, but the wrangle that resulted from conflicting rural, suburban, and urban ideas about nature and culture decided much about the shape of the modern South. This book tells that story.

Finally, while this book challenges historians' thinking about urban expansion, it also pushes the boundaries of southern environmental history as a field. By taking the environment of rural places and people seriously as actors in metropolitan expansion, we see not only new (and perhaps unlikely) rural environmentalists but also a different kind of environmental debate than most southern environmental historians have recognized. When we see that, as Baker puts it, "the rural persisted among the urban," the result is a history that repositions decision making and the cultural impact of reengineering landscapes of the fringe South back into the story of the Sunbelt itself.

James C. Giesen
Series Editor, Environmental History and the American South

Bulldozer Revolutions

A More Rural Metropolitan History

Roy Harris emerged from the backwoods of East Texas in the fall of 1958 to challenge Floyd Patterson for boxing's heavyweight title. To sell the matchup, fight promoters flew some two dozen New York City sportswriters to Houston, then drove them north, out from the city, through Conroe, the seat of neighboring Montgomery County, and finally up the dirt road to Harris's home near the town of Cut 'N Shoot, Texas. There the Harris clan filled reporters' ears with tales of vendettas, night riding, and death-defying practical jokes. They told of the time Uncle Jack, in a Samson-like feat of strength, felled sixteen men with an axe handle and of the time Uncle Bob literally cut off a man's head after being stabbed thirteen times. They showed reporters their pet alligators and offered them moonshine. These big-city reporters walked past the sleeping hound dogs and rooting hogs, photographed the barbed-wire-roped boxing ring and the engine block the Harris boys lifted for strength training, and talked with the barefooted and coonskin-capped members of the Harris family. Here their preconceptions were confirmed. Cut 'N Shoot, as its name implied, was a place of backwoods violence and rural grit; a place where "they farm, fish, raise a few piney woods rooter hogs—and fight," and where the forests were so dense that, as Harris himself put it, "sometimes it's noon before it gets to be daylight."[1] The reporters soaked in the backwoods authenticity of Cut 'N Shoot. As Milton Gross of the *New York Post* explained, "No longer do I feel that this is all makeup for one of the most fabulous fight buildups in history. The outside privy is real, the insects are genuine, and so are the people, after their own fashion. They are a back country folk who have suddenly found the outside world thrust upon them."[2] As a backwoods Tarzan, Harris captivated boxing fans across the nation. In the process he reinforced a popular image of East Texas and Montgomery County in particular as a place of primeval forests where natural splendor, rural poverty, and frontier virtues persisted.

Yet even as Roy Harris prepared for his title shot, this rural world was fading into memory. Beginning in the 1950s, Houstonians began purchasing acreage outside Harris County, in neighboring Montgomery County, constructing second homes and lakefront cottages, taking up part-time ranching, and commuting into the city. This trickle became a stream in the 1960s and a flood by the 1970s as the construction of two major highways and Houston's continuing sprawl shrunk the distance between the city and surrounding rural communities. Montgomery County was one of dozens of counties across the South and hundreds across the nation where metropolitan development transformed demographics, politics, society, culture, and landscapes in the decades after World War II.

After losing to Floyd Patterson in Los Angeles in the twelfth round, Harris returned to Cut 'N Shoot with a $100,000 check. Contrary to his backwoods persona, Harris was a shrewd businessman. He invested in local real estate and secured his broker's license before opening an office in Spring Branch, in northern Harris County. From here he led the local development community in repackaging and rebranding the forests of Montgomery County as a privatized recreational and suburban retreat. Even Cut 'N Shoot, culturally and environmentally enmeshed as it was in the Big Thicket, nestled rural subdivisions in among the pines. From his home in Cut 'N Shoot, Harris continued to hunt and fish while selling this lifestyle to Houstonians. Harris saw in metropolitan growth an economic opportunity rather than a looming invasion. A business leader and a hometown hero, he leveraged his local popularity into the job of county clerk, a position he held for more than twenty years. Harris spent the rest of his working life signing off on every parcel of development in the woods he had roamed as a child.[3]

The story of Roy Harris is in many ways the story of the postwar metropolitan fringe. Harris and his town were profoundly reshaped by their relationship with nearby cities, yet few would consider Harris a metropolitan American or his community a suburb. Harris and Cut 'N Shoot were each simply too rural to fit within a historiography whose primary focus is on the flight from the city, the role of race and government policy in propelling it, and its political, social, and cultural implications.[4] The "new suburban history" has done much to expand the popular understanding of suburbs to include minorities, the working class, and other marginalized groups, yet in that history rural people and themes are muted at best.[5] At the same time, stories like those of Harris and Cut 'N Shoot were too metropolitan to fit within rural and agricultural historiography. Historians in these fields generally exclude metropolitan rural places under the justification that they distract from the central rural narratives of out-migration, the growth of state power, and the rise of agribusiness. This has left the postwar rural South as a region caught in the aftermath of historical processes—a place of historical memory rather than historical drama.[6] A rural America dominated by commuters, rural factory workers, recreation seekers, and hobby farmers seems out of place in a subfield focused on the fate of the late nineteenth-century and early twentieth-century family farm. The shadow of the city obscures the picture such historians are trying to paint.[7] Both rural and urban historians, then, have allowed metropolitan rural areas to fall between the cracks.

As a result, we have not made sense of the places where suburban, urban, and rural intertwined; where agriculture, recreation, and development competed for space and local support; and where the Sunbelt confronted the South. Many have followed those 1950s sportswriters in portraying countryside dwellers confronting modern development across a stark urban/rural divide. Doing so misses the adaptation and the opportunism involved in the creation of a distinct, albeit sometimes short-lived, social and cultural world on the metropolitan fringe. This is not to say that the metropolitan fringe remains completely unknown. Journalists, rural sociologists, and geographers have cataloged some of its distinct characteristics.[8] Urban historians have recently followed their lead, starting with a 1996 article in which James Wunsch pushed historians to grapple with the diversity of suburban landscapes. "Suburbanization," he reminded his readers, "did not take place in the forest primeval, but amidst a welter of towns, satellite cities and industrial areas, some as old as the central city itself." This call went largely unheeded by historians, for in a 2009 essay Andrew Needham and Allen Dieterich-Ward observed that "while the new suburban scholarship has succeeded in incorporating suburbs into postwar historiography, it has also implicitly reinforced an artificial boundary that obscures far-reaching effects of metropolitan growth. That boundary lies at the suburban fringe." A major cause of this divide, they argue, is the fact that "rural and urban historians have barely acknowledged the existence of the other, let alone understood themselves as co-investigators on the same social and cultural landscape." If historians were, the authors argue, to integrate the study of city, suburb, and hinterland into a conglomeration they term a "metropolitan region," then the narrative that would emerge would be one of increasing interdependence rather than urban decay and suburban sprawl. Such an approach would also reveal the substantial and meaningful conflict on the fringe.[9]

In the pages to follow, I take up Needham and Dieterich-Ward's challenge that "little historical research has been undertaken to explore the expansion of 'suburban' areas into the rural periphery from the perspective of local residents."[10] Bringing this world into focus requires that we shift the center of analysis from the city to the metropolitan fringe. We must, at least temporarily, put this "borderland" at the heart of the story if we are to fully understand the process of metropolitan growth. Setting the boundaries on such a study, however, raises significant challenges. The metropolitan fringe, like all frontier zones, is a transient, geographically ambiguous thing, for as urban growth expands unevenly outward or is invited inward, depending on your perspective, it pushes the fringe farther into rural areas. Chronological boundaries are just as difficult for the simple reason that finding the pristine countryside before metropolitan engagement is as impossible as finding pristine nature.

Therefore, rather than chasing the fringe, I ground my analysis and narrative in a fixed political and geographic frame: the county. This approach offers a way out of the quagmire of suburban taxonomy that has left the field with an endless cascade of neologisms, each offering a more finely grained model for understanding metropolitan development of particular places that only adds to the general cacophony. It is a field full of *bourgeois utopias* and *technoburbs*, of *boomburbs* and edge nodes.[11] It has *garden cities, satellite cities, edge cities, edgeless cities, edge nodes*, and the *galactic metropolis*.[12] When one focuses on housing developments, there remains a smorgasbord of *picturesque enclaves, streetcar buildouts, mail-order suburbs*, and *sitcom suburbs*, in addition to *manufacturing suburbs*, African American suburbs, and working-class suburbs.[13] As one moves farther from the city center, the density of neologisms seems to increase even as the population thins. Out here are *agriburbs, rurban settlements, rural fringes* and *borderlands, suburbscapes, penurbia, farm fringe streetcar suburbs*, and *wilderburbs*.[14] It is enough to make one's head spin.

This quest for conceptual specificity has punched holes in the cultural image of lily-white suburban Levittowns full of conformist, middle-class nuclear families. Somewhere along the way, however, the law of diminishing returns set in. The publication in 2003 of Dolores Hayden's taxonomy-driven book *Building Suburbia: Green Fields and Urban Growth, 1820–2000* as the replacement for Kenneth Jackson's policy-driven *Crabgrass Frontier: The Suburbanization of the United States*, published in 1985, was emblematic of this shift that prefers splitting over lumping and places developers, architects, and homebuilders at the forefront of suburban history. Scholars have, as a result, generally pushed the lived experience of residents and their communities to the margins. I do not propose that we abandon conceptual models of development, of course, if that were even possible. Rather, this book uses a few of these conceptual tools to illuminate and analyze the history of metropolitan development, not the other way around. It relies on a conceptual frame that historical actors both recognized and engaged with: the county.[15]

A definition of terms, then, is in order. First, *metropolitan*. This study adopts the standard census definition of the metropolis as a core urban area of fifty thousand or more population and the surrounding counties that have a "high degree of social and economic integration" with the urban core. I use *metropolitan fringe* broadly to denote areas within metropolitan counties whose landscapes, politics, and social relations are not primarily characterized by urban or suburban development. The fringe includes rural land uses such as agriculture and forestry, vacation homes and industry. It also includes exurban land uses such as rural subdivisions, recreation areas, landfills, and hobby farms. Because of the cultural baggage and historical debate surrounding the terms *suburb, suburban,* and *suburbia,* I have endeavored to avoid them whenever possible. When I do succumb to the temptation, as I did already in this paragraph, it is to denote a pattern of land-use and settlement primarily consisting of single-family homes in developments that are dependent on cars and usually located outside incorporated cities.

This is a study of metropolitan *landscapes,* a term that admittedly functions as a catchall for the confluence of physical geography (natural and human-made space) and cultural meaning (place) over time. As such, this book is environmental history when it traces what was happening on the ground, in the water, and to the air. It is social history when it describes the shifting political economy and social relations embedded within these places. And it is cultural history when it uncovers the meaning historical actors ascribed to these metropolitan landscapes. Land on the metropolitan fringe was a factor of production and a site for development. It was both the product of and a force in historical change. Landscape foregrounds this intersection between nature, place, people, and meaning over time.[16]

This book takes the reader to a place, the metropolitan county, where together we set up lawn chairs and watch the scramble of activity that was metropolitan growth. Such framing is vital to avoiding the slide back into taxonomy. Roy Harris, after all, never saw himself as building *agriburbs* or *penurbia.* Nor did he wring his hands about the ideal form of housing development. Instead, he got his realtor's license and ran for the office of county clerk. Rural people on the fringe (Harris being only one example) exercised social, political, and economic power through county government and politics as they interacted with developers and new residents, a fact that complicates broader narratives of rural poverty, marginalization, and cultural homogenization.[17]

Framing this study around the county also enables this book to grapple with the various transformations accompanying and often intertwined with metropolitan growth. These counties were rural; they were part of the metropolitan hinterland; and they were a marketable product: the countryside. This study, therefore, has as much to say about agriculture and rural life as it does about housing developments and metropolitan infrastructure.

Cities have loomed large in most accounts of metropolitan development, and rightly so. In the nineteenth century in particular, cities used their economic and political power to reshape, develop, and exploit their hinterlands.[18]

They built infrastructure, marketed commodities, and propelled real estate development. For postwar American cities, however, this type of urban imperialism faltered before the fragmentation of metropolitan governance and environmental regulations. These changes forced cities into political wrangling with suburbs, fringe areas, and governments at all levels over who would get access to resources, who would profit, who would be polluted, and who would pay for it all. These struggles demonstrated that twentieth-century metropolitan power was never as focused or as effective as it had been in the late nineteenth century.[19]

This hinterland relationship also played out in the cultural realm. Developers and rural landowners marketed their regions in a way that appealed to metropolitan tastes and expectations of rural life. Proximity made these counties subject to the gaze of the nation's white, urban, upper and middle classes. These outsiders projected their values and expectations on rural landscapes— sometimes in line with and other times in contradiction to the land's pasts. As Raymond Williams has argued, such conceptions of the countryside are like a window: an observer sees as much of her own character reflected in the glass as she sees of the land itself through that glass. Or, as another recent study puts it, the countryside "looks like the city thinks the country should look." Such visions of the countryside as a place of leisure, health, permanence, and virtue ignored agrarian social history, in which labor, exploitation, displacement, and corruption have often been the rule.[20] Williams's critique provides a starting point for discerning the way urban expectations transformed the countryside. Rather than focusing, as most urban and suburban historians have, on what these middle-class migrants were running from or what their new suburban world lacked in comparison with the city, I place at the forefront what they hoped to get from the bargain: the opportunity to live in the countryside, to put down roots, and to escape the noise and clutter of modern urban life. What they desired, after all, was good in the fullest sense of the word even as it was tainted by its high social, economic, and environmental costs—costs largely borne by others.

These three overlapping stories—the fringe as rural, the fringe as hinterland, and the fringe as countryside—form the analytical heart of this book. The metropolitan fringe also speaks to two broader conversations. The first is the question of southern exceptionalism. Many historians have insisted that the South's cultural identity and racial politics have been and remain distinct from those in the rest of the nation, burdening the region with a unique heritage and a unique guilt. More recent studies challenge such exceptionalist claims. Postwar transformations, they argue, have brought the South into the mainstream of national culture and structural racism—a suburban racism of white privilege.[21] Where one lands on this debate has a great deal to do with where one looks. Those arguing for the end of southern exceptionalism tend to ground their studies in the region's Sunbelt metropolises, where color-blind conservatism, meritocratic individualism, and residential segregation reign.[22] Their opponents, in turn, point to the persistence of social conservatism and racial paternalism in the South's rural areas—areas caught in the shadows of the Sunbelt.[23] This book explores, on a micro level, the changes in southern identity, racial politics, culture, and landscape where the Sunbelt and the rural South meet. Both of the counties I examine maintained extensive ties to southern identity into the 1960s. However, the southernness of each was, by the turn of the twenty-first century, severely in doubt. Each lost many of the cultural and social markers of the region during the postwar period. This process was not exclusively the project of suburbanites and newcomers. Rural people often joined them in recasting their regional identity, obscuring their ties to the racialized power structures and landscapes of the rural South. These new regional identities displaced their interracial but often violent pasts, establishing a whitened, and at times whitewashed, rural social world in their place. The process of metropolitan growth was, therefore, also a process of integrating the rural South into the Sunbelt.

Finally, the story of the southern metropolitan fringe has implications for the way we understand the origins of environmentalism. Adam Rome, Christopher Sellers, and Samuel Hays have each, in spite of their differences, traced the movement's roots back to socially progressive, middle-class, suburban white families angered over the destruction of nearby forests and creeks and the pollution of their air and water. Suburbanites moved close to nature to enjoy health and quality of life. When their suburban dreams seemed threatened, these homeowners mobilized to fight for the beauty and health of their slice of heaven and, ultimately, that of the planet as a whole.[24] From the perspective of the rural South, the problem with their defense of suburban nature lies in the way it collapsed the cornfield, the second-growth forest, the terraced hillside, the old-field meadow, and the improved pasture into "open space."[25] Naturalizing these rural landscapes justified their preservation.[26] Undeveloped land was, by the very use of the word, emplotted as the beginning of the story. Suburban environmentalists cast rural land as Eden doomed to destruction at the hands of human greed. In the process they largely ignored its history and the history of its people in order to embellish the speed, extent, and tragedy of the bulldozer's work. In fact, this work never could eliminate all vestiges of past land uses. The rural South endured, shaping the politics of development and the meaning of the countryside for decades after development began.[27]

These past studies of suburban environmentalism are also of limited use in understanding the metropolitan fringe because they begin with a definition of *authentic* or *true* environmentalism and then work backward to tease out its roots among various strands of half-baked movements and ideologically vague activism. Taking the county as the unit of analysis, in contrast, pushes the history of environmental activism in a different direction. Residents in some counties fought to protect historic landmarks and homes, preserve scenery and agricultural land, prevent development, and clean up litter. Yet many of them did not consider themselves "environmentalists." Their activism had as much to do with aesthetics, taste, and privilege as it did with concerns for pollution, overpopulation, and wilderness. Just as revealing are the residents in other southern fringe counties who experienced all of the prerequisites for environmental activism—septic overflows, flooding, sprawling developments, and air pollution—yet who never joined the environmental movement. They instead turned their energies toward battling county government and forming private governments in an effort to secure passable roads, basic water and sewer service, police protection, and flood control.

ᆼᅠ

To tell this story, I selected two counties that capture the geographic, historical, and cultural diversity of the American South. Like lenses in a pair of binoculars, the difference between Montgomery County, Texas, and Loudoun County, Virginia, works to bring the whole into greater relief. Each was caught up in the growth of its sprawling southern metropolis. One, the nation's capital, straddled the boundary between Megalopolis and the Virginia of Washington, Jefferson, and Lee. The other, the shining buckle of the Sunbelt, straddled the boundary between the cotton and timber of the South and the cattle and oil of the Southwest. The energy industry fueled Houston's prosperity. Federal spending fueled Washington, D.C.'s prosperity. Each attracted educated, white-collar workers from outside the South.[28] The population of the region that made up Houston's metropolitan area grew from 936,000 in 1950 to 2.9 million in 1980. Over the same period, the Washington metropolitan area grew from 1.5 million to just over 3 million.[29] Even as they grew, each city struggled to cope with white flight. In Houston, aggressive annexation policies kept many of the new suburbs paying city taxes. As a city caught between two states and entirely dependent upon Congress for its political fate, the District of Columbia never had the option to annex surrounding territory. Its population peaked in 1950 at 802,178, at which point 35 percent of that population was African American. By 1975 that figure was 70 percent.[30]

Outlying counties became the proverbial Canaan for this exodus from urban blight, crime, pollution, and integration. Both Loudoun County and

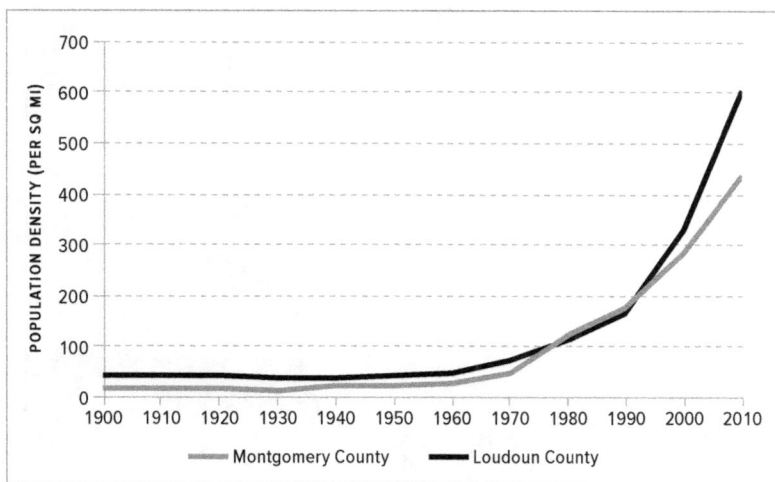

Population density in Montgomery County, Texas, and Loudoun County, Virginia.
Richard L. Forstall, ed., *Population of States and Counties of the United States: 1790–1990*
(Washington, D.C.: GPO, March 1996), 158, 166; U.S. Census of Population and Housing, 2000,
American FactFinder, Census.gov, accessed April 5, 2017.

Montgomery County were located in the path of this development. The distance from the White House to Leesburg, Loudoun's county seat, is a mere thirty-six miles. From Houston's city hall to Conroe, Montgomery's county seat, is thirty-nine miles. This proximity made urban growth possible. The timelines for both counties are almost identical. Both counties saw the first influx of development in the 1950s, the first large-scale subdivisions in the 1960s, and runaway growth beginning in the 1970s. The population of Loudoun County more than doubled between 1960 and 1980. The population of Montgomery County did the same by 1970 and again by 1980. The incentives for development were especially strong in Montgomery County, where the opening of two major highways to Houston, the Houston Intercontinental Airport, and Lake Conroe, Houston's reservoir, during the 1960s and 1970s drove up land prices. Developers also leveraged fears that Houston would annex all of neighboring Harris County, subjecting white families there to busing, urban control, and municipal taxation. In Virginia, neighboring Fairfax County faced no such threat from Washington and therefore served as a buffer between Loudoun County and the city. This fact, combined with Loudoun's relatively undeveloped transportation networks, limited its attractiveness for large developments until the construction of Dulles Airport in 1962 and the accompanying extension of urban sewer services opened the floodgates of growth.[31]

Within these two counties, metropolitan development proceeded as a series of struggles over the ownership, use, meaning, and value of local landscapes.

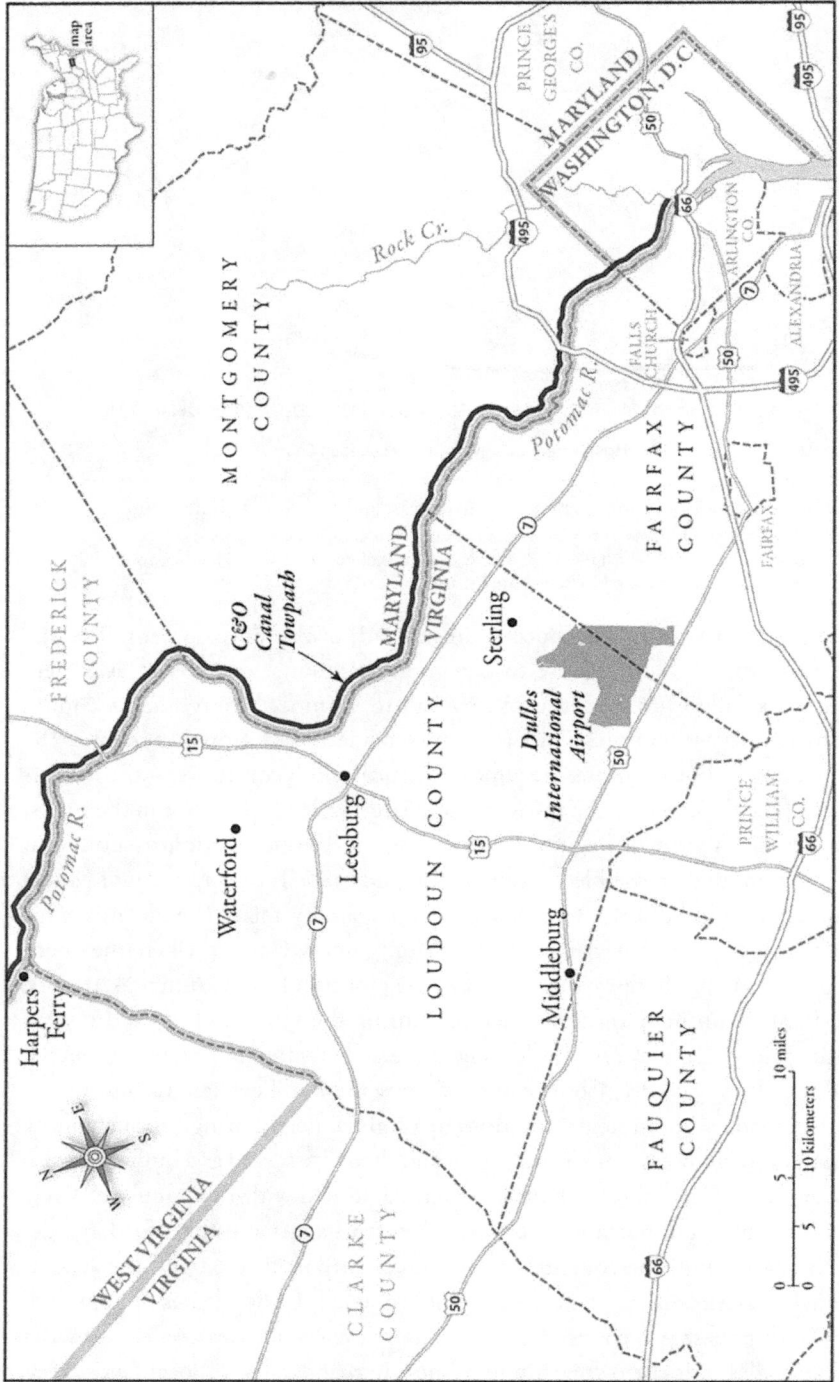

Map of Loudoun County, Virginia.

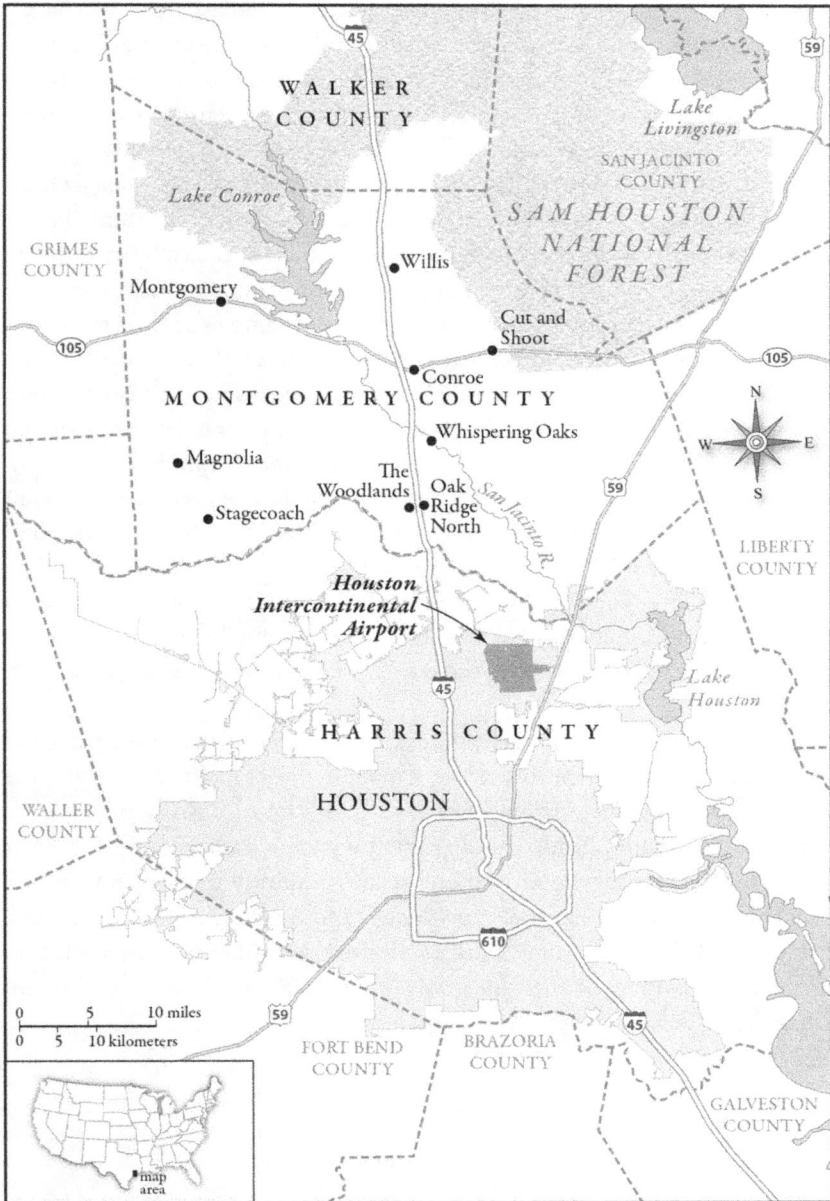

Map of Montgomery County, Texas.

Therefore, this study is arranged into five thematic chapters. The first chapter examines changing expectations of access to the land and the role of landowners and local politics in redefining that access. The second chapter turns to agriculture and its overlapping cultural and economic transformations from production oriented to leisure and consumer oriented. Metropolitan growth bound agriculture and rural life more tightly to the city even as many continued to rhetorically portray them as alternative ways of life. The third chapter shifts to a focus on the development of hinterlands, specifically, attempts to construct reservoirs and the way that these projects connected cities to outlying counties. Such projects were the most obvious examples of cities refashioning their hinterlands, yet, as this chapter demonstrates, these particular cities did not enjoy anything approaching imperial power over their hinterlands. The final two chapters turn to the local politics of housing development and land use. In Montgomery County, residents organized within their communities to put forward local solutions to the failure of developers and government to protect their new homes and landscapes from trash, floods, and sewage and to provide basic services. These residents sought to carve out a stable suburban space within these rural landscapes and political structures. Within Loudoun County, in contrast, a subset of newcomers joined blue-blooded locals in organizing to preserve and protect the county's historic structures, open spaces, and farmland.

This eclectic mix of chapters demonstrates the importance of the rural and agricultural past to the history of the expanding metropolis. By treating the fringe as its own object of study, rather than as watered-down suburbia or as a tainted rural world, historians can more fully appreciate what development meant both to those who arrived and to those already there. It was on the fringe that the battle lines over growth and land use were drawn. It was here that the Sunbelt and the rural South confronted each other. Finally, it was here that the intertwining of rural life and white privilege was most pronounced. Let us head, then, out into the metropolitan fringe.

CHAPTER I

Clearing the Backwoods

A band of men sit around a campfire on a muggy autumn night in Depression era East Texas, their ears straining in the darkness. The last rustle in the underbrush has faded into the din of the forest. Unused to the strain, the newest member of their clandestine fraternity begins to grind his foot into the dirt and scratch his neck in an attempt to remain focused. The men wait. Suddenly, their ears pick up a mournful bay echoing through the pines. Having caught the fox's scent, the hounds take off. Their masters close their eyes in rapt attention to the sounds of the chase. Each traces the path of the hounds by their voices as the canines range over creeks, across pastures, through farmyards, and past abandoned lumber camps, chasing the tireless fox to utter exhaustion. Each hound bears the weight of its master's expectations. Sometimes the hounds tree the fox, or the fox goes to ground. Other times, to their master's shame, hounds in turn grow weary and slump to the ground. Either way, at the crack of dawn, the men break camp, setting out across the countryside and gathering their hounds before beginning the day's work.[1]

By the middle of the twentieth century, the American tradition of hilltop foxhunting could be found from New Jersey to Oklahoma and in most rural areas in between. The sport put down particularly deep roots in the Piney Woods of East Texas. According to *Texas Game and Fish*, "nearly every farm boy has at least one good hound tied out back of the barn."[2] Farmers, rural laborers, small-town professionals, and even big-city lawyers sat together around a campfire or gathered at organized meets. Hilltop foxhunting combined the excitement of the chase with the shadowy meetings, private rituals, and code of conduct of a secret society. The sport brought together men across the lines of class and race in a particular nocturnal subculture. It did not necessarily unite them. The demands of deference and subservience continued to hold sway, even among the pines, yet the achievements of one's hounds gained a man grudging respect, if not honor, across racial lines.[3] Foxhunting made extensive claims on the land. It required a landscape without fences, hunting preserves, or housing developments. It depended on sympathetic or at least apathetic landowners to tolerate the hounds. Montgomery County, Texas, with its extensive timber company holdings and open-range laws, was a haven for the

County Commissioner T. J. Peel foxhunting in Depression-era East Texas.
Courtesy of the Heritage Museum of Montgomery County, Texas.

sport. By the 1950s, the sound of baying hounds had echoed across the woods of Montgomery County for over a hundred years, unconstrained by the property lines on file at the county clerk's office.

Foxhunting was only one of the access claims locals made on the woods in Montgomery County. Whether the hounds chased foxes or raccoons, whether rambling sportsmen sought mourning doves or a secluded fishing spot, county residents and a growing number of Houstonians looked to these woods for recreation, as well as part of their livelihood. Custom, at first reinforced by the law and later in opposition to it, opened private woodlands as a recreational and hunting commons. The county's open-range law protected the right of residents to forage their cattle and hogs on any unfenced land. Local custom protected poaching and hunters' freedom of movement. Popular opinion sided with fence cutters over fence builders. These persistent rural land uses and expectations stymied developers' and rural landowners' attempts to package and sell timbered landscapes to meet the growing demand for home sites. Consumer expectations, reinforced by local advertising and national culture, had little room for roaming herders and hunters and the social and environmental relationships they had forged in the piney woods.[4]

The open woods would not last. Between the 1950s and the 1970s, rural landowners, regional boosters, and timber companies, with the aid of the Texas Agricultural Extension Service, the San Jacinto Soil Conservation District (later Montgomery-Walker Soil and Water Conservation District), and the Texas Forest Service, reconfigured and redefined rural land use. They enclosed it, intensively managed it, and increased its profitability. Some thinned, culled, sprayed, and fenced to produce more lumber per acre. Nearly two-thirds of the county's forests—or nearly half of the county's land area—was under these types of modern timber management practices by 1955. Others fenced, stocked, and patrolled in order to open the woods for recreation to paying customers. Economic prosperity, improved highway systems, and expanding leisure time all stoked consumer demand to get out from the metropolis and into the woods. For rural communities faced with economic stagnation and out-migration, chasing recreational and tourist dollars became a fervent passion and an economic necessity.[5]

These transformations are a well-documented part of the region's rural history. Their impact on metropolitan development, however, remains unexamined. Most suburban narratives, as Christopher Sellers points out, paint the suburban development process as one of either "nature erasing" or "city building." The former casts rural areas as nature crushed under the wheels of American greed and consumerism. The latter paints these areas as a blank canvas to be painted by the city as dictated by urban infrastructure needs and market cues. Both approaches have little interest in the history of these developing rural places. Only recently have suburban historians begun to draw attention to the environmental history of the metropolitan fringe.[6]

Bounding, managing, and controlling the forest were prerequisites for housing development. Developers cleared subdivision roads and building sites, cultivating the forest landscape to match consumer expectations. Yet rural practices could not be bulldozed away as easily as the collapsing sharecropper cabins and the thick underbrush. These businessmen sometimes worked alongside and sometimes built upon the efforts of local boosters, rural landowners, and timber companies to eliminate the entrenched rural land-use practices that threatened to spoil their developments. Local interests strove to eliminate such practices in order to realize the economic benefits of development. Creating a commuter's wooded paradise meant clearing the road of roaming cattle and clearing the woods of trespassers. Creating a hunter's paradise meant protecting game species from the wasteful hunting of locals and Houstonians who refused to pay for the privilege. Carving a wooded suburban landscape out of the woods meant not just bulldozing; it meant protecting the woods from southern land-use practices. Between 1950 and 1970 a coalition of landowners and business interests closed the woods. They enacted stock laws, overturned the culture of benign neglect surrounding game laws, and closed off much of the countryside. In the process, they opened this land for the housing developments that would dominate the landscape by the turn of the twenty-first century.

The central issue was one of power. Who would manage the forest, and who would be allowed access? Landowners and developers worked to shore up private property rights and to reshape the land for their own profit and for the use of suburban newcomers. Those opposed to this vision responded with the tools common to peasant movements across the world: poaching, arson, and trespass. While the landowners never achieved total control over the forest, they accomplished their aims. They reshaped the county's wooded landscapes from inhabited to habitat, from managed to natural, and from production to recreation. As the forest grew back in the decades after the Great Depression, covering the signs of past rural uses, these landowners and developers transformed the county's open woods into wooded nature. Suburban newcomers had little cause to think that it had ever been anything else. These newcomers, along with their children and their pets, claimed the woods for their own enjoyment. The forests that had sustained open-range hogs and cattle and generations of pothunters became an amenity packaged and sold by developers. They became suburban nature.

ℰℐ

This political, social, and cultural world was rooted in the county's particular landscapes. The county's northwest section includes a slice of fertile "black waxy" soils that cover much of the land between Dallas and Houston. These areas, along with the county's north-central bottomlands, were amenable to intensive farming. The bulk of the county's land lies in a transitional region between the Big Thicket in the east—with its poorly drained lowlands and its sandy, loblolly-pine-filled uplands—and post oak forests beginning in the west. The county, like most of East Texas, is subject to searing heat and rapid flash floods and therefore endures erosion, leached soils, and ruthless agricultural pests.[7]

A series of booms and busts drove much of the county's history. During the antebellum period, the county was at the cusp of the cotton frontier. The promise of cheap land and quick profit drew southern migrants to its thick forests. These southerners brought with them a system of agriculture and animal husbandry based on a scarcity of labor and abundant uncleared land. With the work of their slaves, they put small sections of the forests into production, sending eight thousand bales of cotton to Galveston each year by 1860.[8] The rest of the woods became the home of free-range cattle and piney woods hogs. These semiferal animals trampled across the open range, gorging themselves on acorns, roots, and small animals and evading the wolves, bears, cougars, bobcats, and alligators that persisted in the nineteenth-century woods of East Texas.

Extractive timber replaced cotton cultivation as the primary industry beginning in the 1880s as northern capital and new rail lines sparked a fifty-year cutout. The timber companies brought with them low-paying jobs, sawmills, and company towns.[9] The discovery of oil near Conroe in 1931 marked the beginning of another wave of frantic speculation and windfall profits. Almost overnight, Conroe became a boomtown. The local population mushroomed from 2,500 to perhaps as high as 15,000 within thirty days of the strike. Oil provided jobs for displaced timber workers, taxes for county coffers, and profits for those lucky enough to be holding title to nearby land. Crude would underwrite booster dreams well into the 1960s.[10] Behind the drama of oil, the timber industry continued to exert a powerful influence. The county had the third highest number of timber workers of any county in the state in 1940. This number went up over the following decade, leaving the county at the number one spot by 1950.[11] In the loblolly-pine-dominated forests of Montgomery County, Texas, logging reinforced and expanded a patchwork quilt pattern of landscape use that included small farmsteads, forest grazing land, dense thickets of scrub hardwoods and pines, and better-established second-growth pine forests.

&

The free movement of livestock sparked the first battle in this campaign to reappropriate the woods. Under the county's open-range system, cattle and hogs roamed freely across property lines, finding food and water wherever they desired. Landowners bore the responsibility for fencing cattle out of their fields, roads, and homesteads. This was a legally sanctioned practice with deep roots in the state and region. The open range had long been a pillar of Montgomery County's rural economy, social structure, and backwoods culture. Locals assumed access to the woods into the 1950s. Backwoodsmen roamed through the timbers, often on horseback, searching for hogs and cattle to mark and castrate. In the winter, after the animals had fattened on acorns and other mast or grasses, locals would capture and butcher some before setting fires to clear out the underbrush and thereby improve next year's forage. For the county's rural labor force, company forests provided supplementary income and subsistence that made low wages from work in the timber and oil industries economically viable. While a handful of prosperous farmers raised cattle and hogs on the range, it was the part-time farmer who depended on it most.[12]

The open range bent under the federal government's enforcement of cattle dipping for Texas fever in the late 1920s and early 1930s, but it did not break.[13]

The system provided a safety net for the county's rural laborers during the decades of depression. Many continued to keep cattle and hogs on the open range after World War II. As one resident remembered, it was normal to see a backwoodsman on horseback, rifle in hand, blocking traffic on the highway as his hounds drove a herd of free-range cattle across the countryside to market. By the 1950s, however, the system's persistence had as much to do with social expectation and cultural values as it did with agricultural production. Most of the county's rural poor were finding a far better salvation in the jobs available in "heavenly Houston."[14]

Conflict over the open range has been a perennial fixture of southern history. Most states left the counties to decide whether to operate under a stock law or fence law system. Counties in the more developed agricultural regions generally adopted stock laws as part of the Reconstruction era consolidation of planter power over free laborers or as a part of turn-of-the-century efforts to improve the management and therefore profitability of capital-intensive farms. In both cases, wealthy landowners believed fence laws to be a barrier to their prosperity. In contrast, most of the heavily timbered counties in the Deep South remained under fence laws well into the twentieth century.[15] Montgomery County had its share of fence law opponents. The Texas Forest Service, timber companies, business-minded farmers, the Texas Game and Fish Commission, and the East Texas Chamber of Commerce all generally favored closing the range. Each of these groups had an interest in exerting greater control over the woods and in managing the impact of livestock on timber, pasture, and wildlife. Yet these groups had chosen to work for such laws behind the scenes rather than risk drawing the ire of backwoodsmen who were known to cut fences, light fires, and threaten violence when their rights to the woods were challenged. Into the early 1950s, the power of enforcement rested with those protecting the open woods.[16]

In Montgomery County, few dared question the fence law before World War II. A number of factors, however, eroded the open range's foundation. First, the hardships of the Great Depression and Houston's wartime boom fueled a massive rural exodus in East Texas. Between 1940 and 1945 alone, the number of farms in the county dropped 41 percent (from 2,296 to 1,356) and the average farm size increased 74 percent (from 88 to 154 acres) as farm families and rural youths packed their few belongings and headed for the city. This out-migration significantly thinned the ranks of the open range's supporters.[17] For those who remained, rural life now offered new consumer choices. Backwoodsmen could choose a supermarket over home production, better-paying off-farm labor in Conroe and Houston over hog and cattle herding, and the pickup truck over the horse.[18] Second, changes within agriculture and timber management challenged the open range. Pasture improvement, recreational development, improved cattle breeds, timber monoculture, and farm consolidation each provided landowners with an economic incentive to assert greater control over their land. The timber and pulp industries continued to consolidate processing, mechanize harvesting, divest timber holdings, and hire out harvesting to subcontractors, trends that culminated locally in the closing in 1957 of the county's largest sawmill at Fostoria—a mill that had employed seven hundred people. In a county where 84 percent of the land was in commercial timber production, these industry changes had a profound impact.[19] Third, the spread of paved roads and the county's looming integration into Houston's metropolitan highway system made roaming cattle a more ominous threat to drivers, a fact that the Eisenhower administration's push for highway safety made all the more pressing.[20] This issue in particular undercut voter apathy among town residents—an apathy that had been a bulwark of the open range. Highway safety made rural cattle a town issue. Finally, the immediate push for closing the range came from a nebulous but forceful vision of prosperity and progress that the local newspaper and its allies pushed during the period. While this vision did not explicitly promise suburban development, boosters fought the open range as an obstacle to making Montgomery County open for business.

Roaming livestock first came up for debate in the early 1950s. In August 1951 Conroe voters approved a citywide ban on roaming hogs, citing the pigs' impact on public health. In a small southern town during the 1950s, such public health issues were inseparable from racial control. Immediately after passing the law, city police raided the African American section of town, "discovering" hundreds of backyard hogs. The *Conroe Courier* beamed at the new law's success not at making the city cleaner but at making it more "progressive."[21] Proponents next turned their attention to the countywide open range. Their first petition for an election during the fall of 1952 was rejected by the county commissioners on technicalities three different times. These first attempts called for closing the range to both hogs and cattle. Unlike cattle, which were ubiquitous in the county's agricultural economy and rural culture, free-range hogs were most important to poorer farmers and backwoodsmen, black and white. These people were also the least likely to turn out at the polls because of both their rural isolation and the Jim Crow system of disenfranchisement. Also, in a stock law election, only those who owned real property in the county could vote, adding another layer of exclusion for those most dependent on the range. When proponents submitted a new petition that did not include cattle they secured the commissioners' approval. Unwilling to rouse rural voters unnecessarily, the *Courier* and the chamber of commerce maintained cautiously neutral stances. Each hoped low turnout among rural voters would allow the stock law to carry the day. When the votes were counted that December, the final tally was 705 to 515. The range was now closed to hogs.[22]

Hoping to ride this momentum to complete closure, proponents placed the stock law for cattle on the ballot in September 1953. The rhetoric surrounding this election became much more heated, pitting town against countryside. Stock law proponents beat the drum of progress. They painted the open range as an anachronism in an otherwise dynamic and progressive county. As reported in the *Courier*, proponents had little interest in whether cattle roamed on company timber lands or oil leases. The question was whether "cattle shall be ruled off the highways of Montgomery County." The stock law, they claimed, belonged to the era of the horse and buggy. Roaming cattle were "a hazard not in keeping with the times." A collision between a car driven by a local veteran and a calf in July lent weight to these claims.[23] Defenders painted these claims as a direct attack on rural people who were "striving to obtain an honest living from this good earth by farming and raising livestock." The open range, they argued, was not primarily about class. It was about rural solidarity in the face of town imposition. It was about defending the hardy yeoman from the meddling of "preachers, teachers, doctors, lawyers, merchants, [and] bankers" who wanted to take away his means of economic support and thereby drive him into town or city. Wouldn't it be more just, they claimed, if the townspeople simply had enough common sense to slow down on the highway?[24]

When all the ballots were counted, the open-range defenders carried the day. Of the 2,109 property owners who voted, 905 voted to close the range, and 1,204 voted to preserve it. The *Courier* blamed a low turnout and disproportionate voting by the older generation. The reality was more complicated. For all the rhetoric about the town/country divide, the town vote was decidedly mixed. The combined vote for Willis, Montgomery, and Conroe, the county's three largest towns, was 546 for the stock law, 568 against. Even in Conroe, the heart of the movement for the stock law, it passed by a margin of less than 20 percent. The numbers also demonstrated that support for the open range was broad, with only seven of the twenty-one polling locations voting for the stock law. Stock law proponents underestimated the depth of the county's rural conservatism and the continuing power of claims to yeoman common rights. The majority of voters were unwilling to overturn a long-standing rural tradition in the name of progress and safety.[25]

This was the context in October 1953, when Edwin M. Watson took over as editor of the *Courier*.[26] Watson was driven by a vision of a progressive Montgomery County, but he was a man born a generation too late. A small-town newspaper editor with grand ambitions, Watson styled himself a modern muckraker sent to Conroe to rouse this sleepy town from its slumber. Before taking over the *Courier*, Watson had worked as a police reporter for the *Houston Press* and as an editor for the *Beaumont Journal*. Now, settled in his downtown office, he launched verbal barbs against what he portrayed as an entrenched elite who ran the county for the benefit of the rural minority. He confronted a town that had allowed itself to be bound by the cords of its own indifference. The stock law was an opportunity to rouse Conroe.

In June 1956, now with the full-throated support of the *Courier* and the local chamber of commerce, stock law proponents took up the battle again. They filed another petition with the county commissioners for a stock law election.[27] What followed was a series of legal missteps and procedural errors that delayed the vote for more than five months and brought the pages of Watson's *Courier* to a boil. County officials incorrectly prepared the ballots, failed to give proper legal notice, and enforced voting restrictions with unprecedented vigilance, thereby invalidating the signatures of petitioners. Watson cried foul, accusing the commissioners of stalling. Whether their actions were incompetent or malicious, the result was the same.[28] With each delay, the *Courier* raised the tenor of its protests. Watson launched his crusade against the county's entrenched rural elite. He blasted the good old boys for bending the rules for their own profit and for the benefit of their largely rural constituencies—constituencies that wielded a disproportionate share of political power in the decades before the Supreme Court's *Avery v. Midland County* reapportionment decision. Watson's editorials took the 1953 claim that open-range cattle were dangerous and amplified it, portraying the stock law both as an anachronistic holdover from a bygone era and as a gross exploitation of the common good by rural special interests. The "few cattle raisers," a group he neglected to define in any more detail, stood for a "type of government whereby 'the few shall dictate to the masses.'" Industrial development, improved services, and population growth would not come until the town shook off both the image and the practical dangers of free-roaming cattle. By October, Watson was accusing the opposition of systematically harassing and misleading those who signed the petition. Watson trumpeted, "We will now wage a fight based on truths, not lies; facts concerning the many accidents each week in our county because of the cattle running at large; we will tell how these few people want to continue to have their cattle run on other peoples [*sic*] property behind a quaint old state law of 'free range.'" Where open-range proponents had held the moral high ground by standing on their traditional rights, Watson now seized that high ground for the stock law. Cattle owners were the irresponsible freeloaders. Responsible, car-owning citizens, in contrast, were being denied the right to travel on roads "paid for by taxes from the owners of automobiles."[29]

Watson and his allies mixed this good-government crusade with continued fearmongering about highway safety. As one letter to the editor put it, "As long as stock is permitted to wander as they please zigzagging up and down and across our highways, just so long shall we be partly responsible for the accidents, and the murder committed on our highways where stock is involved." With a flair for the dramatic, Watson warned that "VOTING FOR the Stock Law may be a vote . . . [to] not die an untimely death on our highways." For town residents, the choice was clear. A vote for the stock law was a vote for progress, safety, and democratic rule. A vote for the free range was craven submission to a corrupt rural elite and to the danger of an untimely death on the highway.[30]

Watson drew attention to a very real problem, although he certainly overstated it. The vast majority of timber and oil land in the county remained unfenced, leaving roads open to free-ranging livestock, which often found roadside grasses irresistible. During the years leading up to the 1956 election, the commissioners court received multiple requests to fence major roads to prevent damage to livestock and automobiles.[31] The problem with such requests was jurisdictional. The state ruled that the commissioners court could neither use county money to erect fences along state highways nor establish a separate tax for that purpose.[32] The commissioners could and did, however, act to fence county roads when petitioned and funds allowed.[33] Thus the *Courier*'s general but unsubstantiated claim that "several near-fatal accidents have occurred during the past few years as a result of automobiles hitting cattle on the road" had the ring of truth.[34] The weather also played a role here. It is likely that the worsening drought in 1956 forced many cattle owners who had previously kept their cattle fenced to turn their stock onto the range in desperation to find what grass they could. This would have significantly increased the number of cattle wandering the countryside and therefore would have given the highway safety issue an added urgency.[35]

What, then, of the open-range defenders? A loose coalition of farmers, ranchers, country people, and sympathetic townspeople, these defenders continued to employ rhetoric infused with a mixture of anticommunism, agrarianism, and republicanism. They predictably painted those who would take away their rights and their cattle as representing oppressive government interference, a powerful move in the heyday of massive resistance. They rallied to the defense of the poor and embattled cattle owner who would find himself bankrupted by liability claims made by drivers who hit his stock merely because they were unwilling to "slow down a little for a cow sometime." Wouldn't it be better, one opponent argued, to go after the beer bottle, the real cause of most of the county's auto accidents?[36]

These visions of the county's future clashed in an ugly election during which

Polling Location	1953 Election		1956 Election	
	For	Against	For	Against
Arnold	4	16	10	16
Brantley	7	35	15	30
Conroe (North)	198	107	596	85
Conroe (South)	169	154	446	178
Copeland Chappel	12	11	34	24
Dacus	2	26	2	17
Dobbin	31	16	50	37
Fostoria	14	13	18	9
Grangerland			58	56
Haltom	45	76	40	89
Longstreet	7	49	15	47
Magnolia	73	39	108	28
McRae	2	17	6	24
Montgomery	56	147	101	172
New Caney	20	38	73	36
Oklahoma	37	16	51	11
Pinehurst	29	41	67	50
Porter	30	36	65	19
Security	8	54	17	55
Splendora	24	50	57	22
Union Grove	13	102		
Willis	123	160	204	223
Absentee	1	1	11	14
TOTAL	905	1,204	2,044	1,242

Stock law election returns, 1953 and 1956.
CC, December 15, 1956.

harsh words were common and more than a few threats of violence were uttered. Edwin Watson, for his part, claimed that he took to carrying a gun and requested a police escort when he went to cast his ballot.[37] How much of this was editorial bravado is hard to know. The election results, however, were decisive and uncontested. Where the 1953 attempt had gone down to defeat 905 to 1,204, the 1956 law passed handily, 2,044 to 1,242. The *Courier's* rhetoric drove town voters to the polls. More than twice as many voted for the stock law than had three years previously, while the number of voters defending the open range remained steady. Conroe turned out for the stock law. Where the county seat cast only 367 votes for the stock law in 1953, it cast 1,042 for it in 1956. Without Conroe's participation, the law would have only narrowly passed, 1,002 to 979. Other towns in the county remained divided. Rural areas tended to vote according to the type of agriculture that predominated. More densely wooded areas voted against the law. More progressive farming areas, which tended toward purebred cattle and dairy operations, voted for it. The election also hinted at political changes to come, because areas closest to Houston voted for the stock law. These areas were just starting to be settled by Houstonian gentlemen ranchers and exurbanites and therefore shared Conroe's fears over highway safety.[38] Fittingly, the *Courier* celebrated this victory the following month by printing a series of articles polishing the city's image and celebrating its achievements. The "Miracle City" was now ready to grow.[39]

What impact did the passage of the stock law have? It did not immediately close off the timbered landscape to backwoodsmen. In fact, there is circumstantial evidence that it exacerbated the arson and violence surrounding the open range. The county experienced an unprecedented spike in the number of arson-related forest fires in the months leading up to the stock law election. Admittedly, the drought played a role in this, yet it is also consistent with backwoodsmen's reaction to newly imposed restrictions on their rights of movement.[40] As for highway safety, the passing of the stock law had no significant impact on the number of traffic fatalities in the county. Even a cursory glance through justice of the peace records from the period reveals that drunk driving, not animal collisions, was the greatest danger on county roads.[41] What the law did accomplish was the shifting of the power of the state behind those who wished to fence their land. In this, the law's passage marked the beginning of the end of the county's open woods. By closing the woods to cattle and hogs, the law also accelerated the shift in agricultural production from low-input, small-scale, supplementary farming to capital-intensive, larger-scale farming. The agricultural statistics bear this out. The number of farms with cattle dropped even more precipitously after the passage of the stock law, from 1,214 (38,382 head) in 1954 to 965 (37,056 head) in 1959, just as the number of farms with hogs in the county had dropped after the hog stock law had passed from 762 (8,523 hogs) in 1950 to 589 (4,599 hogs) in 1954. The few livestock that remained on the range by the early 1960s were feral anachronisms in a developing county.[42]

In light of later development, it is clear that the persistence of the open range was incompatible with suburban understandings of property and expectations of privacy and safety within the woods. Suburban fences were built as much to visually demarcate space as they were to control movement. They could keep dogs and children in, for the most part, but they were never expected to keep bulls, hogs, and mounted backwoodsmen out.[43] As we will see in later chapters, the suburban dream these developments sold beginning in the 1960s may have sometimes employed cowboy images, but developers never expected suburban newcomers to actually wrangle free-range livestock out of their picturesque woods. Closing the range was a vital step in the process of purging the woods of its rural history and packaging it as suburban nature. Yet it would be inaccurate to claim that the desire for suburban development was a dominant motivating factor for the closing of the range in Montgomery County. Rather, town boosters cleared the county's highways of a menace to public safety and a barrier to economic growth. The type of growth they craved, however, was the growth of Conroe as an East Texas town, not Montgomery County as a bedroom community of Houston. Yet through their efforts and through the efforts of rural landowners, the second grew out of the preparations they had made in the decade after the passage of the stock law.[44]

ℭℌ

The open range had been the keystone of the county's early twentieth-century backwoods culture. With the range closed, the rest of the system of access and common use began to collapse, just as open-range defenders had feared. Interspersed among their denunciations of meddling townspeople were jeremiads over the potential closing of the woods to recreational access. One letter writer lamented the fact that "a lot of our fishing, swimming and hunting places have been fenced up" because landowners feared being held liable for their cattle. A pamphlet from the same period claimed that while "most of us like to go on an outing, fishing or hunting, . . . if a general stock law is passed THAT WILL BE A THING OF THE PAST." The closing of the range threw into question the longstanding right for locals to hunt, fish, trap, and traverse the woods.[45] For many, the fight had little to do with livelihood. It was about protecting rural people's "God-Given rights" to move across the landscape, to picnic beside a stream on timber company land, to swim in a sawmill pond, to hunt and trap, to fish, and to simply be out among the pines. The stock law reshaped the lifestyle of these people as much as it reshaped their way of life. The stock law multiplied fences and brought No Trespassing signs, transforming the way Montgomery County residents interacted with their forests, their fields, and each other.[46]

Just as stock law opponents predicted, boosters and rural landowners next turned their attention from hogs and cattle to turkey and deer. Here, too, local practice was at odds with modern expectations. Backwoodsmen, sawmill workers, town residents, and even some local ranchers habitually ignored game laws as they roamed the forests during their off-hours looking for sport and food. These hunters shot whatever their dogs could track down. One reformed backwoodsman remembered it as "an open season—on anything." Local law enforcement tolerated the hunting commons. As one state conservationist complained about East Texas in general in 1945, "Disrespect for protective wildlife laws is widespread and this attitude is strengthened by the time-honored system of the open range and large blocks of 'company owned' land." People would regularly poison streams and creeks in the county to illegally catch fish. Poachers shot does throughout the year. The public kept mum about any such transgressions. The woods were open. Local lips were sealed.[47]

Area sportsmen and landowners began to challenge this system during the early 1960s, pushing back against the backwoods culture of trespass and poaching and restoring wildlife populations on their own land.[48] They did so in part for their own recreation and in anticipation of offering paid hunting leases to Houstonians. That doing so secured them greater control over their private property only added to the attraction.[49] Montgomery County's woods needed the attention. Over a century of unregulated hunting and fishing had taken its toll on what would have otherwise been thriving game populations. Turkeys were the first to disappear, the last one being sighted in 1939. Even after a major restocking push, there were only a few hundred in all of southeast Texas by the 1960s.[50] Deer populations, which had already declined significantly by the 1920s, collapsed during the lean years of the Depression.[51] One resident remembered that a person could have gone years without seeing deer tracks in the county.[52] An entire generation grew up squirrel hunting.[53] The county's hundreds of thousands of acres of timberland had little to offer hunters or wildlife seekers in the postwar decade. Few were willing to drive an hour from Houston to pay for the opportunity to shoot squirrel, wily though they may have been.

This was the state of things when Charles Kincannon took on the post of Montgomery County game warden in 1951. An outsider, Kincannon had the unenviable job of enforcing state game laws on an intransigent county that, he later claimed, had "the worst reputation in the state for illegal hunting."[54] In his first years, Kincannon's efforts yielded frequent social snubs, occasional threats, and little else. This resistance was compounded by the apathy and even antipathy of county officials. According to one piece of local lore, Kincannon, patrolling the woods late at night in the early 1950s, came upon a group of men hunting deer with their dogs. He confronted the men and informed them that he would be taking them to jail for violating state game laws. After a few moments of awkward silence, one man stepped into the light and responded, "You can lock us up, but I can't promise I'll stay long. I've got the keys." Kincannon backed down rather than arresting the county sheriff.[55] He ran afoul of local political power again in 1965 when he confronted Justice of the Peace Bo Calfee about his alleged game law violations. Calfee responded by knocking the uniformed game warden to the ground and, as Calfee later admitted to a Houston reporter with a hint of pride, repeatedly kicking him in the face. In response, Kincannon told the *Courier* reporter that he would begin carrying his gun while on duty. As he put it, "It looks like I'm going to have to enforce my own peace around this county from now on." Restoring game populations required the cooperation and support of the local political establishment, which was less than forthcoming at this point.[56]

Rather than wasting his energy arresting poachers whom popularly elected justices of the peace would not fine, Kincannon focused his early enforcement on defending the county's game and livestock from outsiders. Working-class Houstonians, many of them migrants from the rural South, looked to Montgomery County as a place to practice the unrestricted hunting, fishing, and camping of their home regions. Yet Montgomery County was not their home. Some of these blue-collar sportsmen found themselves at the mercy of a double standard enforced by local courts. In one case, three Houston men were fined $700 for poisoning fish in 1953 during a period when locals commonly did the same.[57] In another case, three Houston bricklayers originally from Alabama drove to the county to go squirrel hunting in 1954. Finding no squirrels, they killed what legal documents later described as a "clearly marked" hog that they assumed was feral—a fine distinction of profound legal importance. The three men faced charges of hog theft.[58] In 1954 a group of Houston hunters accidentally shot a yearling cow while illegally deer hunting on a farm near Magnolia. After a lengthy trial and the possibility of imprisonment, they were acquitted.[59] In July 1956 Kincannon secured fines on nine hunters, five of whom were from Houston and none of whom were local.[60] A few years later, three Houston men killed a stray hog while they were trespassing and camping along the San Jacinto River. These men were fined $490 for their trouble.[61] The overall trend in the county courts throughout the 1950s was the selective enforcement of game and property laws against outsiders. Enforcement patterns are consistent with local residents and elected officials continuing to view poaching as a victimless crime and wildlife as a common resource for the people of Montgomery County to harvest.

This mentality was difficult to dislodge. The Chamber of Commerce Game Conservation Committee had struggled to convince landowners of the economic possibilities of game development since the mid-1950s with little success.[62] They only started making headway in the late 1950s, a period when outdoor recreation was becoming a booming industry in Texas and across the nation. Official statistics reported a 50 percent increase in outdoor recreation in the state between 1955 and 1960. The amount of money Texans spent on recreation doubled over the same period. Partially in response to this increasing interest, the legislature placed Montgomery County under the regulatory authority of the Texas Game and Fish Commission in 1959. This gave the commission, rather than the legislature, direct control over the length of game seasons, hunting regulations, and enforcement.[63] Within the year, Fish and Game experts in Austin had identified Montgomery County as a target county for recreation development. With Houston so close, estimates for the income potential of recreation development in Montgomery County ran into the millions of dollars.[64] On January 30, 1961, Eugene Walker, a representative of the Texas Game and Fish Commission, stood in front of a gathering of local landowners to sell them on recreation.[65] He regaled them with tales of rural counties that had turned their local economies around through restocking programs and wildlife management.[66]

Restocking coincided with the establishment of private hunting clubs across East Texas. These clubs fenced and posted their lands, managed the forest for game production, and hired armed guards to prevent poaching. Their operations demonstrated the potential profits to be had in wildlife management.[67] Walker encouraged these landowners to follow suit, developing their piney-woods acres into forests teeming with game. Montgomery County landowners had a great deal to gain from their proximity to Houston, if only they could protect their game from poachers. Walker found a receptive audience. The uncertain future of the local lumber industry during a downturn in the early 1960s pressured landowners to find alternate sources of income from their timberlands.[68] The increasing number of Houstonians buying up acreage for gentlemen ranches, future development, and hunting also generated interest. The local chamber of commerce, eager to launch a new local industry, worked with the Texas Game and Fish Commission, the local soil conservation office, and the agricultural extension office to create a local wildlife improvement association.

This organization took on the unenviable task of refashioning the way locals understood land. When lumber and pulp were the only commodities harvested from the county's woods, the landowners' timberlands could coexist with the backwoodsmen's wooded commons with its grazing cattle and unregulated hunting. This coexistence certainly had its moments of friction, but there was no fundamental conflict. Changes in timber production, wildlife management, agriculture, and law, however, tugged at the tangled knot of open-woods land use, pulling any particular acre toward a form of efficient, specialized production. Cattle that had grazed on the forested open range would gain more weight if bred with more oversight and confined on improved pastures. Cutover timberlands that had been left relatively undisturbed after harvest except by periodic fire were now replanted in rows, thinned, weeded, and sprayed so they would produce the most board feet per acre. While it might not appear so at first glance, producing wildlife and recreation required a similar type of specialized management and control over the land. Over the course of the 1960s and 1970s, local landowners protected and cultivated the game that lived among the pines.

Protection was the most immediate issue. With local law enforcement and courts still largely uninterested in arresting, trying, or convicting fence cutters and poachers, landowners turned to private security to fill the gap. The

Cattleman's Security Association was the most prominent. Serving the counties surrounding Houston, the association offered its paying members, fifty of whom were in Montgomery County, protection from trespass, poaching, and cattle theft. While it was an effective deterrent, putting private security contractors in the woods could have deadly results. One such incident occurred in 1961. Just after dawn on Halloween morning, Jeff Beeson, a fence rider near Grangerland, in the south-central part of the county, was patrolling private pastures in order to keep deer hunters out. When he saw a teenager on horseback riding out of the woods with his hounds, Beeson confronted him. After a few minutes' conversation, the content of which is unknown, Beeson shot the youth twice.[69]

At the same time they were exerting private control over their land, sportsmen, landowners, and businessmen organized to form the Montgomery County Fish and Wildlife Improvement Association. This organization became the public face of the effort to promote the enforcement of game laws, the development of habitat, the destruction of undesirable species, the prevention of pollution, and better communication between sportsmen and landowners.[70] The group affiliated itself with the Sportsmen Clubs of Texas and, working with Charles Kincannon, set about recruiting local landowners to patrol and report any suspicious activity along every county road and highway within the county. While public education and promotion were important, surveillance and control of private land were the central thrust. Members of the group organized to keep people out of their property as they cultivated their acreage for game.[71]

In so doing, they confronted resistance from foxhunters and some deer hunters, both of whom continued to bring their dogs with them into the woods and resented having their sport placed beyond the pale.[72] The sportsmen were right to want dogs out of the woods, for they suppress game populations. Although they rarely catch healthy adult deer, dogs, as an apex predator, create what wildlife biologists term a "landscape of fear." They harass deer and other animals, sometimes to the point of exhaustion and malnourishment. They can kill does and fawns and thereby significantly limit reproductive success.[73] Conservationists and foxhunters during the period understood much of this. Deer populations wreaked havoc on foxhunters' sport, for foxhounds would often abandon the chase in order to hunt the irresistible smell of deer. Deer and dogs could not coexist in the woods. Foxhunters were clear about which had to go. The issue was more complicated for old-school deer hunters who used their dogs, artificial light, fire, and other unsporting methods to kill their targets. These men saw the push to more intensively manage deer populations and establish profit-making leases as an attempt to cut the little man out of the woods and to sell game that was rightfully his to outsiders. Both issues were the cause of more than one instance of local meetings degenerating into shouting matches and walkouts.[74] Conflict boiled over in 1964 as members of the Cattleman's Security Association pushed the National Forest Service and Texas Fish and Game Commission to designate twenty thousand acres of the Sam Houston National Forest, much of which was in Montgomery County, as a game preserve in which hunting would be heavily regulated. In doing so, they would assure themselves large deer populations and thereby lucrative hunting leases on their own properties as deer from the forest would restock their lands. They would have also closed what was quickly becoming the last hunting land open to both local residents and working-class Houstonians.[75]

For foxhunters whose hounds were increasingly being killed for trespassing, this federal land was their only hope of keeping their sport alive.[76] Local hunter Bill Terrell spoke for these hunters in a letter to the editor. Responding to the broader transformations over the previous decade, he argued that "closing the forest would benefit the deer hunter and the turkey hunter," but "what do you good hearted people plan to do for the squirrel hunter, the coon hunter, the foxhunter, the possum hunter, the armadillo hunter, and the many people that just go into the National Forest every year with a gun just to get into the open?" These people, he argued, were the victims of a movement by "the Land Owners that are trying to make a few extra dollars off of lease money."[77] In protest, irate hunters disrupted a meeting that organizers had hoped would demonstrate how thoroughly the county had adopted conservation ideals. Instead, as the *Courier* complained, the meeting "probably set state and federal aid to wildlife projects in this area back about 10 years."[78] Unwilling to alienate so large a group of local hunters, the Texas Fish and Game Commission kept the national forest open to public hunting and pushed the issue of wildlife conservation back onto landowners and local government.

Frustrated in their attempt to secure federal protection of local wildlife, conservation advocates returned to the issue of local enforcement. Traditionally, game violations had been handled at the precinct level by justices of the peace (JPs). Because their reelection depended on maintaining the goodwill of their small segment of the county electorate, these JPs had a strong motive to look the other way when it came to game law violations. Those who enforced these laws did so at great personal and political risk, as Raymond Weisinger found out personally. After daring to fine a local poacher, this JP was himself assaulted and beaten in a local café.[79] Of all the JPs, only Bobby Yancey had a sustained record of filing against poachers. Yancey took it upon himself to crack down on so-called fire hunters—hunters who "jacklighted," or hunted deer at night using artificial lights. These hunters were, he remarked, "a detriment to the county's rural economy, not to mention the sport of hunting." As early as 1960, he began issuing stiff fines. As a personal advocate of wildlife conservation, Yancey was an exception. Most JPs kept their heads down, preferring instead to spend their time handing out speeding tickets to out-of-town drivers who neither voted nor held a personal grudge.[80]

As the movement for conservation gained momentum, Kincannon began filing some of his arrests for game violations with the county judge, W. S. Weisinger, rather than with the JPs. Weisinger, a Conroe businessman, prominent chamber of commerce member, and major area landowner, handed down heavy fines and jail time to game violators as a warning to would-be poachers. In the past, local violators had gotten off with light fines or dismissals, but Weisinger made public examples out of poachers no matter where they were from. The *Courier* did its part to publicize these cases and warned hunters of an "all out crackdown" on game law violations.[81] Between 1960 and 1963, Weisinger handled only three cases related to game, each of which had to do with fence cutting and trespassing. Over the following two years, he handled thirty-eight cases.[82] These included fines (between $100 and $200) and/or jail sentences. Offenses ranged from hunting with artificial light and hunting from a car to hunting without a license and poisoning fish. Increased enforcement was a central factor in transforming the culture of hunting in Montgomery County in the 1960s. Weisinger's actions paved the way for JPs to follow suit.[83]

The records from Justice of the Peace, Precinct 1, located in the northern part of the county, illustrate this shift. This precinct was adjacent to the Sam Houston National Forest and received a great deal of use by hunters and fishermen during the period. In 1960 the precinct recorded twenty-three game citations from four separate instances. Because deer populations in that part of the county were slower to rebound, only one of these violations was for deer. The rest were for hunting squirrel or trespassing. Fifteen of the violations were by Houstonians, and all but one of the remaining cases were against residents of the towns of Conroe and Willis. Enforcement under J. M. Jordy, the justice at the time, was better than some but still reflected a general preference for enforcing game laws against outsiders and town residents rather than locals and a general laxity in enforcement. When James Harvey "Bo" Calfee took over the office in 1963, the trickle of game law violation cases stopped. During 1964 and 1965, the years of the game law crackdown, Calfee logged only two hunting-related citations. Both were for killing a hog, legally an act of theft rather than a game law violation. Given that Kincannon accused Calfee of illegal hunting himself in November 1965, it is little wonder that he decided not to bring such cases to Precinct 1 and that Calfee filed no such charges.[84] When J. P. Bailey took over as justice in 1970, enforcement resumed. Bailey logged forty-six citations during 1970, ranging from arson, trespass, and dog slaying to night hunting, livestock killing, and deer poaching. The majority, twenty-six, were for night hunting or deer poaching. These cases suggest the persistence of these practices and the extent of enforcement efforts. By 1975 the number of citations had declined to four. In light of newspaper coverage and other contemporaneous sources, this decline was likely caused by a genuine decrease in the number of incidents rather than a relaxing of enforcement. In 1980 the office handled twelve cases, including a few trespassing cases and one arson case. By that point, however, the opening of Lake Conroe had drastically changed the area. It was now duck hunters from suburban Houston and Lake Conroe fishermen, rather than blue-collar deer hunters and backwoodsmen, who showed up on the docket books. The game wardens and justices had a far more lucrative target in outsiders who persistently fished and boated on the lake without proper licenses. By 1980 lake-related citations dominated other game citations by more than ten to one. Between 1960 and 1980 the county transformed from local apathy and lax enforcement to reliable enforcement of game laws and the closing of the woods before ending up regulating Houstonians who came to the county for paid recreation.[85]

Improved enforcement and rising game populations provided landowners with the incentive they needed to fence and post their land. A 1964 survey of timber landowners found that 45 percent had purchased fence posts during the past year. By 1969 a study by the local soil and water conservation district found that fences now enclosed 90 percent of the area's unforested land and 75 percent of its forested land.[86] At the same time, the number of hunting leases rapidly expanded. One hundred and fifty local landowners were issuing leases by 1966.[87] The bulk of county land available for hunting was through three large landowners. Champion Paper had made 10,000 acres open to hunting since 1961. Foster Lumber Company had a similar total. Mitchell & Mitchell, a development company with ties to Houston oil money, leased the bulk of the 36,526 acres it bought from Grogan-Cochran Lumber Company in 1964. Each used leases to help balance the books as they further improved the land for either development or timber harvest. By fencing, leasing, and regulating their land, these companies reinforced the boosters' efforts to add game to the list of salable products of the county's woods.[88]

Montgomery County made strides toward developing recreation. Conservationists undermined the position of the backwoods poacher as a local folk hero. As Kincannon boasted in November 1965, "What once was considered as 'running to the law and ratting' now is considered an act that will benefit hunters and land owners alike." Earlier that year he had commented, "When I first came to Montgomery County . . . it would be a rare day that I would get a call or complaint about game violations. Now I get about 25 a day."[89] Statements like this were certainly self-serving, yet the fact that the county court handled only six game-related cases in 1970 offers some evidence that Kincannon and the county judge felt secure in trusting game enforcement to the justices of the peace. That justices were willing to support broad enforcement of the law is, in turn, evidence that voters' opinions had shifted. The strongest support for Kincannon's claims is the deer populations themselves. Deer populations and legal hunting boomed during the period. In 1957 only 375 bucks had been legally killed in the county. In 1964 580 bucks were killed during the first two days of the season.[90] Local conservation organizations continued to call for more fencing, game law enforcement, leases, and education in 1969, but by then the county had turned the corner.[91] Poaching continued as a crime of opportunity in the county's woods, but it now did so as a violation of local norms and customs rather than as a fulfillment of them.[92] In fact, efforts to restock and restore deer populations were so effective here and across the nation that roadside deer became a major public safety issue by the 1970s. Automobile collisions with deer replaced collisions with cattle as the daily threat to exurban commuters. Unlike cattle, however, deer were much more difficult to fence off.[93]

In spite of these efforts, Montgomery County never lived up to its billing as a sportsman's paradise. Rising land prices and metropolitan proximity worked against this. Rather, the county offered convenience to Houstonians looking for a day in the woods and a pair of antlers to hang on their wall. Money from Houston hunters paid the taxes while landowners prepared to develop their woodlands into bedroom communities and recreational developments. In each case, landowners cashed in on these former timber and agricultural lands by appealing to Houstonians' desire for time among the pines.[94]

What place did foxhunting have in this fenced and privatized woods? Little, if any. As early as the 1960s, the large blocks of land foxhunters required were becoming scarce. Landowners, empowered by the shifts described above, were now quick to complain about dogs trespassing and harassing cattle and deer.[95] In a last-ditch effort to save their sport, foxhunters came out of the shadows and claimed a place among the county's legitimate sportsmen. In March 1964 they formed the Tri-County Fox and Wolf Hunters' Association to provide a sheltered, organized, and community-sanctioned version of the hunt. This new foxhunting organization, which met quarterly on a leased 7,300-acre tract of land near the county's northern border, transformed what had been a semi-clandestine activity into a geographically contained, predictably scheduled, and well-publicized family festival. Foxhunting became a county fair, complete with live music, barbecue, and prominent local figures giving lectures about the history and legacy of foxhunting in the county. The meets drew as many as five hundred people, and membership in the association hit 718 by 1966. Yet this surge of interest had far more to do with the celebration of rural culture and heritage than it did with the sport itself—celebrations of a life lived rather than evidence of future vitality. Residents would find other avenues during this period for celebrating the county's rural heritage, leaving foxhunting to fade into local memory.[96]

❧

The damp coolness of a late October morning in 1976 found "foxhunters" gathered in southern Montgomery County. This time, however, a spectator straining to hear the yelp of hounds would have been disappointed. Past fox-hunts had pitched camp in the pine woods of this area. The hundreds of houses now under construction in The Woodlands, a master planned community, made such meetings impossible. These "foxhunters" met in the parking lot of the Rice Food Market. In the past, the fox had directed the hunt wherever it desired as hounds careened through the woods after it. Such activities were a nuisance in southern Montgomery County by 1976. Now the hunters drove themselves through the woods on paved and gravel roads. Their quarry no longer unpredictably crossed fences and disregarded changing property lines. In fact, it was not a fox at all. It was a citizens band (CB) radio transmitter that these drivers attempted to find—a transmitter that could be placed within tightly drawn legal boundaries of property. The organizers of the Copperhead Gap CB Association Fox Hunting Rally were not attempting to recreate the past glory days of foxhunting. It is doubtful many of the participants in what the group termed a "semi–treasure hunt and sports car rally" knew much about its history in the region. As a bellwether of change, however, CB foxhunting is emblematic of how metropolitan Montgomery County retained and reinterpreted fragments of its backwoods past. The thrill of the chase, the excitement of discovering backcountry roads, and the wooded landscapes remained central to the lifestyle even as the woods themselves continued to change.[97] By the mid-1960s the closing of the range and the resurgence of wildlife populations had set the stage for the Montgomery County woods to become suburban nature—a private amenity for homeowners and their children and pets. These people headed out beyond the crabgrass frontier for more than a larger house or a whiter school district, although both were certainly important. They also moved out in order to experience a more wooded and wild brand of suburbanization that offered the romance of discovery and proximity to wildlife along with suburban amenities. These newcomers inherited the woods from the rural South—a woods that had been transformed in a way that met their expectations of what forests should look like.[98]

From the early 1960s these newcomers had been some of Kincannon's most reliable supporters as he fought to protect wildlife. They joined sportsmen in keeping a watchful eye on backcountry roads and called in tips. Early developments in the area sold the county's recreational attractions and residents' proximity to nature as much as they sold the houses and the proximity to Houston. These nature-seeking residents had a vested interest in protecting wildlife and were largely immune to the social stigma locals attached to whistle blowing. They were often incensed at the destruction of their backyard wildlife.[99] By the 1970s tougher game law enforcement had made such cases rare. The *Courier* kept the mystique of the backwoodsmen alive through stories of moonshine, cockfighting, and poaching, but it did so as folklore rather than news.[100] Developers and their customers increasingly had the luxury of imagining the woods as a place without a history, as nature, in spite of decades of poaching, burning, clear-cutting, and extraction. The county ranked second in the state in the amount of saw timber available for harvest. Many of these trees would now fuel a new local industry, suburban development.[101]

With a historical continuity lost on these newcomers, these exurbanites and their children claimed access to the woods surrounding their homes as part of their suburban lifestyle. Kids roamed and hunted nongame animals on the floodplains, common lands, utility easements, and as-yet-undeveloped spaces that surrounded their suburban enclaves. Coming to the fore in the decade after the crackdown on trespassing and poaching, the suburban woods were never as rigidly defined or stubbornly defended as the rural commons had been. Still, for those who lived there, the woods surrounding their homes provided a secluded playground that remained open to them provided they left game animals unharmed and timber uncut and didn't wander past No Trespassing signs.[102] The suburban woods rested on a critical assumption in parents' minds—that the forest was no longer inhabited. Suburban kids were allowed to roam precisely because the backwoods poacher no longer could. Only a depopulated forest could serve as an informal summer camp for suburban youth. In this way, clearing of the woods enabled the suburban experience of nature that followed it.[103]

This continuity between suburban nature and the backwoods commons is most clear in the history of dogs. Newcomers claimed the right to let their dogs run free. The move to the country was not only to bring children into daily contact with nature but also to free the family pet from the constraints of urban life. Roaming dogs were nothing new in Montgomery County. In fact, across rural America, no rural homestead was complete without a few guard dogs or hunting dogs lounging on the front porch. Nor was the affection shown for these pets new to the area. In East Texas many hounds were just as beloved and spoiled as any suburban pet. What changed with suburbanization was the rapid increase in the population and visibility of these animals as newcomers let them loose in the woods and subdivisions. As with so many of the problems caused by suburbanization, from septic tanks and garbage disposal to water supply and drainage, newcomers' attempts to appropriate a country lifestyle at suburban densities overloaded rural infrastructure and environments. Montgomery County, like most southern counties at the time, had no leash law. Even at the height of the movement for game preservation, no local official would think of antagonizing his constituency by trying to pass such an ordinance. The town of Conroe itself only passed a leash law in 1963 after years of vaccination crackdowns, heated debate, and retaliatory dog poisonings. The county took no such actions. As a result, when suburbanites moved to the "country," they let their dogs roam free.[104]

The result was that suburban dogs did far more damage to wildlife populations and caused more problems than foxhunters ever had. The introduction of suburban dogs into the county's woods combined with the frequent dumping of unwanted dogs in the area by Houstonians created a serious problem for county officials. Two factors made the local dog problem especially acute. The area's mild winters limited the role of the climate in controlling populations. The mixture of poor trash removal facilities, increasing housing densities, and pockets of woodland combined to provide the shelter and food that feral and free-roaming dogs needed to survive. New suburban arrivals did not think about such issues. Like the backwoodsmen who preceded them, these people claimed the woods for their animals to roam. They expected the bonds of ownership to protect their animals, while at the same time they defended the need for dogs to enjoy the freedom to act out their animal instincts. Like the piney-woods rooters that roamed the woods before the closing of the range, these dogs lived much of their lives outside their owners' control. Returning dogs to nature frightened away the very wildlife that suburbanites expected to see in nature.

These roaming dogs proved a thorn in the side of local boosters and county officials. For the organizers of the first annual Robbie Williams Golf Tournament in 1968, roaming dogs were an embarrassment. The tournament, held at the new Panorama golf course north of Conroe, was supposed to position the new suburban development to make a bid for a spot on the PGA tour. Unfortunately for investors, the tournament's most memorable event came while a golfer was setting up a crucial tee shot at the eighteenth hole. After a few practice swings, the man was forced to step back from his ball as a pack of roaming dogs raced across the course, yelping and barking as they ran. Spectators were eventually able to restrain the animals while the golfer took his swing, but the damage to both his concentration and the event's prestige was done. Suburban wildlife of this sort clashed with the popular image of stately deer grazing among the pines.[105]

Roaming dogs damaged more than just the county's image. They posed a very real threat to both wildlife and people, to business, and to public health. These problems became acute by the mid-1970s as the number of subdivisions in southern Montgomery County ballooned. Dogs rummaged through trash bags, dug up flowerbeds, chased residents, and occasionally bit children. The problem was not limited to any one development or social class. Joggers and bikers within the county's wealthier developments carried sticks to fend off dogs. Suburban development brought with it citizen complaints of stray dogs.[106] These complaints landed on the desk of the county's already overwhelmed and underfunded sheriff's department and justice of the peace offices. They in turn passed complaints along to the newly launched county Humane Society, started by town and suburban citizens and now foundering under the workload of responding to between fifteen and twenty calls a day. One dog had upward of thirty complaints against him, with no action taken.[107]

The county commissioners were slow to take up such a heated issue. For every resident adamant about dog control there was someone who was just as adamant about his animal's right to roam. After years of stewing conflict, the commissioners passed a strong rabies control order in March 1979. The law authorized county law enforcement to pick up dogs roaming in packs after complaints had been filed. They refused, however, to pass a leash law or a vaccination law. They also did little to fund enforcement of what they had passed. As the county entered the 1980s, it did so with no real solution to the problem of free-ranging dogs. As local Humane Society president Harry Goetzman put it, "Our control is how many animals can survive the streets. Our shelter is the subdivision." In an ironic twist, then, suburban development in Montgomery County filled the woods with far more roaming and feral dogs than had been there during the days of backwoodsmen and foxhunters. In fact, these new dogs were even less controlled and therefore more of a threat than the hounds or the piney-woods hogs that had gone before.[108]

೮೨

This particular brand of suburban nature was most obvious on the ragged edge of metropolitan development. Yet livestock, game, and timber management each also played a role in the planning, development, and settling of

Houston's premier planned community. The Woodlands, a "new town" located in southern Montgomery County, was the brainchild of Houston oilman George Mitchell. Designed during the peak of environmental activism and urban decay in the early 1970s, The Woodlands promised its customers a sustainable, environmentally friendly alternative to traditional suburban development, as well as a new urbanism that would rein in the problems of white flight. Mitchell's team built a suburban city that would contain over seventy thousand residents on seventeen thousand acres of rural Montgomery County land by the end of the century. This land offered a microcosm of the county's historical land uses and abuses. It bore the marks of timber companies, cotton sharecroppers, oil producers, and backwoodsmen. Mitchell acquired the two largest tracts from timber companies—a 2,800-acre tract he received when he purchased the Grogan-Cochran Lumber Company and the 4,300 acres he acquired from the Champion Paper Company.[109] The rest he assembled from over three hundred smaller tracts, most of which had been worn-out homesteads or cutover timberland that unscrupulous speculators in the 1920s had sold sight unseen to eastern investors.[110] More modern land uses also crisscrossed the land. Oil company pipelines, pumps, and storage tanks broke the silence of the woods. Logging roads led past areas of recent harvest where the forest had begun to reclaim the cutover. These more recent uses sat side by side with ruins from late nineteenth-century cotton production and early twentieth-century timber camps. A few range cattle and hogs, remnants of the thousands who had roamed this land before the stock law, grazed in the clearings on grasses that had themselves been brought to the area by settlers centuries before. These cattle competed for browse with resurgent deer populations, which in turn drew hunters to leases and hunting cabins on the land year after year. These deer hunters themselves had only recently displaced the wide-ranging fox and coon hunters who had dominated the area up until the closing of the range and increased fencing made their roaming nighttime hunts untenable. As late as 1951, The Woodlands' forests had been the site of a field trial by the Montgomery County Coon Hunters Association, a meeting with a high-enough profile to draw hunters and their hounds from outside the state, including a dog owned by actor Roy Rogers. The Woodlands inherited this land from the rural South.[111]

The dense understory and uneven growth of this land represented anything but the climax forest ecosystem of the period's ecology textbooks. Neither were they models of the even-aged management that timber companies and the National Forest Service had embraced. Nor were they the backwoodsmen's ideal, as the area had been relatively untouched by fire. The land's history was entangled with multiple land uses, and its past decades were ones of little management. Mitchell added to this history by contracting with Georgia-Pacific to cut trees over twelve inches in diameter on his Grogan-Cochran land in order to raise money.[112] The woods and their history were in turn shaped by the soil. Nearly one-third of the land lay within the hundred-year floodplains of Panther, Bear, and Spring Creeks. These areas were full of palmetto trees, swamp oaks, water oaks, and magnolias. The remaining lands tended to be sandy and were dominated by pines. Taking the forest's history in hand, The Woodlands' alchemists went to work. They used bulldozers, cement trucks, and ad copy to transform third-growth timber, worn-out cotton fields, hunting lodges, and oil pipelines into wooded nature worth preserving.[113]

Advertising for The Woodlands built on earlier efforts using wildlife conservation to attract Houston money. Where boosters in the 1960s had protected game so it could be hunted, The Woodlands protected game so it could be sighted. It offered a form of backwoods ecotourism, promising its customers that they would "live in harmony with nature"—an urban conceit that would have made little sense to locals. As one reporter described it, The Woodlands did not add natural elements to its development; the development was "hewn out of primeval forests." This meant living among the animals of the forest. The development's head of marketing and sales, James W. Rush, made this explicit in a 1976 interview. Rush waxed eloquent to a reporter about looking out his office window "into a squirrel-filled sylvan Texas forest . . . [where] deer meander up, delightfully besmudging the glass with their nose prints." Rush went on to explain, "I have animals, flora and fauna. The rabbit, the squirrel, the deer. I can look out there at any given time and see a species of bird that I would rarely see anywhere else. This is their natural habitat, their home." In The Woodlands, protecting wildlife was not about recreation. It was about nothing less than undoing man's alienation from nature. Here was nature "close enough to touch."[114]

Providing this harmony with nature required a great deal of management— management that had as much to do with suburban imaginings of nature as it did with local ecology. Planners at The Woodlands understood that, when it came to sales, not all animals were created equal. Few suburban residents had any understanding of the complex interconnections that defined the ecosystem of southeast Texas pine forests. For them, and for The Woodlands' planners, contact with nature meant large populations of four types of animals: white-tailed deer, rabbits, squirrels, and songbirds.[115] These four appeared over and over again in journalistic accounts of the development and in the company's advertisements—the symbols of what it meant to have "nature living close by."[116] Fittingly, the deer populations that were the focus of so much conflict during the 1960s now embodied The Woodlands' images of unspoiled nature. This connection became explicit when the project hired Robert Mae-stro, a Texas A&M University wildlife biologist, to advise them on the best way to manage the woodland's fauna. Given his background, it is not surprising that Maestro's report rehashed the well-worn formulas of game management: ensuring year-round grazing through planting nonnative crops for forage, managing the forest in a way that maximized the amount of edge environ-ments, and providing for managed hunting. These practices, in the case of The Woodlands, would allow for "aesthetic contact" with squirrels, mourning doves, bobwhite quail, and deer—the region's four most popular game spe-cies.[117] Not only were these edge species more likely to be seen by suburbanites looking into the woods from their kitchen windows, but they also offered the possibility of setting up shooting preserves as one of the recreational amenities, something Maestro couldn't help but mention.[118]

Conserving the populations of these species provided another justification for the development's innovative drainage plans, which used existing streams and wetlands to handle the area's flash floods. Leaving floodplains undeveloped ensured the presence of wildlife corridors filled with the hardwood species that suburban fauna preferred. The Woodlands' planners picked up where earlier game management strategies left off, cultivating a suburban environment that maintained the wooded aesthetic and game populations, this time as suburban amenities. Nature did not disappear with suburbanization. Developers and their suburban customers continued to manage the forests to ensure they pro-duced the natural experience these newcomers paid for. These newcomers were the heirs of the closing of the range and the restoration of game populations.

What did The Woodlands' residents do with their inheritance? They joined their neighbors in letting their dogs and children loose in the woods. When planners at The Woodlands discussed ways to keep wildlife populations up, roaming dogs were one of their prime concerns. Within a few years of opening, dog complaints outnumbered all other issues at community meetings within The Woodlands. Laurian Dunkerton, a kind-hearted resident who offered to maintain a local pet registry, found herself swamped with twenty-five to thirty calls a day about roaming and stray animals. For all the talk of the commu-nity's aesthetic beauty and world-class recreational amenities, dog bites and overturned trash cans were a daily hazard in The Woodlands.[119]

Local youth did little better. Montgomery County, because of its surging population and its lack of recreational facilities, had the highest rate of juve-nile delinquency in the state. Many parents moved out of the city to protect their children from delinquent youth, yet these suburban kids weren't all right. Rather than being exempt from the problems of juvenile delinquency, places like The Woodlands were hotbeds of them. Vandalism, theft, and destruction were common as the juvenile delinquent replaced the backwoodsman as the unruly figure in the woods. Suburban freedoms left suburban youth and suburban dogs free to roam and free to destroy.[120] Yet the woods themselves had changed. Timberlands had become forests, deer had replaced hogs, and culs-de-sac now nestled among the pines. Suburban nature had arrived.

CHAPTER 2

Cultivating the Fringe

In Montgomery County, pine forests, crude oil, and bottomland soils provided the raw materials for lumber, oil, cattle, and cotton production and the backwoods landscapes and culture that these nourished. In Loudoun County, rich soils, especially in the western part of the county, sustained a prosperous farm economy that produced dairy, cattle, and wheat within lush agrarian landscapes. These land uses ultimately depended on the vagaries of commodities markets. Across postwar rural America, improved transportation, international competition, and capital-intensive agribusiness and timber industries each altered the economic equation, often pushing local production to the economic margins and leaving these areas with landscapes of rural decay. Proximity to the metropolis offered Montgomery and Loudoun Counties a way of escape from these rural trends. Where their forebears had built their livelihoods on extracting from and cultivating the land, the postwar generation increasingly cultivated the landscape, molding it to appeal to urban desires for the countryside. Agricultural landscapes attracted metropolitan investment and propped up rural land values. Fields and pastures, herds and horses became markers of rural identity and authenticity even as their agricultural productivity became marginal to rural livelihoods. This chapter weaves together the agricultural transformations of both Loudoun County, Virginia, and Montgomery County, Texas, as their residents cultivated the land to cater to the expectations and consumer demands of metropolitan newcomers. In the process, the interplay between popular memory and cultural values, on the one hand, and structural and market forces, on the other, reshaped the use, value, and meaning of the land.

Looking backward from the twenty-first century, two historical narratives predominate in the popular memory of agriculture in Loudoun County, Virginia. The first is a Whiggish tale of progressive, educated, and well-capitalized farmers adopting the latest research and building the finest dairy operations in the state. The second narrative is a tragedy in which farmers cultivated their lush pastures and lovingly managed their dairy herds to produce wholesome milk for urban consumers. These republican yeomen and the rich soils from which they drew their competence had settled too close to the city. As the metropolis expanded, urban people colonized Loudoun, with some moving to the countryside, where they complained about the stench of manure, the noise of tractors, and the flies that buzzed around their backyard barbecues. Others moved to the subdivisions that shot up like red cedars in Eastern Loudoun. These newcomers knew little of farming and the rural world that it supported. They demanded the services they had enjoyed in the city, raising taxes to pay for schools and roads, for traffic lights and sewer lines, and for landfills and police protection. They taxed farmers to provide solutions to problems new residents had themselves created. In the face of this onslaught, some Loudoun farmers stoically abandoned their milking parlors and tractor cabs, selling out to developers and going off into the quiet night of Loudoun's agriculture. Others raged against the dying of their way of life.

Each of these stories has deep resonance in local historical memory. Each influenced debates over farmland preservation and the future of agriculture. The former is the central message of the Loudoun Heritage Farm Museum, which protects and interprets this legacy of progressive agriculture among the county's largely suburban population. The latter dominates among preservation groups, fueling efforts in Western Loudoun to protect the remaining fields and pastures from development. In their broad outlines, these narratives make sense of much of the county's twentieth-century agricultural history. Yet by fixating on a particular model of agriculture (capital-intensive, full-time family farms), each of these narratives obscures the simultaneous formation of metropolitan agriculture and the novel landscapes it supported.

Loudoun County's agricultural inheritance was an enviable one. Agrarian prosperity went as far back as the 1730s, when Quakers settled the rich soils of Western Loudoun. In a state where slave-worked plantations practiced shifting cultivation, Loudoun Quakers developed a system of crop rotations and soil building that enhanced the productivity, value, and look of the land.[1] During the Civil War, Loudoun was part of the breadbasket of the Confederacy. In the years following war and emancipation, diversified commercial farming continued to dominate as farmers supplied Washington and the Potomac Valley with wheat, corn, cattle, horses, and sheep. Farmers had felled the overwhelming majority of Loudoun's deciduous forests to make way for agriculture long before the twentieth century, making rural land in Loudoun essentially synonymous with agricultural land. Because its climate and soils were similar to land farmed in many parts of the North, Loudoun farmers adopted many of the progressive cultivation and horticultural methods coming out of northern agricultural clubs and later land-grant universities.

Agricultural prosperity meant that nineteenth- and early twentieth-century Loudoun never attracted the rural industries that were the economic lifeblood of so many rural southern counties. Because of its geology and history of settlement, the county contained strong regional variation. The areas west of Leesburg, most notably within the Loudoun Valley, which ran north to south from the Potomac down through Western Loudoun, were blessed with some of the finest soils along the eastern seaboard. These soils attracted Quaker settlement from Pennsylvania and ultimately supported a more densely populated countryside. Eastern Loudoun, with its poorer soils and history of slavery, had more in common with the rest of the southern Piedmont. In spite of these differences, general prosperity continued into the twentieth century. In the 1920s the county ranked first in the state in corn production and in yields per acre. It was sixth in the number of hogs and fourth in the value of its dairy products. County farmland was both intensively managed and highly productive, making the county fourth in total farm wealth. Agriculture pervaded the county, with roughly three-quarters of its acreage in improved farmland—the highest ratio in the state. Loudoun's agricultural prosperity was widely distributed, with family farms of fewer than two hundred acres dominating. Only one-quarter of these were run by tenants.[2]

Loudoun farmers were some of the first in the state to purchase tractors, automobiles, and binders; to develop and adopt new pasture and feed crops and animal breeds; and to adapt to changing agricultural markets. Where so many farmers across the South were crushed under the wheels of agricultural progress, locals kept their balance atop these wheels, reaping substantial profits as they kept pace with ever-intensifying agricultural practice.[3] Their proximity to the nation's capital fueled the rise of the county's most profitable agriculture sector: commercial dairy farming. That local industry emerged before the turn of the century, peaked just as federal planners were laying down their first sketches of Dulles Airport, and entered its well-publicized twilight as the county population tipped toward a suburban majority in the 1980s. The dairy industry admittedly never accounted for a majority of local farms, yet it attracted the most progressive and capital-intensive farmers. As a technologically sophisticated enterprise, dairy farming exemplifies the interplay between changes within agricultural industry and the transformations wrought by metropolitan expansion. Each impelled local dairy farmers to intensify their businesses, adapt to changing conditions, and, ultimately, sell out.[4]

Railroad access allowed a few enterprising farmers to begin selling cream and butter to Washington in the 1870s. Fluid milk production expanded around the turn of the century, when former Wall Street lawyer and Virginian native Westmoreland Davis took it upon himself to transform the state into the Wisconsin of the South. Davis refashioned his twelve-hundred-acre Morven Park estate in Leesburg into a showcase for the latest breeds, implements, and practices. He took the lead in organizing the Virginia Dairyman's Association in 1907 to disseminate the latest agricultural research and practice to the state's dairy farmers and to promote the industry's interests in Richmond, securing the creation of the Dairy and Food Division in Virginia, which regulated the sale of milk, ensuring that Loudoun farmers who invested in new technologies and more productive herds would be protected from the devastating impact other farmers' contaminated milk could have on their sales. Beginning in 1910, the lord of Morven Park initiated the county's first farm extension programs. Having heard the gospel of progressive agriculture, many responded in faith. In 1911 progressive dairy farmers formed the Loudoun Valley Cow Testing Association to maintain production records and thereby ensure that their feed was going to only the most productive cattle. They formed the Loudoun County Breeders Association in 1916 to develop more productive herds. They imported purebred bulls from overseas, first Guernsey and then, beginning in the 1930s, Holstein. By the end of World War I, milk going into Washington had one of the lowest rates of bovine tuberculosis in the nation. Between 1900 and 1920 milk sales from Virginia rose from $1.8 million to $19 million even as the number of dairy cows declined from 281,876 to 140,368. On September 21, 1920, dairy farmers from across Washington's hinterland formed the Maryland and Virginia Milk Producers' Association, a marketing cooperative. Within a decade it had become the largest milk producer in the state. Northern Virginia was home to an efficient, highly capitalized, technologically progressive dairy industry.[5]

What is most striking in this story is how many of these dairy farmers, not to mention their cattle and expertise, were newcomers. Virginia's best and brightest agrarians brought their talent to Loudoun County. There they joined commuters and gentlemen farmers—prosperous and educated men who took up farming as a modern business and, in some cases, as a leisure pursuit.[6] The industry's success also lured owners of the county's struggling orchards and poultry farms to switch to dairy production.[7] Success bred success as Loudoun attracted the best university-trained farmers and production specialists. Loudoun dairy farmers adopted electric milking machines and refrigeration when they first became available in the mid-1930s. The same was true for artificial insemination by 1946. They adopted tractors, combines, hay balers, and corn pickers. Their pastures were filled with alfalfa, orchard grass, and other high-yield hay popularized early in the twentieth-century Midwest. A grant from foxhunter-philanthropist Paul Mellon, son of the former secretary of the treasury Andrew Mellon, established the Middleburg Forage Research Station in 1949 to provide farmers with the latest in pasture research tailored to their particular soils and climate. Loudoun dairy farmers had deep pockets, often substantial educations, extensive support networks, and easily accessible urban markets. They used these advantages to their fullest.[8]

Proximity to Washington made this dairy industry possible. National government policy, transportation technology, and market forces had divided dairy production into two distinct rings. Inner-ring farmers delivered fresh fluid milk, a higher-value product, to urban consumers. Outer-ring farmers sold their lower-grade milk to creameries and cheese factories. Because of their higher costs of production and higher potential payouts, fluid milk farms had larger herds and more machinery and required more nonfamily labor. Such farms dominated in neighboring Fairfax County during the interwar period and expanded within Loudoun soon after. The same roads that introduced rural folk to the pleasures of town life in the 1920s also, with the adoption of milk trucks, untethered dairy farms from railroad lines. The adoption of bulk tanks and bulk trucks in the 1950s decreased the time and labor it took to bring milk to market and thereby extended the city's fluid milkshed farther into Loudoun County. At the same time, suburban growth in Fairfax was pressuring dairy farmers to sell out and move westward. As early as 1951, these trends left Loudoun with the most grade-A dairies in Virginia (282) and the greatest value of dairy products sold. Loudoun's dairy industry was the heir to a Fairfax industry squeezed out by suburban development. Thus an ominous cloud hung over the dairy boom of the 1950s and 1960s. In the fall of 1961, even as suburban development loomed, Loudoun was one of the state's most prosperous agricultural counties. The dairy industry that squared off against suburban expansion was dynamic and prosperous, capital intensive and technologically sophisticated. Yet Loudoun's dairy industry was bound to Washington, D.C., and its suburbs. Urban milk money underwrote Loudoun's fields and farms. As the metropolis grew, urban developers increasingly looked to those green fields to supply a more direct form of urban consumption.[9]

Thirty years later, the number of dairies remaining in Loudoun County could be counted on one hand. As of 2008 only one remained.[10] Oral histories of farmers recorded by the Loudoun Heritage Farm Museum in the late 1990s and early 2000s reveal the impact suburban development had on the community of memory surrounding agricultural decline. The metropolis looms large. Images of suburban sprawl gobbling up acreage, developers turning quick profits, and assessors driving up tax appraisals overshadowed the more mundane cost-price squeeze that slowly crushed the local farm economy. Their Pandora's box moment was the construction of Dulles Airport, which opened in 1962. The site directly claimed some six thousand acres of farmland. Many of the remaining Eastern Loudoun dairy farmers sold out for large sums of money to speculators. Looking back, the farmers spoke of the opening of the airport as a cataclysm. Curtis Laycock explained, "Things started changing when they put the airport in. . . . The dairy farms started going out in Eastern Loudoun . . . and they just went out like flies. Land values increased. . . . The land values escalated so rapidly after they put that airport in down there they just got swallowed up, you know. And it just came right on up." Looking back from 2002, Laycock summed up fifty years of Loudoun history in that one sentence: "And it just came right on up." When asked how farming had changed in the county, Bob Grubb responded by laying out a line of causation that tied the opening of the airport to the sprawling developments of twenty-first-century Western Loudoun. The airport brought with it high-tech businesses and their overpaid employees. These people could "home on a chunk of nice farmland and they build an enormous mansion. . . . And farmers can be like anybody else. They might be inclined to want that money for their land, so they can sell it off." Another farmer simply explained, "Dulles Airport came in," and that exposed "one of the problems with farming in Loudoun County . . . that we're so close to the metropolitan area." The proximity that had made dairy farming possible was now agrarian Loudoun's Achilles' heel. Edwin Potts remembered, "I was [at Dulles] for the dedication and I stood right in front of John F. Kennedy when he was up there on stage dedicating the airport. . . . That was the end, basically the beginning of the end of agriculture in Loudoun County." County extension agent William Harrison, invoking Caesar's crossing of the Rubicon, explained that "the die was cast when the airport came in here." These farmers saw themselves as victims of forces beyond their control. The federal government placed its airport in Eastern Loudoun, and all a man could do was sell out.[11]

Dulles Airport certainly forced out many Eastern Loudoun dairy farmers. But these Eastern Loudoun dairy farms were hardly robust and healthy to begin with. The postwar decades had been hard on that part of the county. Its soils had always been poorly drained and relatively infertile. Proximity, not productivity, had made these farms profitable. By the 1960s bulk tanks and trucks had eroded their competitive advantage, as Western Loudoun farms could produce milk for the same markets more efficiently. These business realities led many of these Eastern Loudoun farmers to support development.[12] For Western Loudoun dairy farmers, the airport's initial impacts were more subtle. The cows had to be milked twice a day, every day, making Loudoun farmers dependent on day laborers and tenants. These workers were increasingly difficult to find. Edwin Potts remembered, "People started going down there and going to work, and when that happens the farm help is gone." Henry Stowers explained, "There is no farm labor anymore. If you could find somebody, you couldn't afford to pay them a decent wage." Difficulty keeping children and laborers down on the farm was nothing new in rural America. Loudoun's population had remained stagnant from 1860 to the 1950s in spite of in-migration because rural children had left the farm to seek their fortunes elsewhere. Even with German POWs mitigating the labor problem, shortages during World War II accelerated farm consolidation and mechanization. With the end of the war, laborers continued to chase job opportunities in the metropolis. Dulles compounded this problem.[13]

As the number of dairy farms declined, it became more difficult to maintain the service infrastructure required to keep dairy farms running. Agricultural suppliers, veterinary services, herd-testing services, milk haulers, and repairmen also lost customers. As these supporting companies went out of business, dairy farmers had to travel longer and longer distances for basic services. Suburban newcomers, for their part, often brought a more direct type of conflict. As former extension agent William Harrison explained, these homeowners "say they want the bucolic look of Loudoun County and they want to keep the agriculture, but they won't give you the time of day to take a piece of machinery up the road or spray something." Loudoun farmers increasingly felt like strangers in their own land.[14] They saw themselves as highly successful agrarians who knew their business and yet were unable to keep up with the economic pressures from development. "How can you afford to farm land as valuable as land is in Loudoun County?" one farmer asked. "You just can't do it." Under such pressures, developers proved an easy target for farmers' anger. When asked what caused the decline of agriculture in the county, one farmer answered in one word: "greed." James Hamilton explained the process as one where, beginning in the 1960s, "developers come in and run the farmers out." Such sentiments would lead some to join a slow-growth Western Loudoun political coalition. For most farmers, however, the slow-growth movement was too little, too late. Bob Grubb summed up the frustrations of many when he explained, "I'm not a retired farmer. There's no retirement to it. I'm a quit farmer. That's the title that I have accepted."[15]

With all this attention on the airport and suburban development, farmers' narratives rarely connected their perilous situation to rapid changes within the industry. An entirely new milk distribution system took shape in the postwar years in which supermarkets replaced milk deliverymen and paper cartons replaced glass milk bottles. When combined with refrigerated bulk-tank trucks, these changes nationalized milk markets and thereby weakened the ties of proximity that had bound dairy farms to the city. Thus, even as the costs of dairy production on the metropolitan fringe ballooned, the economic benefits of proximity declined. The industry increasingly favored industrialized, confined feeding operations in which large dairy herds, usually over two hundred

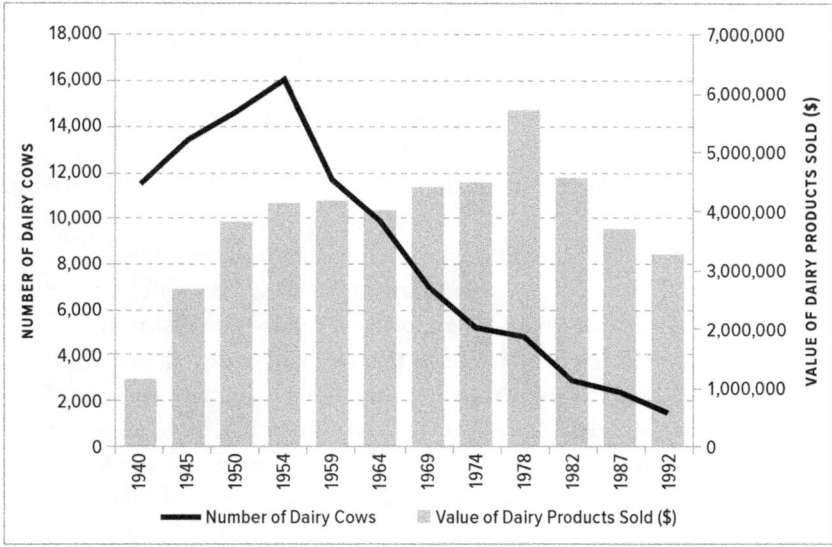

Dairy production in Loudoun.
U.S. Census of Agriculture, vol. 1, pt. 24, county tables 3 (1945), 7.1 (1954), 10 and 12 (1964), and 8 (1969), and pt. 46, county tables 12.2 (1974), 3 and 11 (1982), and 14.2 (1992).

animals, were fed grain and hay that arrived by truck rather than from nearby pastures and fields. In exchange for economies of scale, these operations generated concentrated wastes. Such environmental externalities and economic incentives pushed these operations from the metropolitan fringe out into more isolated rural areas. The landscapes that confined feeding operations created were worlds apart from the pastoral images that had defined Loudoun County and now graced the dairy cartons in the local produce aisle.[16]

Loudoun farmers faced the challenges common to all American farmers in the postwar years. Mechanization, improved transportation, school consolidation, farm consolidation, increased capital costs, regional specialization, the decline of home production, and the exodus of farm children all played out on this local stage.[17] In an effort to stay afloat, Loudoun's most progressive dairy farms focused on their competitive advantage in breeding, producing some of the finest Holsteins in the country. Breeding allowed dairy and cattle farmers to leverage their expertise and industry connections to continue to turn a profit without major changes in their production. This option was outside the reach of most dairy farmers.[18]

The next generation's rejection of farming proved the last straw for many operations. Few farm children were willing to take on the long hours, hard work, crushing debt, and uncertainty of the business, and few Loudoun farmers were willing to wish such a life on their children. Farmland became a retirement investment rather than a legacy to pass on. Rising corn prices in the late 1970s were a temptation too strong for many local dairy farmers, who sold their dairy equipment, put their land in corn, and slept in until dawn for the first time in decades. Industry consolidation culminated in a sharp decline in milk prices from 1975 to 1980 and a federally funded dairy buyout program in 1985, both of which convinced the handful of remaining dairy farmers to cash out.[19]

Jim Brownell's story exemplifies the interplay between these forces in transforming Loudoun's agricultural economy. Brownell and his wife, Mac, chose life on a dairy farm. The grandson of northern Pennsylvania farmers, Jim was born in Washington, D.C. His visits to the family farm during the Great Depression allowed him to enjoy the freedoms and contact with nature of farm life without its drudgery. As he put it, "I was a city boy, no question about that, but every summer I went up to . . . the old family farm, and then I decided I wanted to be outside." After attending the University of Maryland and serving in World War II, he married and spent several years learning the dairy trade while Mac commuted to her job at the FBI headquarters. After searching all across the metropolitan area, they found a seven-hundred-acre estate in Western Loudoun whose owner was willing to lower the price for a young family starting out. Jim and Mac Brownell began farming there in 1959, even as the condemnation letters went out for Dulles Airport. Jim Brownell stayed abreast of agricultural innovation. He had a degree in animal husbandry and had done master's degree work in animal breeding. He rented land across the county and fed his cattle on alfalfa hay he raised himself. He was no romantic, but he maintained a strong attachment to the land. He recalled, "You get a lot of personal satisfaction out of watching your animals grow and watching your crops grow. Like making a beautiful bale of hay or having a good looking crop of corn or a cow that does real well. . . . That's good." Brownell would become a leading voice for farmers coping with suburban growth as president of the Loudoun County Farm Bureau and eventually as a member of the county board of supervisors. From these positions, Brownell embodied southern rural conservatism. He fought to keep taxes low, to limit the expansion of county services, and to slow suburban development.[20]

By the 1980s increasing overhead costs and debt service made holding on to the farm difficult. After decades managing a herd that peaked at 170 dairy cows, Brownell now faced the dimming prospects of passing the farm on to his kids. The oldest son moved to Virginia Beach. Their daughter, Susan's "greatest ambition was to get away from the farm." Their second son, Bruce, also rejected the farm life: "He was born and raised on a dairy farm and he's never milked a cow." He chose instead to become a local developer, spending his energy cultivating subdivisions. The other two sons, Mark and Scott, both put in their time on the farm but eventually left as well. "They got disgusted with all the working and all the hours," Brownell recalled, "and the last one to leave, Scotty, he ran the thing for a while because I was involved in politics. . . . He had finally told [Mac] one day that he just couldn't take it anymore. He just had to quit. The last boy quit, and we left." Mac and Jim seemed resigned to their children's choices. When asked if he hoped one of his children would have stayed on the farm, Brownell replied, "Pretty hard to wish that on them. It's hard to make money farming. . . . You'd like the boys to be farmers, but the figures don't work out." The Brownell family sold out in 1991 but continued to live in the county.[21]

ↂ

An altogether different agricultural regime dominated in Montgomery County, Texas. The postcard image of this, if anyone had bothered to make it, would have shown a lean, grizzled man wearing patched overalls and holding the reins of a gaunt horse, setting off into the piney woods with his hounds to manage his roaming herds of tick-covered cows and semiferal hogs. Another postcard image would have depicted a weather-beaten sharecropper pausing to remove his straw hat and wiping the sweat and dust off his brow before trudging along behind his mule as it plowed the sandy soil in front of his sagging tenant shack. These two images characterized Depression era agriculture across East Texas. As with Loudoun, changes in markets, technology, and production methods made this rural world economically untenable by the 1980s. The backwoodsman and his free-ranging cattle had no place in this new agricultural dispensation. Working in concert with the closing of the woods, landowners took scrub cattle out of the forests and placed them on managed fields. Their shift to pastures, purebred cattle, and registered quarter horses supported the new lifestyle, symbols, and values of the ranch. It propelled the development of a rural social and cultural world in which hobby farming, recreation, and show animals loomed larger than commodity production. This transformation at times reinforced and at times propelled the county's reputation as a home for part-time ranchers, equestrian enthusiasts, and suburbanites looking for a few acres in the country. Newcomers joined locals in casting off the trappings of southern farming and cattle raising. A pure-blooded steer, proudly standing in a lush, green pasture, with a 4-H award and a registered pedigree, a corral behind him, and a pine forest in the distance: this was the aspiration of the county's newest agriculturalists.[22] Cotton fields and cutover pinelands became ranchlands. Montgomery County would become western.

Across the nation, western style and culture reached its cultural zenith

Depression-era cotton agriculture, Montgomery County, Texas.
Courtesy of the Heritage Museum of Montgomery County, Texas.

Depression-era cattle herding, Montgomery County, Texas.
Courtesy of the Heritage Museum of Montgomery County, Texas.

during the 1950s and early 1960s. Western storylines dominated radio and television, pulp novels and Sunday matinees. Cowboy singers climbed the billboard charts. Dude ranching, rodeos, theme parks, and western fashion all exploded in popularity. The cowboy image had strong political currency. Its popularity fueled the rise of national figures like John Wayne, Barry Goldwater, and Ronald Reagan and suffused the dynamic conservative political culture that these men inspired. This collective American myth reaffirmed masculinity and white privilege during a time of Cold War uncertainty and racial tension.[23] For southeast Texas counties, the national popularity of cowboy symbolism and mythology during the Cold War was a locally useful heritage that might cloak the region's southern historical roots, social structures, and power relations under a veil of western nostalgia. In the era of the civil rights movement, national popular opinion associated southern identity with bigotry, ignorance, and social backwardness. In contrast, the cowboy symbolized American individualism, personal freedom, and martial strength. The first was a liability to a nation positioning itself as a global champion of freedom and democracy. The second became a powerful national myth and the symbolic foundation of an ascendant Sunbelt conservatism. Locally, "going Texan" was a means to sell the county to prospective residents and to forge common ground within metropolitan rural communities in transition.[24]

In Montgomery County, western symbols and narratives helped to define the county's position within the expanding metropolis. Historians have long recognized the role urban economic centers have played in reshaping the environments of their hinterlands. Less appreciated is the extent to which cities have shaped the rural culture and identity of their hinterlands.[25] Montgomery County residents crafted a western identity as part of their broader engagement with the metropolis. Rural landowners turned to progressive agriculture and ranching in the post-Depression years both as a way to wring more profits from their land without the hassle of tenants and as a status symbol. They did so with the guidance and cooperation of Houston's agricultural business leaders and the participation of Houston ranch owners. The cultural celebration of ranch life that these changes supported followed a similar pattern. Montgomery County awoke to discover its westernness only when area ranchers with strong ties to Houston brought the celebration of the Houston Livestock Show and Rodeo to the county. Going Texan united small-town and rural residents with suburban and exurban newcomers around a celebration of a particular metropolitan fringe lifestyle. Their children led them through equestrian events, 4-H projects, and the county fair. Like suburban expansion itself, this rural lifestyle was ostensibly color-blind. Like the conservative politics that dominated Sunbelt suburbs in the 1960s and 1970s, it reaffirmed white masculinity, the value of hard work, and the nuclear family.[26] Houston's money, its agricultural leadership, and its cultural gravity accelerated and channeled the development of Montgomery County's rural landscapes into a metropolitan fringe enclave whose residents simultaneously drew much of their culture from the city and defined their lifestyle in opposition to it.

This western identity was, it is true, only one of the popular images of Houston swirling around the city during the 1960s. Houstonians also celebrated their city as a space age metropolis: the home of the Astrodome and NASA's Manned Spacecraft Center. Corporate growth, a powerful business elite, and a vibrant port made Houston a thriving center of commerce and, increasingly, a global city. Migrants from the Deep South and Latin America also continued to place their cultural stamp on the city, driving social conflict across lines of race and ethnicity. Yet for Houston's cultural hinterland, the western image remained the dominant vision of the city, from the ranchers who made Houston one of the nation's busiest cattle markets, to the suburbanites who rode horses on the weekends, to the wildcat oilmen who wore Stetson hats and cowboy boots because they liked the way they let them swagger. The Houston Livestock Show and Rodeo has continued to perpetuate this image into the twenty-first century.

Montgomery County's agricultural economy before World War II was anything but western. Except for a brief fling with specialty tobacco production, some small-scale truck crops, and a few scattered dairies, county farmers endured an often bitter relationship with short-staple cotton production, cattle raising, and timber harvesting.[27] More prosperous landowners followed the southern system of tenancy and sharecropping common across the cotton South. Others grew cotton to supplement the wages from their rural industrial work at sawmills and oil wells. For these marginal producers, the patch of white bolls behind the tenant cabin or homestead often meant the difference between debt and solvency, despair and a sliver of economic hope. The rock-bottom prices and government programs of the 1930s and the wartime labor shortages of the 1940s combined to weaken cotton's hold in Montgomery County. Only 5 percent of the county's land area (a fifth of the county's farm acreage) was in any kind of row crop in 1934.[28] A 1949 study of the county's African American farm families revealed that fewer than half still grew cotton. Those who did averaged only 10 acres and produced less than a third of a bale per acre. County farms harvested, on average, only 26.7 acres of crops.[29] Three-fifths of black farmers worked off the farm for a substantial part of their income, and 80 percent of black families were dependent on some component of the timber industry for their cash income.[30] The declining role of cotton meant that, for the county's poor, agriculture was a supplemental activity.[31]

The results of the county's century-long relationship with cotton and ex-tractive rural industry draw a striking contrast with Loudoun: worn-out soils, empty pocketbooks, and unhealthy people. Schools were ill-equipped, trans-portation was difficult, racism was pervasive, soils were deeply eroded, and off-farm labor was dangerous, unreliable, and not unionized. Pellagra and alcohol-ism were endemic to the countryside. The only comfort on the public health front was that obesity replaced malnourishment as a major health concern beginning in the 1960s. These were the wages of a grinding rural economy that offered tenants and small landholders little hope of a better life. More prosper-ous white landholders, the owners and managers of extractive industries, and those blessed with oil under their land carved out decent lives for themselves. The rest rightly viewed rural life in the county as something to escape. This is exactly what many did.[32]

By the end of World War II, cotton had reached a dead end in the county. Poor soils made the kind of consolidation and mechanization that character-ized the new cotton agriculture economically infeasible.[33] The rural labor force abandoned the countryside to seek jobs in the growing economy of Houston. These migrants did not permanently break the ties that bound them to the county, at least not at first. Their extended families often retained their home-stead as a place of refuge, even as they entered the metropolitan labor market. Montgomery County contributed its share of the rural out-migration that defined so much of southern demographics from the 1920s to the 1960s. From 1940 to 1950 Texas farms had an astounding net out-migration of 45.6 percent, or more than 910,000 people. From 1950 to 1956 there was a net loss of an ad-ditional 276,000 farmers. The highest out-migration rates were in East Texas among the rural landless who had the least to lose. Between 1940 and 1945 the number of farms in Montgomery County dropped 41 percent: from 2,296 to 1,356. The amount of cotton grown dropped just as precipitously. White land-owners used Agricultural Adjustment Administration funds to further shift production from cotton, accelerating the out-migration. By 1955 local farms had a total of only 1,367 acres in cotton.[34]

The decline of cotton's profitability, the out-migration of labor, and mar-ginal soils sent landowners in search of alternative uses for their acreage. They found it in cattle. Modern cattle ranching offered landowners relatively steady returns, improved soils, and cultural prestige without the management issues that went with cotton tenancy. This move was not without precedent. Open-range cattle had a long history in the county. The animals produced by this system, however, were scrub breeds that, while hardy enough to survive in the piney woods, earned their owners little profit. The elimination of Texas fever through federal cattle-dipping programs in the 1920s removed a significant

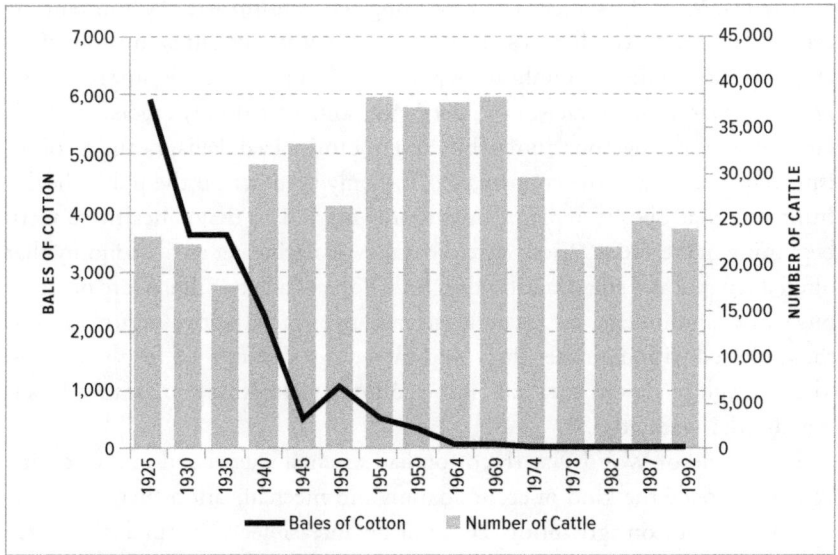

Cotton and cattle production in Montgomery County, Texas.
U.S. Census of Agriculture, vol. 1, pt. 37, county tables 2 and 3 (1935), 2 and 3 (1945),
7 and 9 (1954), 10 and 13 (1964), 8 and 14 (1969), and pt. 43, county tables 12 and 25 (1974),
11 and 25 (1982), and 13 and 14 (1992).

obstacle to more intensive cattle production in the county.[35] The end of the
open range in 1956 removed another by protecting purebred cattle and improved pastures from encroachment by scrub cattle. County landowners
started to realize that, as one local put it, "it is a lot easier to raise cattle than
to farm, and better money too."[36]

Over the following two decades, the farmers who remained in Montgomery County adopted the business practices, the production methods, and the
culture of cattle ranching. In doing so, they transformed much of the county's
landscape and tied themselves more closely to Houston. Landowners and
businessmen from both sides of the urban/rural divide developed parts of
the piney woods into a reflection of neighboring Harris County's pastured
landscapes. The East Texas Chamber of Commerce and the Houston Farm
and Ranch Club were central to this process. Faced with postwar declines in
the number of farms and farmers within its member counties, the chamber
launched the Rural Progress Program in 1952 and the Build East Texas Program
in 1963. Both traced the area's agricultural failings to failures in farm management. Their solution was to ignore laborers and tenants and to teach white
landowners to improve their marketing, expand their conservation practices,
increase production, and streamline their management.[37]

The Houston Farm and Ranch Club was an important ally in this cause.

Houston-area ranchers and agribusiness leaders founded the Farm and Ranch Club as an offshoot of the Houston Chamber of Commerce Agricultural Committee in 1947.[38] Houston's business culture embraced ranching as a status symbol, and many in Houston's business community owned property in the surrounding counties. The city's elite circles, therefore, showed a concern for the health of the ranching industry over and above its economic possibilities.[39] Within a year the Farm and Ranch Club had grown from seven members to thirteen hundred. The group fit squarely within the tradition of scientific agricultural improvement. Montgomery County's extension agent, George Clyburn, and Dick and Fred Nutter, local agribusiness leaders, were on the board of directors.[40]

Montgomery County landowners joined this tight-knit agribusiness community. Some local businessmen used their ranching interests to strengthen their social connections in Houston. Jack Clarke was one example. The owner of a 7-Up bottling company in Conroe, Clarke poured his free time into purebred cattle, establishing himself as a Hereford judge and breeder. He eventually took up prominent positions in the metropolitan ranching scene, spending time as the chairman of the board of the Houston Hereford Club, a director of the Houston Livestock Show, and a member of the East Texas Chamber of Commerce Agriculture Committee. Ranching was a means for county elites like Clarke to enter metropolitan power networks. At the same time, Houston businessmen bought up, managed, and restored properties in the county, giving them a stake in its agricultural development.[41]

These ties brought the Houston Farm and Ranch Club's focus to Montgomery County. In cooperation with area extension agents and agricultural specialists from Texas A&M University, the organization held workshops, field days, and farm demonstrations at Montgomery County ranches on the latest agricultural methods and crops. The club's most significant involvement was in the introduction of improved pastures. Farm and Ranch worked with the East Texas Chamber of Commerce to sponsor pasture tours, develop new pasture management programs, and import improved pasture plant varieties. In one instance, they purchased twenty-five tons of crimson clover seed in Alabama and had it trucked in for club members. The Farm and Ranch Club touted the achievements of the most progressive ranches in the area, stamping its seal of approval on these operations and encouraging others in the area to follow suit. It brought in the seeds and disseminated the knowledge needed to transform Montgomery County's agricultural land.[42]

The environmental barriers to increased productivity were substantial. The temperate climate and rich, basic soils of Loudoun County allowed its farmers to adopt highly productive cool-weather forage crops like alfalfa, timothy, and

orchard grass. The hot and humid climate and more acidic soils that characterized Montgomery County and much of the Deep South required the breeding
and introduction of specially adapted forage species, a process that only began
in earnest after the turn of the twentieth century.[43] Improved pastures were
the keystone of modern cattle ranching. They promised decreased erosion,
greater farm profits, and lower labor costs. Fulfilling these promises required
more than just sprinkling some grass seed on worn-out cotton fields. Modern
ranching took capital, expertise, and machinery. Ranchers first removed scrub
trees and underbrush and then graded, plowed, and disked the land. They then
planted legumes, mainly clovers and species of *Lespedeza*, and fertilized heavily
with phosphorus and lime to raise the soil pH. Once the soil was ready, ranchers had their laborers sprig Bermuda grass or, beginning around 1957, Coastal
Bermuda.[44] Rural landowners maintained control over the local agricultural
education agencies and therefore ensured that their operations would benefit
most from these production changes. Government soil conservation programs,
administered through the local Agricultural Stabilization and Conservation
Service, offered matching grants to subsidize the construction of stock ponds
and the conversion of worn-out cropland or poorly managed forest into improved pasture.[45]

Across East Texas, cattle owners converted land into improved pastures.
In 1949 East Texans planted 177,600 acres, bringing the total acreage in the
region to 712,750. Ranchers in Montgomery and Waller Counties had improved 61,747 acres by 1961. This figure reached 148,000 of the two counties'
211,536 acres of pasture by 1969.[46] Along with new pastures came cattle breeds
that could convert these new sources of protein into marketable weight gain.
Hereford, Angus, and Brahman cattle replaced piney woods breeds, providing increased returns on investment and enabling ranchers to keep pace with
national production trends. With intensive management, yearly fertilizing, a
decent water supply, and a substantial up-front investment, they could realize
greater profitability in both their business and the look and relative health
of their land.[47] Improved pastures allowed grazing for 250 to 280 days a year.
Unimproved county pastures could support an animal unit for every 8.2 acres.
By the late 1950s county ranchers on improved bottomlands averaged around
one animal for every four acres.[48]

Each agricultural commodity carries with it its own distinct cultural and
social world and its own criteria for mastery and achievement. Cattle ranching
was no different. Improved pastures meant higher profits. They also allowed
landowners to claim a new identity as progressive ranchers. Beginning in 1963,
county and regional hay shows sparked strong competition among these landowners as each tried to outdo the others to produce the most nutritious hay.[49]

COASTAL BERMUDA GRASS

PLANTING

Best time to plant coastal Bermuda is in the spring when the soil is warm and moist. Some fall and winter plantings have been successful. Plant stolons in three foot rows, 18 inches apart, either by hand or with a machine.

FERTILIZING

On sandy or loamy soil apply fertilizer in a 3-1-2 ratio for average yields. For irrigated coastal meadow or pasture, apply fertilizer in a 4-1-2 ratio, after each cutting or when cattle are removed for pasture to recover.

Planting coastal Bermuda grass, 1959.
Newsletter, March 1959, folder Newsletters, 1955–59, Walker County SWCD.

Dozens of county ranchers would stake their reputations and their pride on the results of protein tests from Texas A&M University labs. To keep pace with the cattle business in Montgomery County required money, energy, flexibility, education, and land. Adopting new methods proved too much for many conservative ranchers and farmers used to running piney woods cattle in timbered pastures. Extension agent Morris Straughn remembered: "Everybody had to change their whole thinking mode" to stay in business.[50] Improved ranching also meant a new dependence on implement dealers, fertilizer companies, seed providers, and cattle breeders that did not sit well with the old guard. The new agriculture underwrote the persistence of local rural elites. Ranching ran the gamut from a part-time hobby to a full-time job.[51] Ranching paid the bills that came with large-scale landownership in a county with ever-increasing property values. Ranching also gave men like county commissioner Bo Damuth and county judge W. S. Weisinger the time, resources, social connections, management skills, and economic freedom they needed to immerse themselves in county politics. For these men, ranching was as much about status, lifestyle, and local power as it was about agriculture. In Montgomery County, political power and agriculture went hand in hand.[52]

The experience of one prominent Montgomery County family, the Browders, offers an example of this. Judge William Bridges Browder was born in Waverly, Texas, north of Willis, in 1883. A country boy, he eventually earned a law degree and served as a county attorney. After a brief stint working in

Houston during the Great Depression, he returned to Montgomery County to run hogs on the open range and to serve as the district judge of the ninth circuit court. His sons John and Bridges followed in their father's footsteps. In 1947 they started the Browder Brothers Jersey Farm, a progressive operation that boasted the finest dairy cows in the county. The brothers were highly active in supporting local agricultural organizations and kept up with the latest methods. They did so as part-time farmers and ranchers. Bridges spent the bulk of his time in the real estate business in the county, including transferring lakefront land to developers. At different times he served as president of the county Board of Realtors, the local chamber of commerce, and the county planning commission. He also served as president of the South Texas Jersey Cattle Club. His brother, John, worked for twenty-seven years as a research chemist for Humble Oil while also acting as a senior partner in the dairy and serving on various dairymen clubs.[53]

This transition into modern agriculture was much more difficult for those not blessed with the privileges of whiteness. Across the South, government-sponsored agricultural programs, county extension agents, and local farm organizations reinforced local racial hierarchies in distributing aid to white landowners.[54] Montgomery County was no different. A century of racism and exploitation combined with the agricultural difficulties common to all small-scale farmers in the region to limit the options for these farmers. By 1949 only 8 percent of black farmers had over thirty head of livestock, and none had fifty. It was a rare African American farmer who had the resources to attempt the transition into modern ranching.[55] Yet at the same time black laborers did much of the labor that it took to convert the county's ranches to improved pastures. The only black faces that peered out from the quarterly reports of the local soil conservation district were those of laborers. These pictures showed African Americans planting the fields with Bermuda grass sprigs, ensuring the prosperity of white landowners who had access to improved pastures, chemical fertilizers, herbicides, and tractors.[56]

It is little wonder, then, that the vast majority of county blacks left the land for work in Houston. The proportion of black farmers in the county declined precipitously after World War II. African Americans made up almost a quarter of farmers in 1940. This figure declined to 17 percent by 1950 and 10 percent by 1959. By 1969 only 5 percent of the county's diminishing farm population was black. Black families that left their homesteads saw their lands fall into decay, carved up by tax liens and inheritance, and sold off by a next generation that had no ties to the land.[57]

An East Texas businessman summarized the postwar changes in the region: "Yankees have moved South; Negroes have moved North; cotton has moved

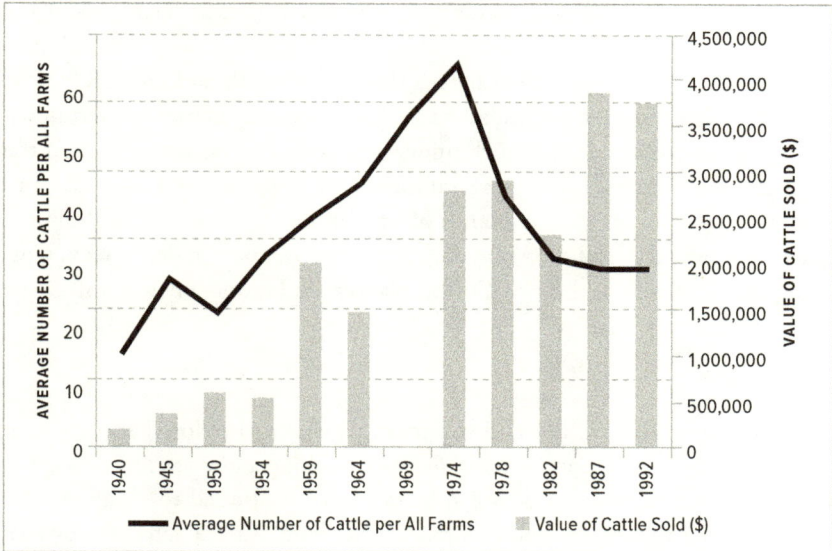

Cattle production and sales in Montgomery County, Texas.
U.S. Census of Agriculture, vol. 1, pt. 37, county tables 1, 4, and 16 (1945), 1, 7.1, and 7.2 (1954), and 1 and 17 (1969), pt. 26, county tables 1, 4.1, and 4.2 (1950) and 1, 10, and 11 (1964), pt. 43, county tables 1 and 12 (1974), 1 and 11 (1982), and 1 and 14 (1992). No data available for value of cattle sold in 1969. Data for 1940, 1945, and 1974 include all livestock and livestock products.

West; and livestock has moved East." These broader shifts brought a measure of prosperity to rural Montgomery County. Mechanization, improved pastures, purebred cattle, and improved marketing combined with out-migration to drive farm consolidation and modernization. The number of farms dropped by a quarter from 1950 to 1964. In the same period the percentage of land in farms increased from 36 percent to 47 percent, and the number of cattle increased 30 percent, from 26,300 to 37,600. Economically, cattle made up a sizable majority of the county's agricultural income from World War II on. Yet even with these changes, Montgomery County did not become a regional leader in the production and marketing of cattle. The industry never surpassed oil or timber in terms of employment, tax revenue, or gross income, but its extensive nature meant that its modernization was the single most important landscape change in the decades before suburban development.[58]

A group of farmers gathered on November 23, 1965, to close the door on Montgomery County's agricultural past. That year there were fewer than three hundred acres of cotton planted in the county out of an allotment of over a thousand acres. With a quick show of hands, landowners put their allotments up for sale. The crop that had defined agriculture in the county since the 1830s was gone. Like sons turning their back in scorn on the freshly covered grave of an abusive father, these ranchers adjusted their Stetson hats, kicked the dust off their boots, got into their pickup trucks, and headed out to their pastures. Montgomery County was part of the cotton South no longer. Ranchers were remaking the county's landscape. Bulldozers rumbled over broken-down sharecropper cabins and the thick underbrush that had begun to reclaim the abandoned homesteads. Tractors contoured and shaped the gullied fields into smooth curves, erasing the evidence of past abuse. A thick mat of Bermuda grass crept over the land, covering the county's cotton past in deep green. Cotton's tenants moved to the city. Cotton planters had found a new commodity, and with it a new identity.[59]

உ

Agricultural modernization and suburban development closed the door on dairy farming in Loudoun County. Yet after reaching a low of 714 in 1974, the number of farms rebounded to 836 in 1978 and continued to climb. At the same time the amount of land in farms spiked from 216,574 acres in 1969 to a high of 228,503 acres in 1978 before sliding downward again. The average size of farms in Loudoun also peaked in 1974 at 310 acres before falling to 273 acres in 1978 and 229 acres in 1982. These three trends reflect the transition to metropolitan agriculture. County land-use policies reinforced this process through large-lot zoning and the passage of the Land Use Tax (discussed in chapter 5), incentivizing rural landowners to dabble in agricultural production to offset some of the costs of landownership. County leaders therefore promoted the type of hobby farming that appealed to exurban and suburban consumers and metropolitan tourists. These agricultural producers sold retail rather than wholesale, focusing on consumer taste rather than production efficiencies. Vineyards, specialty hay, Christmas trees, truck crops, pick-your-own berry farms and orchards, and, above all, horse farms claimed these metropolitan open spaces by the 1990s. Beef cattle and hay production remained the easiest ways to keep one's land in agricultural use. For those wanting to make money in agriculture or to keep their small rural acreages qualified for the Land Use Tax, however, alternative crops offered a popular solution. These metropolitan farmers sold agrarian scenery and experience as much as they did crops and produce. A large number of these farmers were outsiders who had come to the countryside with money to invest and a willingness to embrace new business models. Alternative agriculture was a young man's game and, increasingly, a young woman's game. Where national and state agricultural extension officials generally ignored such trends, the local extension office and county planners rushed to support these new farming enterprises.[60]

Horticulture was not a new pursuit in Western Loudoun. The region was

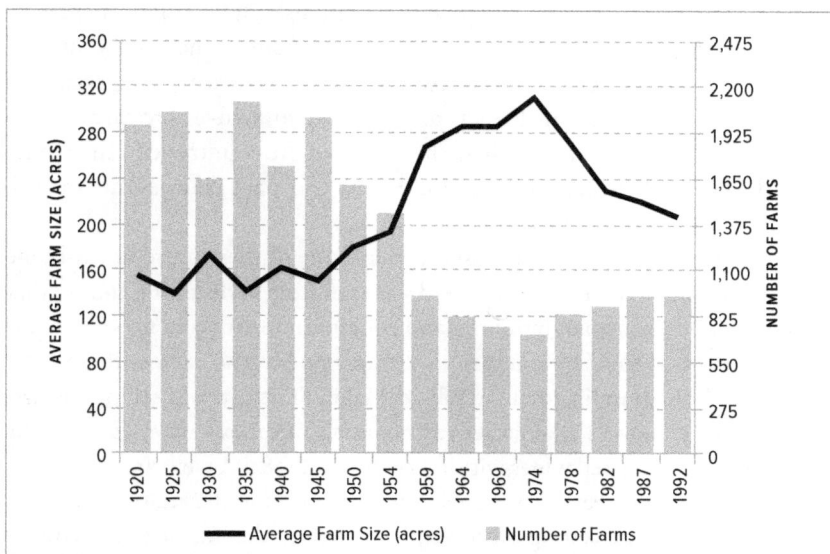

Number of farms and average farm size (acres) in Loudoun County, Virginia.
U.S. Census of Agriculture, vol. 1, pt. 24, county tables 1 (1945), 1 (1954), and 1 (1964),
and pt. 46, county tables 1 (1974), 1 (1982), 1 (1987), and 1 (1992).

part of a thriving orchard belt in Virginia that stretched from Winchester east
to Leesburg and then south, up the Shenandoah Valley through Lexington.
Competition from northwestern growers, the increasing costs of production,
and the scarcity of labor took their toll on the industry in the postwar years. By
the early 1970s there was only one commercial orchard left in Loudoun. Even
as this industry was failing, Loudoun farmers found a new source of cheap
labor: suburbanites willing to pay money for the privilege of agricultural labor.
Pick-your-own orchards and berry patches found excited customers among
suburban families. Nurseries were another popular alternative crop that enabled landowners to market directly to consumers. The number of farms growing nursery and greenhouse products in northern Virginia increased 21 percent
from 1982 to 1987. Sales of their products tripled over the same period, from
$900,000 to $2.7 million as development in the region intensified. Peter Knop
was one example of this type of modern Loudoun farmer. Knop maintained
his day job as an investment banker even as he experimented in a grab-bag
of various alternative crops, including chestnuts, chinchillas, specialty garlic,
and various ornamental plants. "Everyone says it can't be done," he boasted,
but "we're making money." Christmas trees became a staple for this new breed
of farmer. A landowner could plant sixteen hundred trees per acre, maintain
them for seven to eight years with limited labor costs, and sell them for a small

profit while keeping his land in agricultural land use. By the 1990s there were close to seventy nursery and Christmas tree operations in the county, including at least nineteen cut-your-own tree operations. The farmers' markets also expanded. Chip and Susan Planck purchased a thirty-five-acre farm in the county in 1979 as a way to get their children into the countryside. The family opened Planck's Wheatland Vegetable Farms and paid college kids to pick vegetables over the summers.[61]

Grapes enjoyed a prestige and status that none of these more down-home operations could match. Vineyards and wineries were perfect for a county that prided itself on its historic buildings and equestrian foxhunting mystique. It is fitting, then, that the first vineyard in the area opened just across the county line from Middleburg in 1971. Archibald Magill Smith Jr. was selling his first bottles in 1975. Lewis Parker, a retired pharmaceutical executive, became the first to commercially sell wines within Loudoun in 1984. A well-timed drought made 1991 a banner year for Virginia vineyards, putting the region's wines on the national map and setting off the rapid growth of the industry. The county would add more than a dozen vineyards before the turn of the twenty-first century. There were forty in the county by 2014.[62] The impact of this new agriculture was admittedly limited during the 1970s. Berries, wines, Christmas trees, and vegetables did not suddenly transform the economic outlook for agriculture in Loudoun. Nor did these small-acreage operations do much to preserve open space. What they did provide was the germ of an agricultural tourist industry that would, with the increasing availability of Hispanic laborers and the growing popularity of local food, continue to grow into the twenty-first century. They further cultivated an image of Loudoun as a place for Washingtonians to enjoy, if only for a long weekend, the lifestyle of a gentleman farmer.

But what would a Virginian gentleman be without his horse? Loudoun had a long and rich history of foxhunting and horse breeding, and its reputation only grew in the postwar years.[63] When combined with neighboring Fauquier County, Loudoun was one of the most important equestrian regions in the nation—comparable to the Kentucky Bluegrass region; Saratoga, New York; and California's San Fernando Valley. It was not just a place to raise and ride horses; it was a place to breed and train them. The state's largest equestrian training facility, the Middleburg Training Track complex, opened in 1956 and served between 100 and 125 horses every day by the 1970s. Westmoreland Davis's Morven Park estate donated three hundred acres of land in 1968 to found the Morven Park International Equestrian Institute as a national education center for trainers. The Leesburg estate would, beginning in 1984, become the site of the Marion DuPont Scott Equine Medical Center, a world-class veterinary research center. In addition, the site played host to the largest foxhound show in the world. One study in 1986 estimated that the eighty-five hundred horses in Loudoun were worth $21 million, a figure that was only a fraction of the money invested. The equestrian industry utilized an extensive network of supporting staff, skilled laborers, and veterinary services. Horse owners supported feed producers, equipment dealers, tack shops, and blacksmiths. This critical mass of equestrian services brought competitive racehorse breeders to the county. Bert and Diana Firestone purchased a fourteen-hundred-acre stud farm along Catoctin Creek near Waterford in the early 1970s. Originally from New Jersey, the couple raised a number of Derby contenders and one winner, Genuine Risk, in 1993.[64]

Loudoun was well positioned to ride the wave of popularity as an ever-growing number of Americans spent their weekends and weeknights on horseback. By the late 1960s, equestrian sports had become a craze among the nation's middle class. Events ranging from dressage and competitive trail riding to roping contests and barrel racing gained in popularity as urban and suburban families took up the sport. Even foxhunting took on a less elitist air as doctors, lawyers, and other professionals replaced blue-bloods as the most prominent members of the hunts. Nationally, the number of children enrolled in 4-H horse projects exploded from 30,000 in 1950 to 320,767 by 1974. The *Chronicle of the Horse*, the industry's premier publication, headquartered in Middleburg, estimated that the number of horses in the nation doubled between 1963 and 1973. Its editor explained, "Virtually wherever you go, in the country, in the suburbs, and even within city limits, there are horses and ponies, most of them in groups of two or three, on farms, vacant lots and backyards."[65]

Horses were a fixture of the nation's outer suburbs. Within northern Virginia, neighboring Fairfax County had the densest population of these backyard horses. A local survey of the county's three western districts in 1978 estimated that there were eight thousand in the county, with at least half of these stabled at home. The land-use pressures of suburban growth pushed these horse riders into Loudoun County, where they joined with established foxhunting circles and a growing amateur riding culture to make Loudoun the state's leading equestrian county. Horses became serious business. They increased property values and therefore tax revenues, poured money into the local economy, and underwrote the preservation of open space. The horse became one of the most important components of Loudoun's agricultural industry—a fact tightly entwined with recreation and labor, production and consumption, open space and agriculture in a way that would define the countryside into the twenty-first century.[66]

Horses, Christmas trees, vineyards, truck farms, and even emus joined hay, cattle, and horses in the cornucopia of the county's agricultural production.

As late as 2002 just under half of the county's land area was still in some form of agriculture. The county had an estimated 15,800 horses, 294 commercial horticulture operations, 20 Christmas tree farms, and upward of a dozen vineyards.[67] Full-time farmers were hard to find, but part-time farmers were impossible to miss. Agricultural production no longer defined the rhythms and values of Loudoun's rural world—metropolitan growth had taken over. Yet after Ragnarok, there was rebirth. Agriculture became a service industry, keeping up with the ever-changing consumer tastes and preferences of Washingtonian commuters. Rural Loudoun died with the dairy industry. The Loudoun countryside lived on. Montgomery County, Texas, would chart a similar path.

જ્જ

Stan Crawford, a *Conroe Courier* correspondent, captured the complex mixture of memory and forgetting, of piney woods and improved pasture, of national cultural images and local heritage that converged in Montgomery County. In his 1965 article entitled "Cowboy," he described his trip to a ranch in the west-central part of the county. Crawford profiled Garry Sharp, a rancher who had retired here to raise registered quarter horses. Sharp was one of the thousands of Houstonians who fled northward from the sprawling metropolis. As Crawford walked pastures that had, only a decade or two before, been part of the cotton South, his eyes saw only the landscape of a true western. "It is a rustic setting, these rolling, thin-tree environmented hills of western Montgomery County," he explained. "It is an environment that takes you back to youth and dreams of western type adventures and the rugged, individualistic, everyday existence of that once and always Texas Knight in buckskin riggings." He admitted that the heroic cowboy image, with his daring rescues and heroic shootouts, was a child's fantasy that existed only in the movies. Yet even as Crawford debunked this image, he reaffirmed the county's western identity. The real cowboy, he pointed out, was defined not by his bravado but by his simple hard work and self-assured character. Rural life in Montgomery County promised "the city bound soul" the opportunity to carve out his own slice of this western lifestyle with its hard physical labor, its closeness to nature, and its solitude. For, as Crawford put it, "there exists today on ranches hereabouts a slightly modernized way of life directly descending from the days when cowboys were in their glory." Garry Sharp, the modern cowboy, may have ridden the range in his pickup truck and slept outside only a few times a year, but he embodied the plain-spoken, hard-working cowboy. By recovering and reinterpreting local cattle herding as ranching, county agricultural leaders offered migrants like Sharp the opportunity to join in the pursuit of restorative labor, wide-open spaces, and peaceful, if rugged, repose from the hectic business world of Houston.[68]

A combination of factors played a role in crafting and disseminating Montgomery County's western identity. The changes in agriculture and land use already had literally laid the groundwork. Developers and the influx of Houstonians that they attracted reinforced this identity. A subset of suburban migrants came to the county to enjoy a lifestyle that revolved around horses, open space, and country values. Whether it was for a wealthy businessman in the market for a thousand-acre ranch or a commuter searching for peace and quiet on a half-acre in a rural subdivision, the western myth and lifestyle was a valuable amenity. In a telling reversal, Montgomery County's farm population, which bottomed out in 1960 at 1,931, rebounded to 3,199 by 1970—the result of urban and suburban migrants. Over the same period the rural, nonfarm population went from 15,716 to 34,311, an increase of 118 percent. Many of these newcomers joined with locals in the celebration of this rural lifestyle.[69]

This particular vision of rural life justified these newcomers' rejection of the city. For such migrants, white flight was not only a migration *from* urban violence and integrated public space in an increasingly triracial city but also a migration *to* a countryside where the family would be safe, where African American and Latino populations were small, and where kids could learn hard work, discipline, responsibility, and the joy of life in the outdoors. Responding to critics who saw 4-H programs as an anachronism in a suburbanizing county, the *Conroe Courier* responded, "Do you know that many people who move here from larger cities, seek a bit of acreage mainly for their children's sakes?" Moving meant escaping from the corrupting influences of the city and immersing children in the wholesome values of the countryside. Those who moved to the country for the children found common ground with those whose roots kept them in the country. Each believed that raising a hog, a horse, or chickens was a path to maturity. Even as agriculture became less important to the county's economic production, it became ever more significant as a lifestyle choice.[70]

Western horse riding was the most prominent of these activities. Equestrian breeding and riding required more money, claimed more property, and incited more envy than any other recreational activity on the metropolitan fringe. In a world of automobiles, tractors, and all-terrain vehicles, the horse was an economic and social anachronism. This fact only added to its attractiveness. As in Loudoun, equestrian money, land uses, and social life attached markers of exclusivity, class privilege, and status to Montgomery County's rolling pastureland and country homes. Whether they stabled their horses in half-acre rural subdivision lots, rented stalls from rural landowners, or rode on newly refurbished ranches, the thousands of professionals and businessmen who moved their families to Montgomery County replaced productive agriculture with a landscape of status and leisure. As local extension agent Morris Straughn put it, this type of farming was "not making money, [it was] spending money."[71]

Where Loudoun raised Thoroughbreds, quarter horses dominated Montgomery County's equestrian scene.[72] Some local ranchers of means entered the world of quarter horse breeding and racing, selling to racing outfits across the Southwest.[73] Race horses may have drawn the big money, but youth programs made up the day-to-day fare of the county's equestrian scene. Beginning with the Conroe Horse Club, local 4-H groups organized to serve this new horse culture. Members held their first western youth horse show in the spring of 1958 and their first field day in 1960. By 1964 there were four 4-H horse clubs. By the end of the decade, monthly shows were attracting upward of five hundred spectators to enjoy these western-themed competitions. Similar private shows spread across the county.[74] These horse events became widespread by the late 1960s. Horse and livestock ownership was expensive, requiring substantial investments in land, feed, equipment, and veterinary care. These expenses stoked resentment among working-class rural people. One of the reasons for the failure of a major park bond in Montgomery County in 1968 was, in the *Courier*'s words, the fear that it "was inspired and pushed by . . . the horse lovers and owners who constitute an elite minority in this county."[75] In many ways the local newspaper's printing of award lists from equestrian competitions was the society page reborn, a who's who of the county's rural elite.[76]

When developers promoted their recreational subdivisions, they combined the early twentieth-century image of suburban exclusivity, access to nature, and a family-centered home with strong western symbols and equestrian amenities—a suburban lifestyle of the saddle club rather than the country club. One advertisement promised "delightful ranchettes and acreage, a mere 35-miles from Houston, where you can keep a horse, forget about high taxes and crowded neighborhoods, sing or shout without inhibition."[77] Jim Fuller, a prominent local developer, opened his Frontier Hills development in 1965. He described it as a "Big Wooded Western Resort Subdivision" with "a real western atmosphere." At the center of the development, Fuller placed a "western city," a commercial strip done up in the shape of a frontier town. At the subdivision open houses held by the local chamber of commerce, Frontier Hills' table boasted a collection of antique weapons that "helped to tame the savage land." The relics in this collection "were probably used by our forefathers to fend off Indian attac[k]s or by the Army to widen our Frontiers." Residents, though, need not fear that such dangers would confront them. In Frontier

Hills, the frontier was closed. As Fuller's advertisers put it, "Behind these locked gates is your paradise on earth." To complete the western lifestyle package, the development maintained its own stables, rodeo facilities, and miles of bridle paths. Residents could ride across this frontier, embellishing their western fantasies to their heart's content without the fear that any real danger or even unexpected adventure would sneak into their exclusive development.[78]

These amenities lured prospective buyers. Stagecoach Farms, Lazy River, Wigwam Springs, Southern Oaks, Arrowhead Lakes, Lake Bonanza, Tri-Lakes Estates, and Forest Hills subdivisions all opened in the county with equestrian facilities during the 1960s. Southern Oaks promised that "junior can have a horse." Lazy River included its own rodeo arena, riding ring, stables, and bridle paths. Tri-Lake Estates ran its own yearly trail ride and western festival. Even in Oak Ridge North, a more standard suburban development situated along the interstate, residents could secure extra-large lots laid out specifically for horses. Some of these developments packaged horse facilities with western chic; others simply added these facilities to a list of amenities. As the county's equestrian reputation improved, the general caliber of these subdivisions went up. The Reserve, a master-planned subdivision near Lake Conroe, later offered over two hundred lots with stable facilities for as many horses, ten miles of bridle trails, a training track, three arenas, and accommodations for groomsmen and riding instructors. Horses were a major business by the 1980s.[79]

Other show animals also drew a great deal of attention. In reading accounts of 4-H participants, it is difficult to determine where the farm animal ends and the suburban pet begins. Changes within agriculture fueled this confusion. The new economics and technologies of production had disconnected much of the value of these pigs, horses, sheep, and goats from their commodity price. Diversified farming was no longer economically feasible when grocery stores sold meat below the family farm's cost of production. Keeping farm animals, therefore, took on new meanings for children, whether they lived on the suburban fringe or on the farm. Owners kept these animals knowing full well that they would rarely see a financial return on their investment. Agriculture itself became a hobby—a voluntary decision, often in opposition to economic cues, made for lifestyle reasons. For those who raised these animals to show, the motivation was a mixture of economic speculation—for scholarship money—and the emotional connections and companionship that characterize pet ownership. These animals were judged less on market criteria such as their value as breeding stock or as meat and more on their appearance, their pedigree, and the dedication of their owner. The 4-H kids pampered their animals, subjecting them to shampoo, hair spray, talcum powder, and a bevy of other beauty products. One boy whose animals made it to the Houston Livestock

Show brushed his calves' hair three hours a day and quartered them in a room with three large fans and a fogging machine to keep them looking their best. Such treatment turned products into pets, commodities into consumer goods. Their owners, in turn, often defied the line between homestead and subdivision. Many county communities welcomed and even promoted the raising of project animals. Even those whose restrictive covenants expressly forbade livestock and poultry (in order to protect property values) often made exceptions for 4-H. Show animals were respectable.[80]

The county fair, held every March, celebrated the lifestyle and values these residents had chosen for their children. County fairs have been so enshrined in popular culture as part of a nostalgic rural life that it is difficult to appreciate how quickly the Montgomery County Fair expanded beginning in the 1960s. The fair was anything but a swan song for rural life. It was a product of suburban and exurban growth. Its period of most rapid expansion coincided with the first wave of metropolitan development in the county. While only a few area kids had shown animals in the 1950s, many children clamored to take part by the mid-1960s, goading parents to dig deep into their pockets to help their children find a way to keep a show animal. Children who raised a cow or horse, organizers told parents, could not go wrong. Bob Youngblood, a local horse trainer, claimed that caring for and riding a horse was "the closest to life a child can get."[81] The county fair was about growing character, not crops. It was about raising quality children just as much as it was about raising quality animals.[82] By 1974 over thirty thousand people attended annually in a county where the population had just topped seventy-two thousand.[83] Morris Straughn, a local extension agent, remembered, "It was unreal how it grew." The county fair was the "in thing. . . . [I]f you wasn't part of the fair . . . you were on the outside." Participation in the fair served as a litmus test of one's belonging. Stuart Traylor, a lifetime board member, talked about membership in the fair association as a sign that "you've arrived." Straughn explained that participation was "kind of a status symbol," a badge of rurality.[84] The county's 4-H clubs integrated new residents into a western-themed, exurban culture. They held events related to western fashion, horticulture, wildlife, and horses. This new 4-H applied its long-standing commitments to teaching practical life skills, building character, and developing citizenship in rural and exurban youth. Its efforts were largely successful. The county added six new 4-H clubs in 1973–74 and claimed a substantial increase in participation that year. Ervin Kaatz, an extension agent, boasted, "We can visualize a 4-H club or project group in every subdivision in Montgomery County."[85]

The yearly Go Texan celebration that preceded the Houston Livestock Show and Rodeo did more than any other institution to popularize western culture in the city's hinterland. By 1972 Houston hosted the largest livestock show in the world, drawing cattlemen, breeders, meat packers, and equipment dealers from across the nation. From the mid-1950s onward, rodeo organizers sent touring "goodwill ambassadors" across East Texas to raise the rodeo's profile. These delegations came both as emissaries from the metropolis and as prophets calling locals to embrace what had become almost a civic religion of western culture.[86] Montgomery County responded to the call. Ranchers and local agricultural groups joined with the local chamber of commerce's agricultural committee to establish a yearly Go Texan Day celebration in the county seat of Conroe. They held the first in 1965. The United Merchants of Conroe, facing increasing competition from Houston and Harris County merchants with the construction of nearby Interstate 45, jumped at the chance to bring people back to downtown. Ranchers and newcomers saw an opportunity to promote agriculture and rural youth activities. Many suburban residents saw it as a way to integrate themselves into the county's social circles. Some joined in simply for the fun of the show. The yearly celebration of ranching and cowboy culture quickly surpassed the county's other parades and celebrations in scope and intensity.[87]

The Houston rodeo's organizers had begun the tradition of dressing in western wear during the weeks leading up to the rodeo in the early 1940s. Conroe leaders grabbed hold of this and made it their own. Western street decorations went up on the courthouse square starting in late January. Organizers, backed by the *Conroe Courier*, called for residents to wear western gear and costumes throughout the month, even to work. For those unfamiliar with western clothes, the *Courier* published a special guide to instruct incompetent town folk, suburbanites, and uninitiated rural people on how to appropriately display western identity. "Don't mind if the real cowboys smile when you walk by," the editor chided. "Just because they've just slogged through a cow pen, don't you feel self-conscious in your clean boot heels, smelling only of leather." The United Merchants of Conroe carried western wear in their stores to outfit participants. Local horse clubs demonstrated proper western wear to their audiences.[88] Western wear spread beyond just February. Cowboy hats and boots became a year-round symbol of local power and authority. Local Democratic politicians made sure that the *Courier* pictured them wearing these markers of identity and white authority whenever election days came around. Western wear became so entrenched that some outside developers found it difficult to navigate local power structures unless they too donned cowboy hats and boots.[89]

The ceremonies began each year on a Saturday morning in early February. A western band played to set the mood. The parade included the president of the Houston rodeo, L. M. Pearce Jr., and Houston chief of police Herman Short, in addition to the usual hand-waving politicians, banner-toting service organizations, and the high school band. Local 4-H clubs, the home demonstration club, and others spent weeks constructing floats for the occasion. The newcomers' 1966 float, which won first prize, cast their real-life white flight to Conroe as a frontier journey, complete with Conestoga wagon, clanging dishware, and pioneer gear. Residents of the newly opened, luxurious Panorama Golf Club formed the "Panorama Herd," a line of golf carts full of women in cowboy hats. The Conroe Country Cousins, a square-dancing club founded by air traffic controllers who moved to the area in 1965, also took part. The Go Texan parade brought suburban, exurban, and rural people together to celebrate Texas's western identity.[90]

Conroe's shootout, which also took place on Saturday morning, put to shame any of the spectacle that would follow a week later in Houston. On one level, it was a bit of theater for the kids—a chance for the crowds to enjoy a re-enactment of their favorite western movies. Understood in the county's larger cultural and social context, however, the shootout takes on a more complex meaning. The ceremony, symbols, and traditions that made up the shootout hint at the intertwining of the region's southern history with the symbols of its newfound western identity. The shootout assembled local residents to celebrate law and order and the triumph of the white male over the forces of social decay. It also echoed many of the social and cultural meanings of southern lynching, repackaged within the trappings of western culture.[91]

Residents looked forward to the shootout with eager anticipation. During the week leading up to the event, the *Conroe Courier* plastered fictional wanted posters for the "despicable seven" across its pages and posted daily accounts of their movements. The stage was set for a classic western showdown. Anyone who sighted the "bad guys" was supposed to call the "good guys." County sheriff "Cowboy" Gene Reaves, a prominent local rancher and sawmill owner whose local roots went back three generations and whose tenure as sheriff would last until 1980, led his group of western heroes. Reaves's persona was intimidating, to say the least. The *Houston Chronicle* once described him as "lean, rawhide-tough, with a face that has the impact of a fist." He and his fellow "good guys" were clad in white. The showdown began promptly at nine in the morning as the "bad guys," wearing black, rode into the courthouse square to the jeers of a packed crowd. From there, they kidnapped county judge Jonathan Thornberry and bank president Seth Dorbant. As they prepared to make their escape, the "good guys" swooped in and started a gunfight in the street, ducking behind covered wagons and hay bales and eventually subduing the despicable seven. They then marched the desperados up the stairs of the

The "shootout" on the courthouse square in Conroe. *CC*, February 4, 1968.

gallows, constructed especially for the occasion, and pretended to hang them all in front of the crowds, which reached as many as eight thousand people. Houston KPRC-TV and KNRO radio both broadcast the entire spectacle to allow the wider metropolis to participate in meting out justice to these outlaws.[92]

Montgomery County residents celebrated and participated in a stylized, westernized street theater lynching on the courthouse square. The Go Texan celebration demonstrates the power of western symbols and western identity to tie Houston to Conroe and the county's newcomers to longtime agrarians. Historians of lynching in Texas have emphasized the way ritualized violence both rested upon and reinforced a sense of shared historical memory and white identity. In Conroe's shootout, those suburban newcomers who joined the crowds took up a western historical memory and identity. Within the reassuring safety of street theater, these white suburbanites "lynched to belong."[93]

At the same time, westernizing and fictionalizing lynching significantly refashioned its meaning. The shootout spoke to similar social fears, but it did so through cultural performance. Where actual lynching was an act of direct racial and social oppression, as well as personalized violence, this modern western lynching was victimless and therefore lacked the sharp edge of social oppression. Yet western tropes also broadened the message of lynching beyond racial control. Like the conservatism that coalesced across the South and the nation at the time, the event's appeal subsumed racism in a wider appeal to law and order, the reaffirmation of white men's martial strength, and the perpetuation of white supremacy. This appeal had deep cultural roots and strong support in the culture and politics of both the South and the West. As Michael Pfeifer has argued, lynching in both regions shared a commitment to what he terms "rough justice." In contrast to procedural justice, rough justice was personal, violent, and enforced by the broader community. The shootout validated police-sanctioned "rough justice" as a means of preserving the racial and social order.[94]

Many in the county had reason to be attracted to this no-nonsense brand of justice. A civil rights protest at historically black Texas Southern University in south Houston boiled over into racial violence in 1967, confirming some of the worst fears of Montgomery County residents. Houston police responded with excessive force, arresting 489 male students and trashing parts of the campus. Many residents chose to leave Houston rather than face the next outbreak of racial violence. The threat of integration of the city's schools also hovered over Houston's white communities in the late 1960s as civil rights activism among both African American and Latino communities gained ground. Lawsuits against Houston's ineffective freedom of choice integration plan resulted in a 1970 decision that ordered city schools to begin busing. White flight on a massive scale ensued. The Houston Independent School District (HISD) lost thirty-eight thousand students to the suburbs during the 1970s, and the percentage of whites enrolled declined from 49.9 percent in 1970 to only 25.1 percent by 1980. Montgomery County welcomed these refugees.[95]

In an era charged with social tension, when the city of Houston was supposedly rocked with lawlessness, this small-town performance reinforced the belief that, at least on the city's metropolitan fringe, law and order prevailed. These contemporary fears occasionally boiled to the surface in coverage. Coverage also described the "good guys" as "the virtuous forces of law and order." At one point the paper referred to the bank robbers as "punks," a term that owed more to the Nixon era of law-and-order politics than it did to the Wild West.[96] For families who moved to the county to escape busing and the threat of urban unrest, the figure of a white sheriff empowered to exact swift and brutal justice was a reassuring sight. A police force that could handle armed desperados could certainly handle drug pushers, unruly blacks, and juvenile delinquents. By adopting the trappings of a western lynching spectacle, town and rural residents marked out common ground with newcomers and reaffirmed their commitment to a justice system that would act swiftly to punish the guilty and protect residents from urban violence.

If the shootout reassured residents, the yearly trail rides that followed it every year interpreted their exodus before an urban audience. Every year, during the week after Conroe's Go Texan celebration, the Montgomery County and Sam Houston Trail Riders would begin their multiday trek on horseback and by wagon to the Houston Livestock Show and Rodeo. The nearly one thousand riders from the county, a mixture of horse enthusiasts from suburban developments, small towns, and local ranches, slowly made their way back to Houston. Once there, they gathered in the city's Memorial Park with some fifty-four hundred other trail riders from as far away as Western Louisiana. This larger group would then march through downtown in the city's Go Texan parade. The Montgomery County trail rides promised family entertainment, including country dances and barbecues, often with a helping of drinking and carousing involved. These trail riders performed their western heritage on a metropolitan stage. For Montgomery County, the trail rides also advertised their county's western culture to prospective home buyers.[97]

Both Houston and its hinterland had much to gain through this celebration. The trail riders reaffirmed the Bayou City's western identity. Once in Houston, the riders paraded past the fabulous mansions of the Memorial area and through the streets of downtown. As they marched down the skyscraper-lined avenues, trail riders joined the mayor and local officials on horseback in a celebration of a metropolitan western identity bound up in imagery of the

Trail riders making their way to downtown Houston in the early 1970s.
Photo by Geoff Winningham, in William C. Martin and Geoff Winningham, *Going Texan: The Days of the Houston Livestock Show and Rodeo* (Toronto: Herzig-Somerville, Ltd., 1972), 30. Courtesy of Geoff Winningham.

horse and the cowboy. In an increasingly international city whose dramatic economic growth fueled rapid immigration from across the nation and the world, the trail riders asserted a vision of Houston's southwestern heritage. The city, in turn, validated the lifestyle chosen by these rural and exurban residents, inviting them to parade in front of the cheering metropolis. Both rural and suburban residents could celebrate their frontier migration. In completing the ride, as the *Courier* put it, "each boy or girl, man or woman, experiences the same accomplishment in miniature of much longer trips their ancestors made in moving west."[98] In effect, the city signed off on the white privilege and white flight that undergirded this horse culture in exchange for the riders' participation in the city's western festival. Even as they fiercely resisted annexation by the city, these residents basked in the city's yearly celebration of their rural world.[99] The rodeo had begun as an attempt to tie the urban agricultural businessmen of Houston to the agricultural producers of the city's economic hinterland. By the 1960s the trail rides themselves had become one of the most important products the county shipped to Houston. As they paraded down the streets of Houston on horseback, their broad-brimmed hats prominently displayed and their covered wagons in tow, the trail riders tied themselves all the more fully to the metropolis and validated Houston's own attempts to obscure its southern past and continued racial problems.[100]

Within Montgomery County, this ascendant western identity both drew its

strength from and obscured the county's transformation from rural to suburban. The rural subdivisions that developers constructed across the county took
land out of farming, ranching, and forest. They also paved over the markers of
southern rural life. The western-themed subdivision of Stagecoach Farms was
an example of this. A white landowner built the community on top of acreage
that had been farmed by a dozen black families who worked at Swinley's mill in
the 1930s. The owner saw a greater profit to be had in residential development
than in farming. In the mid-1950s he dredged Lake Apache and Lake Hardin
and subdivided the land into large, horse-friendly lots. Open as they were
only to people "of the Caucasian Race," the plots found a ready market among
Houstonians looking for a place in the country. The subdivision boasted its
own home demonstration club and a strong community social life. Residents
voted to incorporate their country subdivision of nearly one hundred homes
into the town of Stagecoach in March 1974. The only evidence of the black
farmers who went before was an old barbed-wire fence among the underbrush
on the outskirts of town. The development of rural subdivisions replaced the
social world of the rural South with a whitened rural world of leisure, 4-H, and
single-family homes.[101]

The shift to improved pastures and ranching in Montgomery County cleared
the way for a set of rural and suburban land uses whose most important product was leisure rather than fodder. Equestrian culture, gentleman ranching,
and country subdivisions together formed an alternative to suburban sprawl.
Montgomery County ranchers opened the area up to a particular brand of
agrarian exurbia that would have otherwise been slow to take root in what
remained a timber-dominated county of recreational subdivisions, lakefront
resorts, and bedroom communities. The popularity of equestrian homesteads
and gentleman ranching in the county accelerated the inflation of land values and the transfer of land from full-time ranchers and rural landowners to
Houstonians. Those who wanted to continue to ranch packed up their equipment and their livestock, made a tidy profit off their land, and bought even
larger acreages farther from Houston. Others simply cashed out and retired
in local subdivisions.[102] The few who could afford to continue raising cattle in
the county did so for reasons that shared a great deal with those articulated
by newcomers. Stuart Traylor, a longtime rancher in the area, summarized his
decision to continue to ranch in the county this way: "We farm because we
like to, that's basically it."[103] Farming and ranching were now lifestyle choices
open to any who had the means to pursue them and containing their own
amenities and values.

Here western myths validated racially and socially exclusive landscapes of
open space and leisure. By explaining these landscapes as a lifestyle choice and

by connecting them to landscapes that had no legacy of racialized slavery, suburban and rural residents obscured the complex history of dispossession and segregation that undergirded these metropolitan spaces.[104] Western culture also provided common cultural ground between locals and newcomers, promoting a set of shared values that defined Sunbelt conservatism: fierce independence, martial strength, and meritocratic individualism. The lack of explicit racism surrounding Go Texan Day allowed residents to reaffirm a strong commitment to law and order, an idealized western past, and white privilege without being labeled bigots or cultural outsiders by the wider national culture. Newcomers could find common ground with these southerners within the values and rhetoric of the West. Western celebrations reinterpreted local values for the postwar world. In rebranding their lifestyles, their town, and their county as western, Montgomery County residents traded their membership in a region nationally portrayed as social pariah for membership in the limitless possibilities of the Sunbelt.[105]

cſɔ

In each county, newcomers joined with local people in articulating a metropolitan fringe lifestyle and identity that rooted white privilege and Sunbelt conservatism within productive rural landscapes. These metropolitan fringe residents embraced the countryside for the status it promised, the amenities it offered, and the image it projected. Their efforts were part recovery and part creation, a mixture that only added to its allure. In the process they molded the metropolitan fringe as an alternative to urban life even as their employment, daily lives, and consumer habits tied it more closely to the metropolis. In terms of agriculture, metropolitan proximity and national consumer values overrode the differences in climate, soil, and agricultural history that had divided Loudoun and Montgomery Counties. Metropolitan development propelled their agricultural convergence in the postwar decades—with beef cattle, pastures, alternative agriculture, horses, and recreation dominating both counties by the 1980s.[106]

Over the postwar decades, these people restored worn-out land and rebuilt or replaced decaying homes—both figuratively and literally fertilizing the countryside with their wealth. Theirs was a project of rural gentrification. Newcomers cultivated their refined countryside on top of a productive agrarian economy. Farmers valued land primarily for its agricultural use; these newcomers valued it primarily as a lifestyle amenity. The former maximized productivity; the latter cultivated aesthetics. Like a honeysuckle vine slowly shading out the tree it climbs, all the while presenting an image of verdant green, these newcomers maintained the look and land-use patterns of an agrarian ideal even as their actions transformed the social relations surrounding their use and the economics that supported them. In their efforts to restore and protect, they reshaped, refined, and sometimes replaced. As the honeysuckle image also reveals, gentrification proceeded with a quiet violence, choking out the growth of the plant it rests on.[107]

CHAPTER 3

Damming the Hinterlands

Metropolitan development proceeded under an assumption common to urban planners and anathema to rural leaders, that outlying communities and their landscapes were hinterlands subject to the needs of the metropolis. As regional centers of economic and political power, cities orchestrated the use, and sometimes the abuse, of whatever resources, landscapes, and communities they found at hand. They constructed power plants and power distribution systems. They opened landfills to house their waste. They dumped treated and untreated sewage into streams and rivers. They built dams to prevent flooding, store water, and provide recreation. As historian Joel Tarr described it, a growing city "extends its ecological footprint deeper and deeper into its hinterland." In the process, cities frequently inundated, befouled, and drained their surroundings.[1]

This form of unilateral urban power over rural places and people, or "urban imperialism," was most pronounced during the early decades of the twentieth century.[2] In the postwar decades, however, postwar metropolitan growth fragmented urban power even as resource demands continued to grow. Urban efforts to secure resources during this later period were characterized more by contingency and obstruction rather than by imposition and exploitation.[3] Where cities had earlier, with the support of states and particular federal agencies, imposed upon their hinterlands, postwar infrastructure projects became enmeshed in a tangle of federal, state, and regional agencies and environmental groups.

Reservoir construction provides a prime example of this type of blunted urban imperialism. In Montgomery County, Texas, reservoir development proceeded only when the city of Houston partnered with the state-chartered San Jacinto River Authority (SJRA), whose leadership represented the interests of the watershed even as it remained economically dependent on development. Houston's demand for clean water propelled the inundation of Montgomery County bottomland, yet it was the SJRA that ultimately dammed the San Jacinto River, thereby opening the county to recreational developments. In contrast to this Texas example, Washington, D.C., carried a unique burden as it developed its infrastructure. Legally, the District of Columbia was a ward of the federal government. Decisions about its growth and development were not made at city hall, for none existed, or within the councils of urban boosters, although they spoke their piece. Decisions were made in the halls of the Capitol, where southern congressmen oversaw the city's growth. Indeed, the federal/city relationship was as important as the urban/rural relationship in shaping this metropolis. Debates over the proper development of Washington's primary water supply brought the U.S. Army Corps of Engineers, the Department of the Interior, Congress, the president, regional planners, landowners, and environmental activists into the struggle to reshape the "nation's river." Loudoun County's position within the Potomac watershed—upstream, above the fall line, and just outside the metropolis—thrust it into national debates about dams, water pollution, and environmental policy.

While the SJRA successfully dammed the San Jacinto River in 1973, the Corps failed to dam the Potomac between Washington and Harpers Ferry. In each case, metropolitan fragmentation dampened the power of cities and their allies to impose on their hinterlands. Yet this fragmentation by no means freed outlying counties from the impacts of urban growth. Their choice was not between rejection of or engagement with the metropolis. Rather, it was a question of how they would engage and to whose benefit. In the final accounting, it is these relationships themselves, rather than reservoirs and recreational subdivisions, that were the greatest testimony to these counties' integration into the metropolis, for the construction of Lake Conroe on the San Jacinto and the rejection of the Seneca Dam on the Potomac were metropolitan decisions about the proper allocation and development of a regional resource. Rural history, politics, and landscapes were at the center of these metropolitan stories.[4]

જી

The first act in Loudoun's drama opened with an electric utility company. Rapid development in Maryland and northern Virginia along with the proliferation of air conditioning in the 1950s sent the Potomac Electric Power Company (PEPCO) in search of a site for a new coal-fired power plant. Cold War security concerns dictated that the site be outside a potential nuclear blast zone. Economic imperatives required that it be close enough to suburban customers to minimize transmission costs, yet far enough out to minimize development costs. Logistically, it also had to have rail access to coal mines in West Virginia and a reliable, high-volume water supply for cooling. This triangulation led PEPCO to the northeastern corner of Loudoun County. The company signed an agreement to buy 519 acres of Potomac River frontage at Sugarland Run on August 3, 1955.[5]

This was big news in the crossroads hamlets of Loudoun County. The previous decade had brought a trickle of exurban commuters and gentlemen farmers to Loudoun. The potential impact of PEPCO's six-hundred-megawatt power plant was of a different order of magnitude. Its 120 employees and investment—between $70 and $100 million—would be an economic windfall, nearly doubling the value of the county's taxable property. This money would mean new schools, better roads, and improved services without any increase in property tax burdens. Local and state officials rushed to support the project. The Loudoun zoning board, the county board of supervisors, the Virginia State Corporation Commission, and the Virginia State Water Control Board had all signed off by the first week in November 1955. The District Public Utilities Commission did so by the end of the month. The plant was scheduled to open in 1958. All that remained was the Congressional Committee on the District of Columbia. The committee scheduled a hearing for November 10, 1955.[6]

The county's place in the Potomac watershed brought PEPCO to its doorstep. The plant was designed to draw the water for its steam turbines from a watershed that already connected these upstream communities to Washington. The contamination of the Potomac below Washington spurred PEPCO to look northwest rather than south or east. Yet the plant potentially threatened water purity upstream from the capital. The water that would fill its boilers and turbines entered the Washington aqueduct some two dozen miles downstream before mixing with the city's sewage effluent in the Potomac Estuary along the riverfront of the capital. This November hearing pitted the Loudoun site against a rival site in neighboring Montgomery County, Maryland. Each argued before a congressional committee why it should secure the economic benefits of integration into Washington's metropolitan infrastructure.

Washington's water supply and water quality were the responsibility of an unlikely pair of governmental entities. The perennially underfunded Interstate Commission on the Potomac River Basin (ICPRB) acted as the region's toothless watchdog over the river's water quality.[7] The Corps of Engineers, the nation's politically powerful and well-funded water management agency, was responsible for the district's water supply. Each kept a keen eye on upstream development that might compound the river's already significant industrial pollution issues. District engineer Col. Ray Adams and representatives from the ICPRB each testified before the congressional committee that the PEPCO plant placed the city's water supply in jeopardy and thereby posed an imminent threat to the security and continued growth of the nation's capital.[8] There was reason to be concerned. Like so many postwar cities, Washington was awash in poorly treated sewage released from sprawling suburban developments and aging urban infrastructure. The capital region depended on Potomac River intakes above the fall line at Great Falls and Little Falls for the majority of its drinking water. The district treated its sewage at the perennially overloaded Blue Plains plant before releasing it into the Potomac. Much of the city continued to use combined sewer lines that routinely washed untreated sewage into the river during heavy rains. Fairfax County and Alexandria each flushed sewage directly into the river. Striking a note that would continue to resonate over the next two decades, a 1954 ICPRB report called the Potomac below the fall line a national disgrace. There millions of gallons of sewage lapped against the shores within sight of the austere monuments and halls of power of the most powerful nation on the planet.[9]

The topography and hydrology of the capital region compounded these problems. As it winds its way between Maryland and Virginia, the Potomac rushes through the Blue Ridge Mountains, across a narrow Piedmont plateau, and into the coastal plain. After cascading over Great Falls, fourteen miles upstream from Washington, the river enters the Virginia Tidewater region. Here the meandering Potomac River fans out to become the Potomac Estuary. During winter snowmelts and spring rains, the river overcomes tidal forces and wind to drive estuary water toward the Chesapeake Bay. When the river's flow slackens in summer and early fall, these forces push water from the estuary back up to the fall line at Little Falls, just north of the District of Columbia. During these times, the city's waste putrefied in the Potomac Estuary, a body of water one ICPRB report referred to as a "natural sewage lagoon." Here fecal material dotted the surface of the water, bubbling continuously with decomposition like some sort of vile witches' brew as catfish swarmed to eat their fill. During the summer it took as many as forty days for water to move downstream a mere fifteen miles and one hundred days to clear the estuary altogether. At these times, nitrogen-fueled algae blooms covered the water with a thick green mat. The resulting eutrophication, combined with the continual silting of the estuary caused by upstream erosion, took a heavy toll on the ecology of the river. Poor water quality also severely limited its recreational uses and marred the city's public image. Yet this pollution did not directly threaten metropolitan water supplies. Rather, the estuary served as an omen, a ghastly spirit of Christmas Yet-to-Come sent to warn Washington of the future above the fall line if the metropolis did not mend its ways.[10]

This was precisely the danger the Corps and ICPRB saw in the PEPCO plant. In his testimony, Colonel Adams drew special attention to the problem of heat pollution. If the Loudoun power plant raised the temperature of the water significantly during periods of low flow, he argued, the river would act as an incubator for bacteria growth, algae blooms, and noxious smells. The figures provided by the Corps of Engineers predicted that the plant might raise the

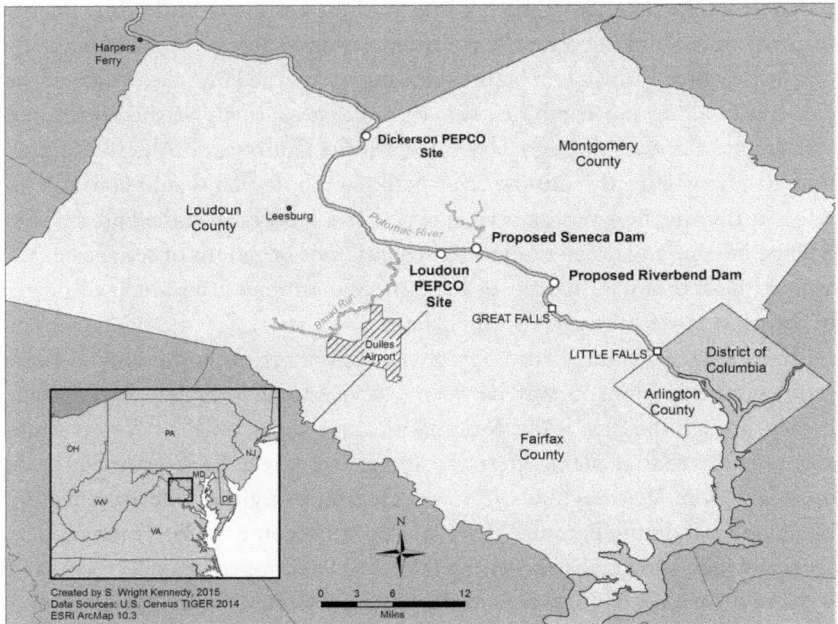

Loudoun County's place within the Potomac watershed.
S. Wright Kennedy, 2015.

water temperature as much as fourteen degrees at the site. If two medium-sized industries located within ten miles of the PEPCO site and discharged organic wastes into the river, these wastes would combine with the heat pollution to create significant water quality issues. The PEPCO plant was, in Adams's words, a "door opener to further industrial development which would pollute the stream immediately above the point where the District takes its drinking water." The ICPRB agreed, calling the potential for industrial development "a possible serious menace to the Potomac River." Such prognostications collapsed the distance that had hitherto separated Loudoun from Washington.[11]

From PEPCO's perspective this scenario missed the point. The utility was struggling to keep pace with surging electricity demand within the city's expanding residential suburbs. Its leadership had little interest in promoting industrial development in Loudoun. Yet as the hearing continued, evidence mounted that the industrialization of Loudoun's Potomac waterfront was a very real possibility. The construction of a power plant and the running of coal trains would significantly depreciate surrounding land, encouraging nearby landowners to demand that the county rezone their land for industry so that they could recoup some of its lost value. Local businessmen were also pushing for rezoning. As part of the deal to purchase the land, PEPCO had contractually obligated itself to assist the members of the land syndicate that owned the five thousand acres surrounding the power plant to secure industrial zoning. Such a request would be hard for the county government to deny, as it would mean more tax revenue for little extra cost. These facts added weight to Adams's warnings.[12]

The Corps had reasons to oppose the PEPCO plant beyond concerns over water quality. Washington's water supplier was also the nation's foremost dam builder, funneling generous congressional appropriations to watershed development projects across the nation. The Loudoun PEPCO site had the ill fortune of being only a few miles upstream from one such proposed project. The $31.7 million high dam on the Potomac at Riverbend was the crown jewel of a fourteen-dam system whose projected costs reached $234 million. The Riverbend Dam would provide hydroelectricity and flood control, trap silt, and even out the river's flow during the summer months. It would also create a reservoir stretching forty-two miles upriver to Harpers Ferry, inundating thirty-six thousand acres, fifteen thousand of which were in Loudoun County. The Corps estimated that 111 residences and 20 commercial buildings would have to be purchased, most on the Maryland side. In exchange for this loss of land and tax revenue, the Corps promised inexpensive electricity and recreational development that would bring industry and tourists to both counties.[13]

Fierce regional opposition, spearheaded in Virginia by Senator Harry Byrd and Representative Howard Smith, had thwarted the Riverbend Dam in 1945, leaving the plans on a shelf collecting dust as Washington's population continued to surge.[14] By the time of the PEPCO hearing, a decade later, some within the metropolis were calling for a reassessment of a high dam on the Potomac, now primarily to provide water supply and pollution abatement. These yellowing pages, therefore, proved a significant obstacle to a Loudoun PEPCO plant—a fact that incensed Howard Smith.[15] Did Colonel Adams really believe, he demanded, that Loudoun "property must stay in status quo indefinitely . . . because it might cost some more to build a dam at some future time?" As Smith saw it, the Corps was obstructing development in Loudoun to keep the way clear for a dam that public opposition had already rendered "a pipe dream." He wanted Loudoun to benefit from metropolitan development without having to face the dams that so often came with being part of a metropolitan watershed.[16]

A different strain of argument against Loudoun's PEPCO plant came into play that further complicated the battle lines between county and Corps. Many within both Loudoun and Washington hoped to preserve the Potomac waterfront from both industry and reservoir development. This nascent coalition wanted to develop Loudoun as part of Washington's backyard. The

Washington Post added its weight to this position, insisting that industrialization in Loudoun County "would be a serious mistake" not because of potential pollution but because of the loss of what was becoming known as "open space." The growing metropolis needed access to undeveloped land for parks, residential development, and recreation. Loudoun was, in the paper's words, "probably the choicest undeveloped land in the area." Claude W. Owen of the National Planning Commission agreed. The area was a "beautiful backdrop for the Nation's Capital that should be used for open recreational space and low-density residential developments." Exurban development here would be an act of preservation.[17]

Loudoun's boosters chafed at the metropolitan condescension that suffused such arguments. These men were just as opposed to the growth controls that came with preservation as they were to inundation. A group of fifty of Loudoun's most prominent citizens—stalwarts of the agrarian old guard—made their opposition clear in a letter submitted for the PEPCO hearing. "We do not believe it is the manifest destiny of Loudoun County to become a satellite of Washington, and to be restricted exclusively to agricultural pursuits forever; or to be, as one District of Columbia newspaper regards us, Washington's backyard. We feel," they continued, "that we have a right to grow up, to become a community of diversified interests." Loudoun's political leadership insisted on their freedom to benefit from metropolitan development even as they claimed the power to determine the shape and impact of that growth. Loudoun's bar association, chamber of commerce, and farm organizations joined in lobbying for the power plant's construction as a means to that end.[18]

They failed. The Senate Special Committee submitted its report on December 16, 1955, concluding that the construction of the PEPCO plant in Loudoun "would serve as a bellwether for further industrial development in the immediate area of the plant" and that such industrialization would threaten metropolitan Washington's present and future water supply. In addition, the committee members agreed with the Corps that Washington's need to dam the Potomac made a Loudoun PEPCO plant unacceptable. PEPCO would later build the plant upstream, in Montgomery County, Maryland.[19] Congress and the Corps, stewards of the nation's capital, reached into the city's watershed and prevented the construction of a metropolitan power plant. They wielded their power to limit the county's economic and environmental ties to the city in the short term. In so doing, they also protected the county from the environmental degradation that would have come with heavy industry. They sequestered the county's Potomac riverfront.

Even as the plant's construction began, suburban growth just outside the District of Columbia continued to pressure Congress and the Corps to develop metropolitan water supplies, control floods, and abate pollution. Water quality in the upper Potomac Estuary worsened as septic tanks and spotty treatment plants proliferated. These sewage systems oozed organic and chemical pollutants into creeks and streams across the Potomac watershed.[20] Following the passage of the Federal Water Pollution Control Act of 1956, the U.S. Public Health Service held a series of conferences on the Potomac's water quality, setting a goal of 80 percent treatment for the region's sewage. The following year, the newly formed Washington Metropolitan Council of Governments (WMCOG) joined an increasingly active ICPRB in coordinating region-wide studies of the river and its problems. Identifying the source of the pollution was never the issue. The question was how to clean up a river subject to the overlapping claims of dozens of local governments, state governments, and federal agencies. On top of this jurisdictional fragmentation, the limited technological capabilities and prohibitive cost of secondary sewage treatment also hampered efforts. This left dilution as the ideal solution.[21] Channeling the Cold War era spirit of technological optimism, the Corps and its allies renewed their calls for large dams, now with the stated purpose of providing the flows of water needed to overpower the estuary's tidal action. Since the "estuary behaves like a toilet bowl" during the summer months, "what may be needed is a good flushing." This radical simplification of the natural systems and pollution issues of the Potomac River sidestepped jurisdictional and technical difficulties and placed the Corps at the head of metropolitan efforts to clean up the river. The Corps, in turn, selected Loudoun to be the storage tank above Washington's toilet of an estuary.[22]

Any further action on the dam awaited the completion of the Corps' study, submitted in 1962. During the intervening years, Loudoun's attention was focused on the development of an altogether different piece of metropolitan infrastructure—a project that, once again, threatened the purity of Washington's water supply. Beginning in 1958, the Civil Aeronautics Administration, forerunner to the Federal Aviation Administration, purchased ninety-eight hundred acres of farmland, much of it through eminent domain and three-quarters of it in Loudoun, as the site of Dulles Airport.[23] The airport and the development it would propel threatened to add a substantial pollution load to the Potomac River above the city's water intakes. Planners proposed that the waste bypass the river altogether.[24] The proposed forty-one-mile-long pipeline would carry sewage from the airport north across the Potomac into Maryland and then southeast, eventually arriving at the Blue Plains treatment plant in southern Washington, D.C. Northern Virginia congressional representatives Joel Broyhill and Howard Smith saw in this a golden opportunity. They sponsored a bill expanding the capacity of the airport's sewer pipe, opening over

90 percent of it to paying customers across the watershed. This Potomac Interceptor appealed to a broad range of interest groups. To its sponsors, the interceptor was a pork-barrel project. To the ICPRB, environmental groups, and city residents, it was a way to clean the river. To the city, it opened the door to a truly metropolitan sewer system and more paying customers for its sewage treatment plant. To developers, the interceptor meant sewage services for suburban projects that would have otherwise relied on unpopular and often faulty septic tank systems that failed in the region's clay soils. To developing counties, it meant avoiding some of the most egregious environmental costs of sprawl. Even the Corps supported the project, which was designed to be inundated and therefore posed no threat to a future Potomac dam. The bill passed on June 12, 1960. What began as a piecemeal solution to airport pollution became a federally subsidized metropolitan infrastructure project spurring suburban development in Eastern Loudoun. Where cities had so often built aqueducts to pipe clean water from faraway watersheds, Washington built a catheter to drain suburban sewage to the city's treatment plant at Blue Plains.[25] The final gravity-fed system was designed to carry 150.62 MGD, or an estimated 300 gallons per person per day by the year 2000. Federal taxpayers assumed the financial risk, providing a $3 million grant and a forty-year, $25 million loan guarantee. Without this federal involvement, regional sewage lines would not have reached Eastern Loudoun until there were enough residents to justify the expense, a benchmark regional planners did not expect the region to hit until the 1990s. Designed to mitigate the environmental impact of impending development, the Potomac Interceptor became a major force in propelling the arrival of suburban sprawl to Loudoun County.[26]

Even as the county coped with this suburban influx, the Corps continued to call for a high dam on the Potomac. Upstream communities had lined up to oppose the Riverbend project in 1944. Now, in the early 1960s, the WMCOG, the region's dominant regional planning agency, came out in support for the project. Metropolitan politicians at every level were willing to inundate upstream communities if doing so provided clean water to their constituents.[27] The Corps adapted its proposal to meet these metropolitan demands. It abandoned the Riverbend hydropower project and instead proposed a more modest, eighty-four-foot-high dam four miles upstream at Seneca Creek, just below the rejected PEPCO site. The Seneca Dam would ensure the region's water supply until the year 2010, flush out the Potomac Estuary, provide recreation, trap silt, and cut annual flood damage in the D.C. metro area in half.[28] At a hearing in Leesburg on June 5, 1962, the local chapter of the Izaak Walton League (a conservation group), garden clubs, county officials, and a crowd of residents reiterated their unalterable opposition to the plan. When, after four

Potomac Interceptor under construction within the Chesapeake
and Ohio Canal on the Maryland side of the Potomac River.
Department of Sanitary Engineering, Washington, D.C., *The Potomac Interceptor: Symbol of Metropolitan
Cooperation* (Washington, D.C.: September 1968), 20. Noman M. Cole Jr. Collection, C0066, Special
Collections Research Center, George Mason University Libraries. Courtesy of D.C. Water.

hours, Col. Warren Johnson, the district engineer, informed those present that
his recommendations were already being printed, Loudoun residents walked
out, disgusted at what garden club members described as the Corps' "shocking, stubborn and dictatorial disregard for the economy and the people of
Loudoun County."[29] Yet this apparent local unity obscured growing divisions.
Local political and economic leaders focused their opposition on budget issues. The dam was expected to displace 460 families, destroy farmland, and remove $214,000 from the tax rolls of counties on both sides of the river.[30] Such
estimates did not take into account the five thousand acres along the Broad
Run watershed in Eastern Loudoun that local planners had set aside for industrial development. Tax money generated by these properties was vital to paying
for the services demanded by suburban newcomers living in the homes that
Dulles Airport and the Potomac Interceptor had brought. This land had ev-
erything businesses required: sewer connections, reliable water supplies, roads,
a nearby airport, and access to Washington. The dam would transform the
area into a series of small, isolated peninsulas requiring numerous bridges and
expensive sewer connections. It would also transform the area's pastoral fields,
the ideal location for suburban office parks, into a landscape pocked with
thousand-foot-wide mudflats.[31] As county supervisor J. Emory Kirkpatrick explained, "We find it incredible that one agency of our Federal Government can
create our problem of new population, other agencies join us in providing the
utilities and transportation to give us the industrial land which will help us care

for that new population and then a third agency of the Federal Government plans to inundate the entire industrial area." Loudoun was simultaneously enmeshed within both the Washington metropolis and the grasp of "Washington."[32] The county's earlier opposition to the Riverbend Dam had been rooted in the defense of the agrarian countryside *from* industrial development. Much of its opposition to the Seneca Dam, in contrast, was rooted in the defense of the agrarian countryside *through* industrial development. Loudoun supervisors' first barb thrown at the Corps' plan demonstrated this shift in local priorities. "We are unalterably opposed to [a Potomac dam]," they explained, "because we want no interference with the growth that is now taking place in the county."[33]

Suburban newcomers, for their part, joined conservationists and garden clubs in their opposition under the auspices of the Broad Run Citizens Association and the Sterling Civic Association.[34] They organized under the banner of NIMBY (not in my backyard). Development was already transforming riverfront farmland into prized country lots.[35] National political trends came to their aid. Across the nation, environmental groups attacked large dam projects for being expensive, destructive, and unnecessary. Within Loudoun and across the metropolis, the mobilizing potential of environmentally destructive suburban growth combined with the well-rehearsed arguments against the Corps' rampant and seemingly irresponsible history of inundation to stir up wide-reaching opposition to the Potomac Dam at Seneca.[36] These environmental preservationists worked under the regional umbrella of the Organization of Citizens for a Better Potomac River Basin. Their arguments painted the Corps' plan to flush the estuary as a symbol of the Corps' technological hubris, environmental irresponsibility, and aesthetic insensitivity. Rather than attempting to flush away Washington's filth, these groups demanded that the region clean up its pollution at the source and thereby protect the river, the estuary, and Chesapeake Bay.[37]

Historical preservationists and recreation advocates also rallied to protect the Potomac riverfront. The Seneca project threatened to flood 29 miles of the 184.5-mile Chesapeake and Ohio (C&O) Canal, a ribbon of Maryland riverfront the federal government had purchased in 1938. The Corps and its public utility allies had derailed a 1957 congressional bill turning the site into a national park. Coming on the heels of the defeat of the Echo Park Dam in 1956, the Corps had reason to fear that a C&O park would prove an immovable obstacle to the Seneca project.[38] Loudoun was caught up in a larger metropolitan and even national battle over the appropriate use of rivers, a fact that a Loudoun newspaper hailed as proof that opposition did not come from "backwoods hicks, apple-knockers and stump-jumpers who just don't understand progress."[39]

The expansion of federal power and employment rolls propelled the Washington metropolitan area's rapid development during the period. It is fitting, then, that a decision by the president should ultimately determine the fate of the Seneca Dam. In a special message to Congress on February 8, 1965, Lyndon Johnson committed his administration to ensuring that this "river rich in history and memory which flows by our nation's capital should serve as a model of scenic and recreational values for the entire country." Johnson declared that the Potomac would be clean enough to swim in by the early 1980s.[40] To accomplish this, he placed Secretary of the Interior Stewart Udall, a man with impeccable environmental credentials, at the head of the newly created Federal Interdepartmental Task Force on the Potomac. The task force's interim report, issued the following year, and the Department of the Interior's more extensive 1968 report reiterated the Corps' claims about the need for improved water quality and the danger of future water shortages, yet it rejected the Seneca Dam, calling instead for the construction of smaller, upstream dams. Water quality would be improved through better treatment rather than dilution. The Department of the Interior and its allies had finally ensured that Loudoun would be free from inundation, yet at the same moment they demanded their pound of flesh. This new report recommended the federal acquisition of some 68,815 acres of land along both sides of the river for a national park. This project would, Udall explained, transform the Potomac into a recreational and environmental haven stretching from Cumberland, Maryland, to Georgetown. Here was the vision of Loudoun as Washington's backyard reborn. Such a park would mean the federal appropriation of much of the county's riverfront property to serve the recreation needs of the metropolis. Environmental politics may have saved Loudoun from the Corps, but they also ushered in a new set of expectations about the appropriate use of the Potomac watershed and, ultimately, Loudoun's place within the metropolis.[41]

Not all within Loudoun were opposed to this vision. By 1968 the county was enmeshed within the politics of sprawl. Local elections pitted developers and working farmers, both of whom were committed to maintaining high property values, against exurbanites, gentlemen farmers, and preservationists for whom the protection of open space was paramount. Many in the latter group saw in this federal purchase an opportunity to lock up a large swath of the county's undeveloped land. It was increasingly obvious that the county supervisors lacked both the tools and the willpower to limit the pace of development. Government-purchased green space offered a solution to the county's growing sprawl problem. The National Park Service, after all, would never be as intractable in its land purchases nor as obstinate in its planning as the Corps would have been. Yet for the preservationists' opponents, a national park along the Potomac represented another in a long line of attempts by the federal government to seize and refashion parts of Loudoun County to meet the needs of the metropolis. Negotiation over this project continued in Congress and the executive branch for another five years, largely outside the hands of county residents.[42] Ultimately, Udall's sweeping plans and the resistance they inspired from conservatives in Congress spurred more moderate voices to secure passage of a bill creating a smaller, 5,250-acre park along the Maryland side of the Potomac. The C&O National Park was signed into law by Richard Nixon on January 8, 1971.[43]

As for the Seneca Dam, the Corps had shelved the project in August 1966 once it became clear that Johnson would side with the Department of the Interior.[44] With a new national park nestled against the banks of the main branch of the Potomac above Washington and Congress passing extensive environmental legislation, the Seneca project would never again see the light of day. The Corps, for its part, adapted to this changing political landscape, further transforming itself into one of the nation's primary water-pollution watchdogs by the late 1970s.[45] As for the metropolis, improved connections among water systems, conservation measures, improved sewage treatment, and the opening of an upstream reservoir near Bloomington, Maryland, in 1981 ensured that the metropolitan area has thus far never lacked clean water.[46]

All told, Loudoun County faced six potential metropolitan infrastructure projects between 1944 and 1971. Of these six, only two made it from the drafting table to the northern Virginia countryside. Once there, Dulles Airport and the Potomac Interceptor both bent the county's trajectory toward a position as the new suburban frontier. While the impact of the four failed projects—the Riverbend Dam, the Seneca Dam, the PEPCO plant, and the national park—is less immediately obvious, each also reinforced a particular integration into the metropolis. Rather than acting as an agent of environmental declension within its hinterlands, Washington, through the Corps and Congress, actively prevented the degradation of Loudoun's environment through the construction of the Potomac Interceptor and the relocation of the PEPCO plant. Yet the final result of this preservation was to keep the way clear for suburban development. The PEPCO plant provides a clear example of this type of unintended consequence. Its defeat prevented the industrialization of Loudoun's Potomac waterfront. The Corps' failure to push its dam through in turn prevented its inundation. In August 1960 PEPCO announced that it would open its Loudoun land as a riverfront park. This former site of Loudoun's industrial dreams would host a golf course, a swimming pool, a boat ramp, and nature trails. It provided a recreational amenity for thousands of acres of suburban development. Unfortunately for the county, developers' dreams of suburban homes materialized faster than Loudoun boosters' own dreams of industrial development in Broad Run, leaving the county scrambling to pay for suburban services. When the county finally did secure substantial business development in the 1990s, it would come in the form of high-tech office jobs, not polluting industry. Preservationists had hoped to transform the county into Washington's backyard—a place of beauty, nature, and recreation. The sum total impact of metropolitan involvement in the county did not fulfill this vision either. Rather, metropolitan growth made the area a land of backyards, a county whose suburban homes housed the growing numbers of workers commuting in to government offices, military contractors, and technology firms in Fairfax County.

෴

Compared to the Potomac, the San Jacinto River is a rather underwhelming body of water. Its West Fork meanders southward ninety-eight miles from Walker County, Texas, through central Montgomery County, to the Harris County line. There it meets the sixty-nine-mile-long East Fork, which drains the eastern third of Montgomery County. The combined river then winds another twenty-eight miles toward the Gulf before entering the Houston Ship Channel. The San Jacinto is a fickle river. During hot, dry summers, it is little more than a creek trickling between steep, sandy banks. A sudden downpour or slow-moving tropical storm, however, can quickly transform it into a raging torrent whose floodwaters fan out over the county's bottomlands. Indeed, the flow of the West Fork fluctuates between 1,290 and 9,700 MGD in normal years, but floodwaters can produce 71,100 MGD flows. Dry spells like the 1956 drought can reduce it to almost nothing. In spite of this unpredictability and potential hazards, or perhaps because of them, southeast Texas boosters had long searched for ways to tame, harness, and profit from the San Jacinto. When in the summer of 1930 local booster J. W. Harris looked out on the river's sandbars from his home in Honea, a few miles west of Conroe, he had visions of locks and dams, of barges moving upriver, bringing prosperity with them. He was not the last to dream such dreams.[47]

It was an article of faith in the American South that dams were a one-way ticket to prosperity. Dam building mobilized federal and state resources to power factories, electrify the countryside, produce cheap fertilizer, control flooding, and provide water for drinking and irrigation.[48] The San Jacinto held great promise for this kind of development. After passing through Montgomery County, the river flowed into what was becoming the nation's largest concentration of chemical production and oil refining and one of the nation's busiest ports. Houston's industries grew thirstier every year. Between 1947 and

1963 the number of manufacturing plants in Harris County grew from 779 to 1,987, with value added from manufacturing ballooning from $256.9 million to $1.57 billion. So too did the metropolitan population, which grew from 528,961 in 1940 to 1.4 million by 1960, just missing 2 million by 1970. Both industry and municipal populations relied almost exclusively on well water until 1953, causing declining aquifers, subsidence, and salt infiltration. Montgomery County was upstream from a dynamic metropolis that was literally sinking because of its thirst.[49]

Urban water demand brought parts of Montgomery County under threat of inundation. Yet the county's experiences diverged from those of Loudoun in three important ways. First, where Loudoun's preservationists and boosters were caught up in a national debate over the Potomac watershed, damming the San Jacinto was a regional affair. The federal government had little direct involvement in the watershed north of the city after World War II. This left local boosters and rural landowners, Houston's political leadership, and a state-chartered river authority to hammer out the river's future. Second, where the rhetoric of environmental preservation constrained Potomac development by the mid-1960s, discourses of resource conservation and economic development propelled dam construction in Texas through the 1970s. This allowed the SJRA leadership to position their organization as an advocate for the watershed even as they built a reservoir for Houston. Finally, unlike Riverbend or Seneca, the SJRA constructed Lake Conroe. As with the Potomac Interceptor, the lake spurred housing development within the county. This development raised questions about exactly who controlled the lake and who had the right to access it—questions that echoed the struggle to enact stock laws two decades earlier.

Four groups and their economic interests propelled the Lake Conroe drama through its twists and turns. County boosters wanted the San Jacinto to provide local industrial development and therefore personal and regional economic prosperity. Ranchers wanted to develop the watershed to prevent flooding and protect their soils from erosion, both of which would improve the productivity and value of their land. Houston's political and business interests—one and the same during this period—sought industrial and municipal water supplies to shore up the city's economic growth. Between 1951 and 1973 these three groups courted, cajoled, and, at times, castigated the SJRA, a state-chartered entity with ultimate control over most of the watershed. The SJRA interposed itself between Houston and its northern neighbors, blunting the city's attempts to exert power over the region's watershed. Yet at the same time, the SJRA's limited financial resources left the authority dependent on Houston. The SJRA had to do its own courting, cajoling, and castigating. Its ultimate partnership with the city transformed Montgomery County and its position within the metropolis. In the process, the SJRA brought prosperity and development, accelerating suburban growth and binding the county more tightly to the city.[50]

All of this was still over the horizon when in 1937 a handful of rural land-owners and businessmen in and around Conroe put forward the idea for the SJRA. Obie Etheridge, a local lawyer and owner of the *Conroe Courier*, led the effort. Etheridge had spent much of his childhood in the arid lands of southern Wyoming and northern Colorado. While there, the story goes, he became enamored with the way government-funded reclamation projects pumped economic vitality into dry, weary lands. He hoped similar projects might do the same for his adopted hometown. Etheridge and company convinced R. A. Powell, their state representative, to guide the project through the state legislature. The SJRA's enabling legislation included the standard laundry list of conservation goals: limiting erosion, combating flooding, promoting reforestation, increasing wildlife populations, and, where feasible, constructing "a series of small dams along the San Jacinto tributaries and impound water which could be sold to municipalities, industries, and agriculture." The SJRA's jurisdiction included the entire watershed outside Harris County. The authority's goals reflected its founders' belief that the development of both soils and water would secure for the watershed a golden agricultural and industrial future full of cattle, crops, dams, and factories—a Texan's totems of progress.[51]

The SJRA could wield substantial power with limited local oversight. The state legislature armed the SJRA's appointed board with eminent domain powers and made it responsible only to the Texas Board of Water Engineers (TBWE) in Austin. What the legislature withheld, however, was money. Only after pleading from the SJRA's board did the legislature provide it with a ten-year grant of half the ad valorem taxes within its district. This amounted to $110,000 per year during years when the state collected the tax. This money was, in the words of a later SJRA board president, "ridiculously inadequate to do anything consequential." Montgomery County boosters had handed over their county's water future to an entity insulated from local public opinion and increasingly desperate to secure revenues.[52]

World War II provided the SJRA with its first break. The TBWE selected the SJRA as an institution to help meet Houston's wartime demand for industrial water. In July 1942 the TBWE granted the SJRA the right to 165,000 acre-feet per year from the San Jacinto River with the intent that it would deliver that water to vital ship channel war industries. Heated conflicts between the SJRA and the city over who would control this water supply compelled the federal government to step in and construct two canals to deliver the water. The SJRA's failure to compromise led the TBWE to replace the SJRA's entire board—an act with long-term implications for the SJRA and the region. Where the earlier board had represented the interests of Montgomery County and the surrounding counties, the new board's members hailed from Huntsville, Baytown, Conroe, and Dickinson—from both the watershed and the areas of potential downstream water consumption. The board would retain a similar form for decades thereafter. After 1943 Montgomery County would never have more than two members on the board of six, and all of them were from Conroe.[53]

Walter G. Hall of Dickinson, Texas, took the reins of what had been, in his words, "nothing but a paper organization" in 1943. Hall brought to the position extensive political connections and a deep commitment to conservation. His upbringing on a farm near League City and his experience in agribusiness convinced him that soil conservation, flood control, and reservoir development would contribute to the long-term prosperity of the watershed, not just the metropolis. Hall's SJRA would be the impartial arbiter of regional development, unifying the region through conservation. Under his watch, the SJRA outlined a bold program that sought nothing less than the total development of the watershed.[54] He publicly unveiled this master plan in the summer of 1945. The SJRA proposed twenty reservoirs of various sizes spread across the compact watershed. Conroe boosters were pleased. While they understood that much of this water would flow to industries on the Gulf Coast, they took seriously the SJRA's portrayal of the areas north of Houston as "ripe for further industrialization." Agricultural landowners, for their part, brightened at the mention of flood control and continued soil conservation work.[55]

That same year generous financing from the Federal Works Administration allowed the authority to purchase one of the two wartime canals that carried water from the San Jacinto River to the shipbuilding and oil industries east of Houston.[56] After the TBWE granted the SJRA control of another 165,000 acre-feet of San Jacinto water in February 1947, the SJRA had the water supply, the transmission systems, and the customers it needed to stabilize its revenue stream and begin taking on debt.[57] Hall commissioned engineering studies of the proposed dams and stepped up the SJRA's soil conservation work. He stopped short, however, of approaching Houston to help finance these plans. With the completion of its master plan in 1951, Hall stepped down, leaving the SJRA poised to provide flood control, water supplies, and industrial growth.[58]

Conroe boosters clung to promises of local industrial potential throughout the 1950s and early 1960s. Conroe was upstream. Nature had given the town a prior claim to water from the San Jacinto.[59] The SJRA's response to these local claims is telling. At a November 1954 speech, Hall promised that "the people of Montgomery County can have an adequate supply of surface water to meet any future needs . . . [if they] are willing to pay for it." Montgomery County, however, was not able to fund the sjra's ambitions. Houston could. These simple financial realities would make the metropolis and its ship-channel industries the primary consumer of sjra water.[60] In order to placate the county, the sjra passed a resolution in early 1955 committing itself to providing "a substantial supply" of water at a fair price to Montgomery County from any dams the sjra might build there.[61] It was an easy promise to make and an important piece of rhetoric that allowed the sjra to stand with local boosters even as its planners traced contour lines on maps of Montgomery County, outlining reservoirs full of water destined for a thirsty city.

The task of building these reservoirs fell to a home-grown Montgomery County businessman. Winifred B. (W. B.) Weisinger joined the sjra board in 1951 as a replacement for his older brother, William Samuel (W. S.) Weisinger, who had been elected Montgomery County judge.[62] The Weisinger brothers were the scions of a family whose roots in the county and extensive land-holdings went back into the nineteenth century and whose influence in local politics and society was unparalleled. W. B. Weisinger's biography reads like a Sinclair Lewis caricature. Leaving the family farm a few miles west of Con-roe, he opened a local car dealership and became a leader in the chamber of commerce. He was a Lion, a Mason, a Shriner, a Methodist, a board member of the local bank, a trustee of the Real Estate Development Fund of the Montgomery County Industrial Foundation, and the owner of the local TV and radio stations. Where Walter G. Hall's background had led him to promote the authority as a regional conservation organization, W. B. Weisinger's business background, his local political connections, and his personal ambitions led him to promote recreational development—development on Houston's dime—as the county's new growth industry. This became the sjra's guiding conviction during his nearly two decades at the helm, from 1954 to his death in 1973. Conservation, regional development, and local industrial growth faded in the light of this singular goal. Houston's water needs would underwrite the sjra's construction of a reservoir in Montgomery County—a reservoir that would attract Houstonians and, in the process, fill the pockets of county landowners.[63]

Weisinger had cause for optimism. Subsidence and rising pumping costs were punishing Houston for its dependence on well water. In June 1943 Houstonians approved a $14 million bond, part of which paid for a reservoir on the San Jacinto River in northern Harris County. When it opened in December 1953, 12,240-acre Lake Houston became a distribution point for future surface water developments.[64] Yet a 1955 Houston Chamber of Commerce report predicted that the city would need additional water as early as 1960. "It . . . is essential," the report concluded, "that immediate steps be taken to [secure] a new 'firm' supply of not less than 200 [MGD] . . . within five years. Any unnecessary delay will jeopardize the industrial growth of the entire area."[65] And then the drought came. From 1950 to 1956 the state experienced the lowest rainfall levels on record. Between July 1950 and March 1957 the average flow into Lake Houston was less than one-third of normal. Houston was in the market for new water supplies.[66]

The city was blessed with something few cities had: the luxury of choice. Houston lay within fifty miles of four rivers: the Brazos, the Trinity, the San Jacinto, and the Neches. These rivers combine to drain two-fifths of Texas. Houston's problem was not where to find water but which water source to tap first. In a city of grand ambitions, it is not surprising that officials chased more distant and uncertain sources first, leaving the San Jacinto for later.[67] Houston could persistently spurn the SJRA's courtship for the simple reason that the city could take the SJRA's water for granted. No other municipality within the geographic bounds of the watershed had anything like the resources needed to fund an SJRA reservoir. Nor would the state allow any reservoir development that did not include provisions for water to go to Houston. Geography and politics conspired to make the SJRA dependent on Houston. So long as the city was willing to accept the slow inflation of land prices in the watershed, Houston's political leaders could keep the SJRA waiting for as long as they could do without the water. The SJRA, on the other hand, depended on Houston's money to move even a single one of its fourteen proposed dams from the drafting table onto the landscape. The SJRA needed Houston more than Houston needed the SJRA, and both sides knew it.[68]

The board began this troubled courtship in August 1952 with the SJRA's first proposal to the city, which Mayor Oscar Holcombe flatly rejected.[69] When drought led the Houston Chamber of Commerce to call for a San Jacinto reservoir in 1955, SJRA board members picked up their briefcases full of yield studies, contour maps, and engineering reports and drove the forty miles south into downtown Houston.[70] They fared little better this time. Nor did they make any progress in 1957, when they made the same presentation twice more.[71] By this time the authority was in the awkward position of searching for buyers for twenty-five MGD of water the year after a record drought. Still no one was interested.[72] With the changing of mayoral administrations in January 1958, the SJRA's board members screwed up their courage to make their proposition to Mayor Lewis Cutrer.[73] The Cutrer administration had its own plans. In an unprecedented move, the mayor made a grab for Trinity River Authority (TRA) water. Compared to the SJRA, the TRA was a massive organization. Created in 1955, it covered seventeen counties from Dallas to the Gulf of Mexico. The TRA had more water to sell, a greater financial base, and greater political influence. It was also adamantly opposed to Houston using any water from its territory. The Trinity River was the primary water supply for much of East Texas. Towns up and down the Trinity joined Dallas and the TRA in condemning what they viewed as a brazen water grab by the Bayou City. Pride and boosterism certainly had a great deal to do with the ink spilled over the issue. So too did the allocation of a scarce resource. If Houston secured interbasin rights to Trinity water, it might use this power to limit both water use and upstream pollution, placing Dallas's future development in a stranglehold. Houston certainly had grand plans for the Trinity. The proposed Lake Livingston would blanket eighty-three thousand acres of East Texas pine woods, making it much larger than any of the SJRA's proposed reservoirs. It would hold more than twelve times as much water as Lake Houston and would be cheaper per acre-foot than either the future Lake Conroe or Lake Houston. A TRA contract was simply a better deal for Houston's water users—if they could get it.[74]

Fearing their time was running short, the SJRA made a final plea for the Houston City Council to abandon its Trinity proposal. The SJRA offered eight reservoirs on the San Jacinto, developed in increments as needed, totaling 570 MGD.[75] While its water was significantly more expensive, the SJRA's selling points were water quality and recreation. Ironically, given its origins, the SJRA used Montgomery County's relative lack of industrial development as an argument for placing a dam there. Pure water flowed downstream through the still-rural watershed to Houston. In comparison with this "pure" and "unpolluted" water, Trinity water posed, in Weisinger's words, "a serious threat to the health of more than a million people of Metropolitan Houston and . . . [to] one of the finest recreational areas in Texas [Lake Houston]." Weisinger shamelessly appealed to Houston's pride. Why, he chided, would Houston invest so much money to bring in water that even Dallas had "emphatically rejected" for drinking water during the last drought? Like the Potomac Estuary, the Trinity River was Dallas's sewer, full of paper mill discharges and industrial wastes, polluted runoff and untreated sewage. Would Houstonians really drink water that Dallas residents flushed down their toilets? Wouldn't it be better, he argued, for the city to fund the SJRA's plan for "a chain of lakes, stretching like pearls around the San Jacinto watershed"? The counties to the north would, with their investment, become an area of private resorts, profitably developed by Houston businessmen, and public parks, owned and operated by Houston for its residents. The area would become Houston's backyard. These lakes would provide more than an amenity; they would fuel a $100 million industry. The SJRA estimated that the lakes might bring as much as ten thousand jobs and a 20 percent increase in tourist expenditures to the metropolitan area.[76] The SJRA portrayed the

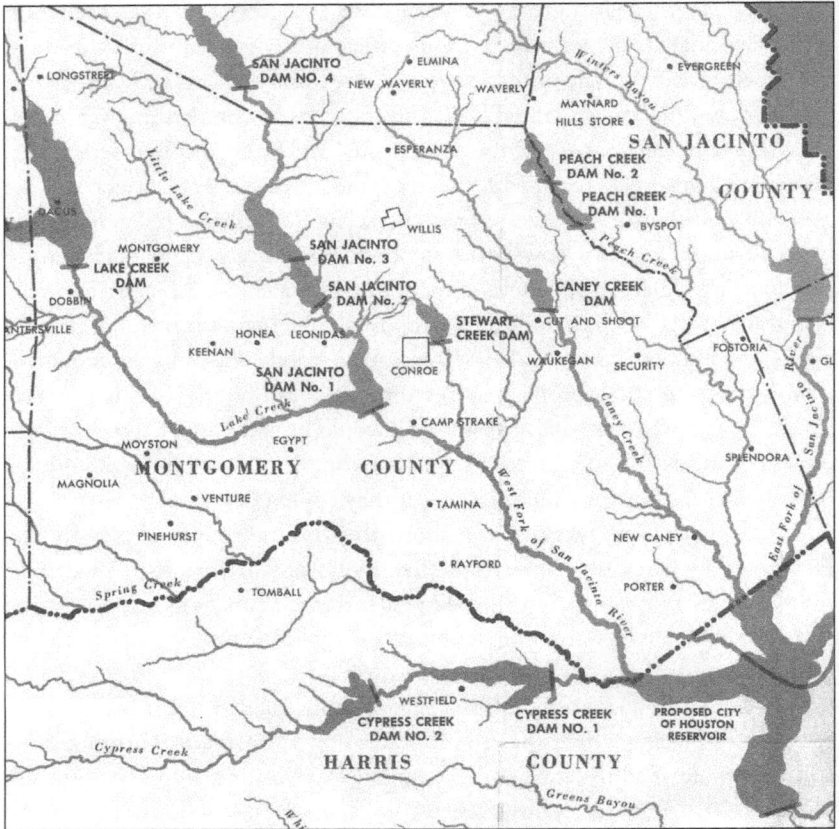

SJRA's map of proposed reservoirs, 1957.
SJRA, *Master Plan: Report for the Full Scale Development of the San Jacinto River*
(Conroe: San Jacinto River Authority, 1957). Courtesy of SJRA.

watershed as "one integrated agrico-industrial unit," a "community of interest" that required a "close partnership" between Houston and the SJRA. In creating this image, Weisinger echoed Walter G. Hall's vision of the watershed. Unlike Hall, however, Weisinger admitted the subordination of this hydrologically defined community to Houston's interests. The SJRA offered Houston the San Jacinto River watershed as a water source and as a recreational hinterland.[77]

Enthusiastic editorials from Houston newspapers and the continued support of the Houston Chamber of Commerce focused political pressure on Mayor Cutrer to adopt the SJRA proposal. Confident that the mayor would see the light, the SJRA board submitted an application to the TBWE for a 350,000-acre-foot reservoir located on the West Fork of the San Jacinto, just west of Conroe.[78] Negotiations with both the SJRA and the TRA dragged on into the fall of 1958. The Houston City Council filed a permit for a dam on the Trinity in October of that year. The mayor had chosen to pour the city's resources into the Trinity project, but it continued to string the SJRA along in the hope that, with only a small investment, it might secure San Jacinto water as well. Houston paid the piper and therefore called the tune within the San Jacinto watershed. The SJRA proposal for the Lake Conroe site came before the Texas Water Board in January 1959. There county landowners discovered just how much its courtship of Houston had changed the SJRA.[79]

As these farmers, ranchers, and timbermen saw it, the Lake Conroe proposal represented a fundamental shift in the SJRA's loyalties, placing the distribution of water for downstream customers ahead of its conservation mandate. These men arrived in Austin as if to plead with a wayward child. The resulting hearing did not pit an expanding imperial city against its rooted agrarian hinterland. The city watched quietly from the sidelines. Nor, as with Loudoun, was it a case of NIMBY activism by locals hell-bent on protecting their land from government appropriation. These men had been schooled from birth in the use of government projects and programs for personal benefit. Nor was it a defense of nature against commodification. These men believed that the San Jacinto needed to be controlled and developed. Rather, the hearing over Lake Conroe was a family dispute. Both the SJRA leadership and landowners shared the conservationist goal of efficiently protecting and developing natural resources for the economic good of future generations. At issue was whether the SJRA existed to develop the soils and water of the San Jacinto River for those in the immediate watershed or whether it existed to appropriate the river's water for the benefit of Houston and the SJRA's bottom line. Did the San Jacinto River define a community of shared interests and shared natural resources, as Hall had believed, or did Houston and its needs define the watershed as part of the city's hinterland? Montgomery County landowners clung to the former, even when the SJRA board made it increasingly clear that it had accepted the latter.

The landowners' feelings of betrayal were understandable. Under Walter G. Hall the SJRA had partnered with the San Jacinto Soil Conservation District (SJSCD), an organization managed by local landowners, to improve the county's pastures and farmland. The SJRA purchased and rented out soil-terracing equipment and supplies to landowners at cost. Landowners used these tools to complete terracing, retention ponds, and other erosion-control methods prescribed by the district's soil scientists. By 1956 the SJRA supported thirteen contractors and twenty-two bulldozers working full time in the district. Some 3,380 landowners had signed up by 1956. They represented 1,426,093 acres, or 31 percent of the total farm and ranch land within the SJRA's boundaries. This arrangement was a boon for rural landowners, allowing them to increase the productivity and value of their land, to provide water for their livestock, and to free themselves of the downward spiral of cotton agriculture. Even as the SJRA was defending its dam projects, its employees continued to average 650 hours a month of conservation work.[80]

The SJRA's pond construction program best exemplifies the watershed vision that the SJRA and rural landowners shared at the beginning of the 1950s. With the SJRA's support, landowners constructed stock ponds and small reservoirs (from half an acre to thirty acres) across the watershed. These lakes held flood-waters and runoff that would otherwise have muddied and silted Houston's water supply. The captured water, after supplying cattle and providing rec-reation, then infiltrated the county's aquifers while it made its way south to Houston, filling the city's wells, mitigating the city's subsidence problems, and fending off saltwater infiltration. Investments upstream benefited the water-shed as a whole. While landowners certainly understood that some of the SJRA's lakes might eventually have to be larger, they expected future development to fit within this broader conservation framework. Rural landowners' experience of the SJRA led them to assume that the authority served their interests.[81]

They were shocked to discover in January 1959 that the SJRA planned to place a 350,000-acre-foot reservoir in the middle of some of the most produc-tive pastureland in Montgomery County—the very pastureland that the SJRA and SJSCD had spent the last decade improving. Ranchers organized the Asso-ciation of Submerged Landowners and Operators of Montgomery and Walker Counties and collected signatures protesting the reservoir. The SJSCD and the local Farm Bureau sent in letters of protest. A half dozen representatives arrived in Austin to state their case before the TBWE on February 16 and 17, 1959. Ar-thur P. Terrell and W. Bryan Shaver represented the submerged landowners, and Luther Hall and W. S. Gibbs represented the SJSCD. They fomented no grassroots protest. They made no claims about the sacredness of the land or its right to remain natural. These opponents accepted as a given that the San Jacinto ought to be dammed and its water put to productive work. What they opposed was the size of the reservoir and its placement. They objected to the SJRA's construction of a reservoir for Houston.[82]

They began with the land itself. Where the Texas Water Board saw empty space, these men saw land that was "open, improved, and in a high state of production." In a county comprised mostly of sandy timbered uplands and poorly drained bottomlands, the SJRA planned to flood "a highly fertile, well developed, and thickly populated area." SJSCD and SJRA investments in this land had made these pastures up to three times more productive than land in other parts of the county. In response to these claims, SJRA lawyer Jack Ayer brought into question the very idea that floodplains and pastureland could ever really be improved. Whenever each landowner mentioned the quality of his land, Ayer asked him how much of the land was cultivated in row crops. The answer was little to none. Ayer then asked the landowner how often his land flooded. Each landowner admitted that much of his land lay within the floodplain. This was all that the board needed to hear. The state charged the board to reject any proposal that proved "detrimental to the public welfare." Inundating a floodplain did not meet this standard.[83]

The landowners' second argument struck closer to the heart of the matter. They claimed that the SJRA was squandering tax money that was supposed to have gone for "erosion, flood control, forestry and recreational purposes" on urban reservoirs. The authority was prepared for this. W. B. Weisinger rattled off conservation statistics from the stand, celebrating all that the SJRA had accomplished in cooperation with the SJSCD. He bragged that the authority had $160,000 invested in the conservation work. Then one of the opponents' lawyers asked him to compare this figure with the SJRA's yearly income from water sales to Humble Oil, its largest downstream customer. Weisinger did not recall the figure. The reality was that industry, not soil conservation, covered the SJRA's bottom line. The Lake Conroe proposal, in SJSCD leader W. S. Gibbs's words, "defeats our concept of conservation." Gibbs and the other landowners had embraced the county's role as an agricultural hinterland, but they could not accept that the SJRA would drown their lands to construct a reservoir for the city—a reservoir they suspected was designed to serve "recreational and land promotional purposes." Luther Hall, revealing a flair for the dramatic, ended his testimony by quoting a conservation textbook whose pages cautioned that "nothing is more priceless than soil."[84]

These arguments focused on one central question: Why *this* dam on *this* site? The 1951 authority master plan had included two small reservoirs with a combined storage capacity of 158,000 acre-feet beneath the proposed reservoir. As the SJRA funded more engineering studies and continued its intense negotiations with Houston, the plans changed. The SJRA proposal submitted to the Texas Water Board on December 19, 1958, called for a single reservoir west of Conroe that would cover both these sites with a greatly increased storage capacity of 380,430 acre-feet. Landowners claimed this large reservoir had "no relationship to the various so-called Master Plan[s]" of the SJRA.[85] The fact was that the Lake Conroe dam site was where the engineers said the dam should be. It had steep hills, good base soils, and a watershed large enough to fill a large reservoir. When the SJRA realized that Houston was unlikely to pay for more than one reservoir, its proposals honed in on the single most cost-effective site for water storage. These reasons were sufficient to justify the choice before the Texas Water Board.[86]

The hearing marked a turning point in the relationship between the SJRA and Montgomery County. The SJRA, with Houston's support, secured approval for its reservoir. On the other side, agricultural landowners found themselves locked out. In a county where personal connections and face-to-face conversations were both form and substance of political power and masculinity, the SJRA had insulted these men. Weisinger did not even make the time to lay out the SJRA's plans to Luther Hall, who was an SJSCD board member, a major landowner, and Weisinger's brother-in-law. Hall only learned that some of his land would be under the lake from Weisinger's mechanic. These meetings left landowners complaining that "we have the distinct impression that steam-roller tactics are being employed to construct a lake which will injure us." The Texas Water Board's refusal to move the hearing to Conroe reinforced these suspicions. Local landowner Albert Myers summed up the landowners' feelings when, at the hearing, he explained, "Before you take their land away, [landowners] just like to be asked." After sitting listening quietly to the landowners' complaints, the Texas Water Board thanked the men for their time and got down to the business of reviewing engineering specifications—the facts and figures upon which the county's future would turn.[87]

In comparison with Loudoun's public opposition to dams on the Potomac, Montgomery County landowners appear strangely ineffective. They staged no rallies. They chanted no slogans. Loudoun County farmers had powerful allies in Senator Harry Byrd and Representative Howard Smith. The ranchers' state representatives, in contrast, lined up alongside the SJRA. Where Loudoun protestors articulated a preservationist defense of the county's historical landscapes, agrarian beauty, and agricultural productivity, the ranchers held fast to conservationist assumptions that natural resources should be developed for their economic benefit. The ranchers viewed conservation as an issue best handled by white landed elites and trained experts. These men shared the same social world and were tied to the same landscape. They submitted their case to the TBWE and grudgingly accepted its decision.

Houston, however, left the San Jacinto project up in the air, choosing instead to sign a $74.5 million contract with the TRA on September 14, 1959. This sent the SJRA scrambling to prepare for another hearing before the Texas Water Board in the winter of 1959. The SJRA gained a major bargaining chip when Houston decided to transport Trinity water through Lake Houston. Trinity water was dirty—a fact that the SJRA never tired of reminding anyone who would listen. The addition of Trinity water into the system would degrade the quality and therefore the value of the lake's water, one-quarter of which was owned by the SJRA. This became the legal grounds for the SJRA blocking Lake Livingston. As the hearings dragged on into the new year, the SJRA was sanguine that its hardline approach would bear fruit even as city leaders and Houston newspapers denounced the SJRA for "hijacking" the hearings and holding the Trinity project hostage.[88]

The SJRA stonewalled in Austin while board members continued their negotiations with Mayor Cutrer. Finally, on March 12, 1960, the city and the SJRA signed a five-year contract. Houston agreed to purchase twenty-five MGD of SJRA water that the city did not need for $228,000 per year. This money was to be used solely for the construction of a dam on the San Jacinto, the plans of which were subject to the city's approval. The city further agreed to not put any Trinity water into its municipal water system for twenty-five years. This ensured that future municipal water supplies would come from the San Jacinto. In exchange for these concessions, the SJRA dropped its objections to the TRA permit.[89] The *Houston Post* smelled a rat. Under the headline "Money Settles Muddy Water of River Fuss," the paper snidely remarked that "the waters of the Trinity River cleared as if by magic" once Houston signed its $1.14 million, five-year contract.[90] Through shrewd negotiation, the SJRA got what it wanted out of the city. Houston had the money, but it did not have all the power. With a modest yearly payment, the city quieted the SJRA and bought the city room to maneuver in the future. With the TBWE approving the SJRA's contract on May 5, 1960, the SJRA returned to Montgomery County with the money and the legal authority to begin Lake Conroe. Nine years later SJRA contractors broke ground at the Lake Conroe dam site.[91]

Financing and purchasing the lake site had proved a far more costly endeavor than either the SJRA or Houston had expected. When the money from Houston ran out in the spring of 1965, the city's agents purchased somewhere close to 70 percent of the required land. A $2 million loan from the state kept the purchases crawling along.[92] Houston, embroiled in its Lake Livingston project, made the SJRA wait another two years before signing another contract on April 14, 1968. This final deal gave Houston a two-thirds interest in Lake Conroe in exchange for its accepting two-thirds of the cost. By this point, the SJRA had already invested $3.9 million into the project, most of it borrowed money.[93] Delays had inflated cost projections from $13 million to $18 million. Most of this increase came from mushrooming land prices. Land acquisition stirred up the usual battery of heated condemnation proceedings, tense negotiations, and accusations of price gouging and dispossession. The SJRA had purchased its first parcel in April 1959 and was still condemning land into 1971. During that period, prices rose from $200 to $300 per acre to $600 to $1,200 per acre. A signed contract with Houston made this a future resort area in a rapidly developing county, a fact landowners leveraged in their negotiations.[94] Even more important than how much landowners got was whom these metropolitan payoffs went to. Whatever conflict the sjra may have had with rural elites, it brought large sums of Houston money to the area to the benefit of landowners, speculators, and county tax rolls. The landowners who held out and thereby received the largest sums for their land represented a cross section of county power brokers—including both the dam's strongest opponents and its greatest allies. Men on both sides of this divide used their knowledge of the local power structures and the legal system to ensure that they would be well compensated for their property. Three of the dam's most fervent opponents forced condemnation hearings in 1969. Luther Hall, Dick Calfee, and Allen Monroe received $925, $1,000, and $1,050 per acre, respectively.[95] These figures were lower than the prices paid by speculators for prime lakefront land, but they were still far higher than those paid to landowners who sold out earlier. These landowners were smart businessmen, as well as conservative agrarians. They held out for their price. The sjra paid it as Houstonians grumbled.

When it came to financial windfalls, sjra officials also joined in. W. C. McClain, a Conroe businessman who had been on the sjra board until 1956, purchased an interest in two tracts that would become lakefront land. C. W. Curry, the sjra's general manager, got in on the act in 1962, buying thirty-seven acres near the lake for $190 an acre. "I was fortunate that I was able to buy that land," he brashly told a Houston reporter in 1969. "One of these days that land will be worth a lot of money." Most of the public attention focused on the Weisinger family. The clan had deep roots along the San Jacinto River east of Conroe. Patriarch John Michael Weisinger had managed a four-thousand-acre cotton plantation in the area, complete with a general store and two dozen cotton tenants. When the elder Weisinger died, he left this land to his eleven children, who included county judge W. S., sjra president W. B., Ruth Mae, who married local rancher and dam opponent Dan Madley, and Nancy Beth, who married Luther Hall. Each of these families owned future lakefront land.[96] As early as 1959 the *Houston Post* was all but leveling charges of graft at the Weisingers, accusing the sjra head of increasing the size of the lake to ensure that some of his family's acreage would end up as lakefront land.[97] Russell Jolley, a board member from Houston, declared, "I think it wrong and completely indefensible for any board member to deal in land on the lake." In his own defense, W. B. Weisinger explained, "You can't throw a rock any-whe[re] up here in the Conroe area without hitting a Weisinger. . . . [T]here are more than 30 of us. . . . [T]his land has been in the family for 75 years—that's not speculation."[98] To those who criticized his management of the sjra, he responded, "[My] conscience is clear. . . . What I do is in the best interest of the San Jacinto River Authority."[99]

Ownership of lakefront land was indeed a family affair. W. S. Weisinger

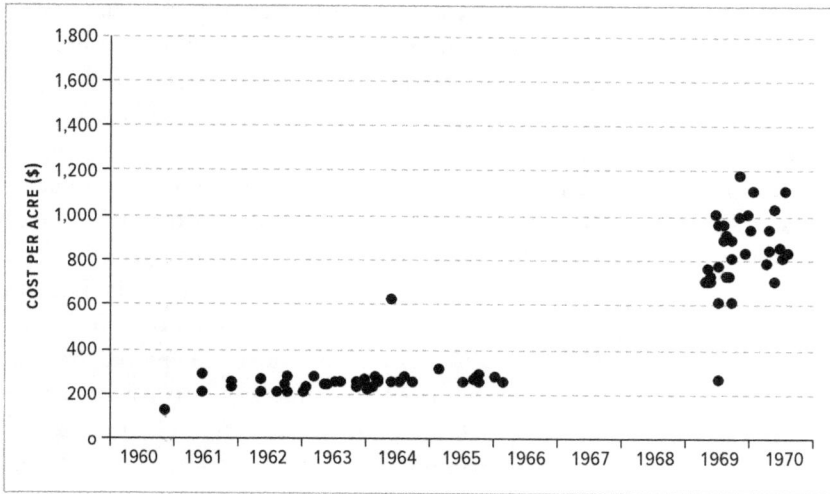

Land purchases made for Lake Conroe.
Data from the eighty-two property purchases for which I secured complete data.
Folder Land Acquisition, Lake Conroe, box 405, sjRA.

had 2,034 acres; Dan Madley owned 3,147 acres; and the Weisinger estate, W. B. and W. S. Weisinger trustees, owned 1,200 acres. For Houstonians, all of this meant paying these well-connected landowners ballooning prices for inundated lands. W. S. Weisinger, for instance, got $513,221, or an average of $765 an acre, for land that he had either inherited or purchased over the previous decades. The real money was in lakefront land. Dan Madley was left with over 1,500 acres of lakefront property. W. S. Weisinger retained 1,334 acres. These two men and former county commissioner T. J. Peel combined to sell 1,470 acres of lakefront property to the Berton Land Developing Company of Houston for $9 million, an average of over $6,000 an acre. Lake Conroe was the center of a real estate boom. All around the lake, developers were paying between $4,500 and $6,000 an acre for land that had, only ten years before, rarely sold for more than $300. Many lots on the lake sold for between $15,000 and $25,000 even before the lake filled. The city's investment in Lake Conroe proved immensely profitable.[100]

It would be easy to join Houston newspapers in crying foul at these windfalls. Sniffing along a cold trail of alleged graft and corruption, however, would distract from the larger point. The dictates of engineering within the criteria of maximizing the efficiency of raw water production for Houston were sufficient to place a large dam at the Honea site. As sjRA board member J. B. Stratton put it, "Of course I know a dam can't be built near Conroe without one or more of the Weisingers being affected, but engineers will make that decision, not I or Mr. Weisinger."[101] Once the dam was slated for the Conroe area, land-owners made the most of the city's investment. That local white elites profited most is a reflection of the pervasive and persistent social and racial inequities of the rural South rather than a shocking revelation of personal moral corruption. Both cattlemen and Conroe businessmen were descended from frontier oppor-tunists. They continued in the paths of their forefathers. They held valuable acreage, added to it when they had opportunity, fought for the highest price they could get, and enjoyed the profits that resulted. The city and the SJRA gave rural landowners a good hand to play, and they knew how to play it. This was the prerogative of those with the financial resources to hold out. The SJRA's intermediary role blunted Houston's imperial ambitions and ensured that dis-placement would fill the pockets of these Montgomery County landowners.[102]

Uncovering what smaller-scale landowners and tenants did is far more dif-ficult. As the cotton and timber economy declined, the children of most non-elite rural families in the area had sought employment in Houston or outside the state. A few decades of this type of migration meant homesteads divided among multiple heirs, many of whom were no longer living in the area. Such families, many of whom were African American, were in a poor bargaining position. If a land speculator could get one family member to sell, he could then sue to force the others to sell the property at auction, usually allowing him to purchase the rest of the land at a bargain price. Tenants had no bar-gaining power at all.[103] Evidence is scarce as to how the area's African American population viewed the coming of Lake Conroe. One scrap that remains comes from Dorothy Reece, who remembered that most of New Home, an African American community, "disappeared beneath the waters of Lake Conroe—the school, the churches, the homes and the old landmarks."[104]

As 1972 drew to a close, the SJRA completed its land purchases, cleared the future lakeshore, and flooded the local timber market with trees harvested from the lake site. The gates closed in January 1973. At this point the SJRA began a new chapter in its history. Its involvement in soil conservation work, which waned over the previous decade, now shut down entirely. The authority freed itself to take on the various management responsibilities that came with the lake and its developments. In consultation with the Texas Water Quality Board, the SJRA licensed sewer and septic installations and monitored wa-ter quality. It regulated marinas and charged license fees. It took the lead in regional planning and oversight for lakefront development. In consultation with the Texas Parks and Wildlife Department, it stocked and managed fish populations. It entered the wastewater business to serve new developments. The authority became, in short, a metropolitan water utility.[105]

Cliché though it may be, the county really was never the same again. The

Grading land for the construction of Lake Conroe, ca. 1972.
Courtesy of SJRA. Additional photos are available at www.sjra.net/lakeconroe/history.

first thing the lake provided was something Loudoun County had sorely missed. The Gulf States Utility Company in Beaumont, Texas, selected the town of Willis, just east of Lake Conroe, as the site for a $50 million, gas-fired power plant. Opening in 1970, it used San Jacinto water, padded local tax rolls, and became a major employer.[106] Recreation was even more important, as lakefront developments were a booming industry in postwar Texas. Explosive growth around Austin's Lake Travis and Dallas's Lake Ray Hubbard convinced speculators and developers of Lake Conroe's economic potential.[107] The lake met all the criteria of a recreational paradise. It had excellent fishing, beautiful vistas, clear water, piney woods ambience, and gently sloping shorelines that, because the lake had no flood storage capacity, would remain usable year-round. It was also less than an hour's drive from downtown Houston. The dam's opponents had feared this very thing. They prophesied that the lake would replace "an existing agricultural economy" with "a lake dwelling citizenry which will lower the moral, political, economic, and educational standards of our established society." Lake Conroe, they warned, would become a place of frivolity, moral laxity, and consumerism.[108]

This, of course, did not prevent rural landowners from cashing in on Vanity Fair by selling their land to Houstonian developers who rushed in to claim the lakefront. Twenty-six separate developments had broken ground by May 1973, ranging from modest weekend homes to full-service resort communities. The august names of some of these developments speak to their aspirations: Point Aquarius, Roman Hills, Corinthian Point, April Sound, and Walden on Lake Conroe. Demand for lakefront land combined with the SJRA's stringent sewage regulations to drive up prices. On the lake, deed restrictions, underground utilities, security systems, concrete drainage, and streetlights were all standard. Lakefront nature was part of the appeal, but luxury and privacy were the most important amenities these developers offered.[109] Through their advertisements and site design, developers cultivated the illusion that the lakefront existed in a social vacuum, separate from the rural landscapes upon which the SJRA had done its work. These developments maintained guarded entry gates, built private boat ramps, and enforced trespassing laws in order to protect their customers—a group that included many of the county's leading citizens.[110] Developers and residents maintained these Lake Conroe resorts for those with the money to enjoy them.

Despite this local windfall, there was no assurance that the broader community would have access to the lake. There was not a single publicly owned park or boat ramp on the lake from its opening in January 1973 until October 21, 1976. Who had allowed this to happen? Part of the blame lay with the county residents themselves. County voters had persistently opposed increasing taxes, soundly defeating county park bonds in both 1954 and 1968. They had assumed that the SJRA and Houston would provide free parkland on the lake. Montgomery County was being tapped for the economic good of the metropolis. Membership in the metropolitan community should, county residents believed, carry with it provision for the county's recreation needs.[111] Legally speaking, this was accurate. The SJRA's enabling legislation charged it with providing recreation opportunities, a commitment the authority had frequently reaffirmed.[112] During contract negotiations in 1968, SJRA officials had insisted, in spite of Houston's protests, on a clause that committed both parties to providing four parks on the lake totaling eighty acres.[113] Such provisions were crucial to validating the SJRA's claims to serve the interest of the watershed. Yet the SJRA chose not to go through the hassle and expense of acquiring parkland by condemnation, especially with Houstonians already grumbling about the money being paid out for land and flood easements. As an SJRA official explained it, "We just kept putting off buying land for parks. When we got to the end we had no money." At the 1969 dam groundbreaking ceremony, W. B. Weisinger had told the crowd that the lake would "be unsurpassed as a recreational playground for our citizens." This promise rang hollow for those who found themselves locked out of Lake Conroe.[114]

Heavy rainfall during 1973 filled the lake faster than anyone had expected. This placed the access issue in a pressure cooker, as county judge Lynn Coker fielded phone calls from irate residents demanding to know how they would get access to "their" lake. Coker sent off a formal complaint to both the SJRA and Houston's city hall reminding them of their contractual agreement. He was told, quite simply, that there was no money. Whatever sympathy Coker may have had from the board had disappeared when W. B. Weisinger died in June 1973. The board elected J. B. Stratton, a banker from Baytown, as the SJRA's new president. Stratton refocused the board's attention squarely on the authority's economic health and security. Where Weisinger had a vested interest in the county's economic development, Stratton viewed requests for parks as proof of the county's ingratitude. Stratton's SJRA was a public utility with water contracts to fulfill.[115]

For real estate interests, public access sullied the carefully crafted image of Lake Conroe as an exclusive retreat from the urban decay, crime, pollution, and heat of Houston. The developments were surrounded by a natural landscape of peace and leisure. Deer and squirrels were to be the only visitors appearing out of the woods to greet the newcomers. The trash, noise, and decidedly unpicturesque character of blue-collar fishermen undermined this advertising image and therefore threatened profits.[116] The county ultimately hammered out a deal with the National Forest Service to construct a seventy-three-acre park site on the northern end of the lake.[117] It also succeeded in building a boat ramp at the end of FM 830, a state road that now dead-ended into the lake, over the loud and well-funded opposition of a recreational subdivision and nearby landowners.[118] Both projects took years to complete. The FM 830 site, the county's first publicly owned access point, did not open until October 1976. The conflict was not so much about the absolute lack of access, as there were privately owned boat ramps open to the public soon after the lake filled. It was about perceptions of exclusivity.[119] Lake Conroe existed for the benefit of the metropolis, the authority, and those who could afford to live in the lake's exclusive developments. In its early years Lake Conroe earned its reputation as a "spa of [the] wealthy."[120]

∽

It is impossible to construct a reservoir without sparking resistance. Appraisal hearings and eminent domain proceedings distill each homestead into a dollar figure. Contour lines, mysterious yet exacting and inexorable, divide the landscape between water and land, between public lake and private shoreline, between condemnation and windfall profits. Engineers remove homes to make a home for tamed waters. It is little wonder that historians have found dam construction so tempting a subject. These great engineering feats exemplify the power cities have over their hinterlands. Yet as both of these case studies demonstrate, narratives of imposition and resistance, of imperial cities and the subjected countryside miss much of the story. Within Montgomery County, many were complicit in the lake's construction, using their knowledge of local power and landscapes to reap substantial profits off the city's water needs. The story of Lake Conroe is, in part, the story of the sjra and its transformation from a rural conservation organization to a dam builder fueling a regional development boom to a full-service metropolitan water utility. It is also a story of recreational development. Urban and state money built the lake. That money also fueled the creation of what amounted to a metropolitan enclave in the heart of Montgomery County. For many Houstonians, Montgomery County became a place to spend a weekend or to buy a summer home and forget the troubles of urban life for a while. The Conroe Chamber of Commerce and most local landowners could not have been happier.

Different agencies of the federal government and environmentalists each claimed some of the spotlight in the drama over Washington's water supply. Loudoun County's location along the Potomac and its proximity to the city drew it into the fray. The question was never *if* these relationships would change the county. It was always *when* and *how*. Even though the Corps of Engineers failed to dam the Potomac, the resulting national attention brought the county into the metropolitan orbit as a place of recreation, leisure, and subdivisions all the same. Loudoun residents found their county enmeshed in a half dozen overlapping metropolitan geographies, from the Potomac watershed to the electric grid, from transportation networks to waste disposal. Each of these drew the county into Washington's metropolitan metabolism. The nature of these connections, however, remained an open question. As with Montgomery County, the history of Loudoun's metropolitan integration was contested, environmentally contingent, often fragmentary, and dependent as much on regional power structures as on national politics. The environmental and metropolitan politics of water and pollution reshaped the metropolitan landscape and bound fringe counties to the metropolis. "Don't dam Loudoun!" began as a slogan of farmers resisting urban attempts to appropriate their land and water. It ended as a slogan used by those who had fled the city to enjoy life in the country and by those hoping to use industry to protect the farming that remained from suburban development. Even without the construction of the dam, metropolitan expansion transformed Loudoun. In this, the two counties had a great deal in common.

CHAPTER 4

Settling the Forest

Writing for a published collection of local histories in 1980, Tip Eckel recounted her family's trek from Houston out to Montgomery County. Where Texas's original frontier families had come by oxcart and wagon, her people "made the arduous trip from southwest Houston to Conroe in a caravan consisting of two cars, a recreational vehicle, an Allied moving van, and a pick-up truck. Braving the many hazards of 16 wheelers and fast cars," she continued, "the harrowing trip across the county line took approximately 45 minutes." Once they moved in, the family "bravely faced the daily hazards of life in the country, fighting off attacks of giant cockroaches, termites, ticks, snakes, and other dangers." There were even worse things in store, as many neighbors "were surprised to find that they had a home on a lake—or even in a lake—when it rained." The rural "natives" also took their toll. Suburban frontiersmen faced "vicious attacks of tire slashing, broken window-shields, and mailbox beatings." Local youth, who were themselves "seeking new frontiers, blazed trails through the golf courses and made 'doughnuts' on the greens in their trucks." The Eckel family took all this in stride, as the lot of those "settlers" who had the gumption to leave "the security of the big city to help settle Montgomery County." Like so many others during the period, the Eckels abandoned life in the city and set out in search of a better life on the metropolitan frontier.[1]

The Eckels joined journalists and historians in connecting white flight to the American celebration of mobility and the search for new opportunities on the frontier. Their careers may have kept many Americans tethered to cities, but improved transportation and the promises of leisure, access to nature, security, and social homogeneity lured urban professionals to the countryside. Such people left the city to escape urban violence and integration; they left in the hope of better school districts for their children; they left to escape high taxes and secure greater personal freedoms; they left to be closer to nature. This constellation of push-and-pull factors that brought the nation's middle class to the metropolitan fringe has been well documented. What suburbanites found there, however, remains unclear. Historians have analyzed the form of suburbanites' settlements, explained why they moved, and demonstrated the way this "suburban secession" undermined the urban core. Yet historians' stories generally leave off just as suburbanites move in. Consequently, we know far more about suburban dreams and developer promises than we do about suburban life.[2]

As a result, historians have underestimated the challenges that came with purchasing homes carved out of rural landscapes. We have assumed that white privilege was sufficient to guarantee the fulfillment of these suburban dreams. Some suburbanites did achieve these dreams, but not without struggle. Many did not. On the metropolitan fringe, suburbanites often looked like either hapless victims or triumphant frontiersmen. Historians whose sentiments lie with decaying urban cores understandably have little stomach for such tales of either suburban tragedy or suburban triumph, for they have painted the entire project as a manifestation of the failings of American culture and society. Their narrative of suburbanization as an abdication of white America's responsibility to the nation's cities is both useful and accurate, as far as it goes. Suburbanites rejected the city and its problems, rejected school and residential integration, and rejected the tax burden that urban services and the urban community placed on them. They abandoned the city and therefore should be held accountable for its failings. Yet as morally satisfying as this interpretation is, it is not sufficient to explain the metropolitan fringe—a place where rural people, landscapes, politics, and social structures constrained the shape of suburban life. The professional skills, financial resources, and government subsidies suburban migrants brought with them did not guarantee them success. Metropolitan expansion outside Houston was more a hard-fought campaign than a victory parade. One might even call it a Wild West of shoddy development, fly-by-night developers, naive suburbanites, and a county government barely keeping up. As such, it bore little resemblance to the seeming order and inevitability of a creeping "crabgrass frontier."[3]

Environmental historians have led the way in cataloging the suburban debacles that new residents faced. They have done so to emphasize the role these hazards played in propelling the national environmental movement. This chapter builds on their work, but with a different end in mind. Adam Rome traced the evolution of national environmental policy in response to suburban environmental destruction. Christopher Sellers explained grassroots opposition to air and water pollution as a defense of a shared suburban nature. Newcomers to Montgomery County, Texas, faced many of the same problems— septic overflows, flooding, pollution, and sprawl. Their responses, however, do not fit well within the "roots of environmentalism" argument. Nor do they align with Loudoun County's preservation culture as described in the next chapter. Suburban failures in Montgomery County reveal the contingency and peril involved in transforming a rural place into a metropolitan place. Here the "crabgrass crucible" did not forge a new environmental movement, but it did forge the landscapes and government of a metropolitan county. The obvious and traumatic failures of local housing developments inspired little in the way of grassroots environmental activism. Instead, newcomers poured their energies into managing suburban private governments, demanding passable roads, opposing unscrupulous developers, and prodding an underfunded and unresponsive county government into action. Where, nationally, environmental activists cut their teeth on such protests, locally, newcomers advocated for increased government regulations and improved services without drawing into question the broader national commitment to economic growth, consumerism, and development. They shored up their tenuous suburban landscapes without becoming environmentalists.[4]

Suburban Montgomery County received three inheritances from its rural predecessor: timbered landscapes, a weak rural government, and environmental hazards. Suburbanites claimed the first inheritance with vigor. They little noticed the second until the third exposed their fragile ties to the land. Only then did they begin to refashion the rural government to meet their needs, appropriating new government structures and claiming their share of federal money and programs.

Montgomery County was dominated by a good old boys system of governance in which landowning rural white Democratic elites used their positions to keep taxes low, services sparse, and political favors flowing to supporters. These political leaders enjoyed a relatively stable relationship with the timber and oil companies that operated within the county. These interests were most concerned that the local government would keep taxes low and do nothing to disrupt their labor supply. Local politicians were happy to oblige. By the time suburban expansion reached the county, timber harvesting, cattle, and oil, the three iconic pursuits of East Texas, were each well represented in the area economy. Battles between cattlemen and businessmen flared up from time to time, but a progrowth boosterism and economic opportunism largely subsumed what antidevelopment agrarian conservatism there was in the region.

The Eckels saw themselves, only partially in jest, as bold new frontier settlers colonizing the rugged Montgomery County wilderness. For all the obvious problems with this self-image—the county was certainly no wilderness—it contains a kernel of truth. In moving beyond the city limits, these migrants abandoned the services and support that the city had provided and took upon their shoulders the task of constructing new settlements within rural Montgomery County. Not all succeeded.[5]

&

Montgomery County was dominated by forests. The county's first white settlers had seen the thick pine uplands and swampy hardwood bottomlands as a nuisance and a barrier to progress. These slave-owning migrants from across the South girdled and burned the trees to make way for cotton agriculture. The arrival of railroads and northern capital following the Civil War set off a timber boom. Companies snatched up tens of thousands of acres of old-growth pine forests and spent the next century cutting, processing, and shipping loblolly and slash pine timber to market. Armed with steam skidders, cross-cut saws, and axes, timber workers extracted wealth from the countryside. As extensive as this cutting was—it was a rare copse of pines that escaped—contemporary conservationists were overzealous in painting the pine belt as a wasteland of dry brush, decaying stumps, washed-out soils, and raging fires. The county's landscape was, instead, a patchwork of small agricultural homesteads and timberlands in various stages of growth, from the open scars of recently cut acreage to the established canopies of loblolly and mixed hardwood areas uncut for decades. These forests were perpetually in transition. Loblolly saplings sprang up quickly, growing two to three feet per year in their early stages and reaching eighty feet in height within fifty years. Frequent fires, rooting hogs, grazing cattle, and hardwood growth often made the process of reforestation frustratingly slow and inefficient in the eyes of timber company managers. Yet in spite of these obstacles, industry experts were complaining by the early 1960s that the county's forests were growing back far faster than companies were harvesting them. In 1961, as housing developments were beginning to go in, 584,600 acres, or 84 percent of the county's land, was commercial forest in every stage of growth. By the late 1960s Montgomery County remained a state leader in the amount of saw timber available. These woods were available for suburban use.[6]

Postwar demand for weekend cottages, country homesteads, and housing developments drove up the price of timbered acreage. Between 1948 and the mid-1960s property values across the county shot up from $50 per acre to anywhere from $300 to $1,300 per acre, largely through Houston's market influence and the potential for lakefront development.[7] Timber companies responded by selling off their holdings and shifting their operations to harvesting by contract, leaving new landowners to develop or continue to sell timber according to the dictates of the housing market. Developers from within the county and from Houston flooded the market with rural subdivisions and lakefront weekend cottages. By the summer of 1957 Conroe had eighteen new subdivisions in the works or completed. More than a dozen rural subdivisions were in various stages of planning and completion as early as 1961.[8] The pace picked up over the next decade as Interstate 45 connected Conroe to Houston in 1962 and U.S. Route 59 did the same for the eastern part of the county soon after; the city's new jet airport broke ground seven miles south of the county line that same year; and Lake Conroe's construction seemed to be just over the horizon. Each of these infrastructure projects connected the county to Houston's fantastic growth. Between September 1963 and March 1965 developers filed forty-seven plats for thirty-three private subdivisions. The number of recorded subdivisions continued to balloon in the following years, reaching 208 by 1967 and 250 by 1969. These homes filled quickly as the county's population nearly doubled from 26,800 in 1960 to 49,500 by 1970. It would climb to 128,500 by 1980.[9]

Because Houston and Harris County had an ever-expanding supply of sprawling subdivisions to offer, Montgomery County's real estate market depended on the articulation of distinct amenities. The preferred sales pitch promised both the convenience of suburban life and the recreational options of weekend and vacation living among lofty pine forests. This was in stark contrast to the oppressive heat, the flat topography, and the stifling humidity of Houston's coastal plain. Developers promised their customers a life in the forest. As one Houston developer put it, their goal was to transform "a rugged Montgomery County Wilderness" into "a scenic subdivision." One exurban family literally built their house around a pair of stately pine trees. This shifted the way locals understood the value of timberland. Landowners had measured its value in board feet; developers now did so in terms of location, aesthetics, and amenities. A tract of Montgomery County timber, no matter its volume, that had good road access, a scenic view, or large trees, no matter their species, was worth far more as a site for recreational development than it was for timber or pulp. Where timber companies had extracted trees, developers now used trees to frame their development. They now saw (and sold) the forest for the trees.[10]

The local chamber of commerce worked with Houston newspapers to advertise Montgomery County's woods as an unpopulated recreational paradise. As part of a series of special inserts in the *Houston Chronicle* in 1963 and 1964, boosters literally sketched their imagined landscape of leisure. A deer with a full head of antlers prances across the southern part of the county, leaping as a hunter attempts to bring it down. Just above this, a bikini-clad water skier waves as she races across the countryside. To the northeast, a golfer poses after his tee shot and a fisherman reels in his catch. The new developments are numbered on the map, but they are not the focus. This is not primarily an advertisement for modern housing, exclusive school districts, or low taxes. Nor does it claim for the county any sort of economic dynamism; quite the opposite. The only hint at the county's industrial and extractive economy is the outline of the Conroe Oilfield, geographically confined to one small section of the map. The drawing focuses attention on the stately pines and rolling hills that made the county's topography so distinct from Houston, a point made explicit by the recording of elevations. The map, and the dozens of pages of advertising it introduced, articulated a vision of life that combined recreation with "gracious" suburban living among "the natural beauty of the pine trees, rolling hills and beautiful lakes." This drawing promised Houstonians a wooded county without rural industry, agriculture, or people—a backyard landscape tailored to meet suburbanites' needs and desires.[11]

Reality was more complicated. Developers and speculators inherited a diversity of wooded landscapes, each with a unique soil profile, ecological makeup, history of logging and fire, and legacy of past management. Signs of past use were obvious to locals. They were far less so to newcomers, who read the landscape through the advertisers' claims. No matter how dramatic the past bulldozing, burning, chemical spraying, and girdling may have been on any given plot of timber, developers obscured the impact of past use. An advertisement for former Grogan-Cochran Lumber Company land is emblematic of this point: "There are tracts clear of all timber and undergrowth. These are slow movers. More in demand are the tracts studded with stately pines and cleared of all undergrowth. And there are tracts with the tall pines, all the hardwoods, and undergrowth just as in the heart of the Big Thicket. These are the choices. And with due respect to Mother Nature, she didn't give mankind any more choices betwixt the Atlantic and the Pacific, save for the desert areas." Each of these particular works of "Mother Nature" were the result of the past timber management performed by Grogan-Cochran, its labor force, and any backwoodsmen who had burned and run cattle on this part of the forested commons. Developers managed the landscape they inherited, preserving some elements and removing others, in order to craft something they could sell to home buyers. Much of the county's cleared land went into ranches, ranchettes, and country homes for equestrian hobbyists. Timbered acres usually went into recreational subdivisions and bedroom communities. Developers wielded the bulldozer with a relatively light hand, ensuring that developments highlighted the stately pines and winding creeks that complemented the summer-camp lifestyle. They repurposed logging ponds and stock ponds or dug new ones. Developers appealing to a more distinguished clientele played up the county's

A promotional map of Montgomery County published in the *Houston Chronicle*.
"Conroe: Texas' Most Beautiful City for Family Living," *HC*, September 15, 1963, special insert,
HC staff / © *Houston Chronicle*. Used with permission.

magnolia-filled lowlands as a connection to a romanticized plantation past of
leisure and status. The diversity of the forest's appearance became a boon for
real estate developers. The landscape's scars became product differentiation.[12]

The Arrowhead Lakes development is emblematic of this marketing of a
suburbanized nature. The brainchild of local real estate magnate Jim Fuller, the

development combined Native American exoticism with the timbered land-scape to create a recreational suburb. Chief Ec Cho Nawny of the Coushatta Indians was on hand to greet Houstonians as they visited the subdivision and imagined themselves boating on Moosejaw Lake and shopping in the replica Indian marketplace. The land's historical ties to tribal hunting lands only added to its "natural beauty." Here, the advertisers boasted, was "one of the last locations within a 50-mile radius where Houstonians may relax in an atmosphere designed by nature to provide complete retreat from the fast pace of the workday week." They would do so with the recreational and sub-urban amenities that "discriminating" Houstonians had come to expect, such as horseback riding, swimming (in a pool built in the shape of an arrowhead), boating, fishing, and over three hundred acres of woods. Jim Fuller, like most Montgomery County developers, did not bulldoze nature and replace it with a faux pastoral landscape. Instead, he sold the county's second- and third-growth trees as suburban forests. These developments protected some trees to preserve the forest feel. They never attempted to preserve the ecology of the forest. Nor did they take seriously the environmental limits that came with the county's soils, climate, and topography.[13]

⁍

For all the rhetoric, these homes were enmeshed within the political and social world of East Texas and within the climate, soils, and hydrology of the piney woods. Developers incorporated the woods into their built environments to great effect. They were just as successful in using the county's weak government for their own benefit. Local conservatism ran deep. The fervent anticommu-nism of locals was overshadowed only by their shrill defense of individual liberties, their devotion to segregation, and their unflappable commitment to the prerogatives of business opportunism. Locals liked their taxes low, their services sparse, and their government to leave them the hell alone. The county earned high marks with the East Texas Chamber of Commerce year after year for its balanced budget and low debt load. The courthouse gang ran the local Democratic Party, and the local Democratic Party ran county government. Political power was held by a mixture of cattle, timber, oil, and other business interests. The county judge and the four county commissioners, each of whom exerted independent control over the infrastructure of his precinct, formed the county's executive leadership. The commissioners acted as ward bosses. Along with the sheriff and the justices of the peace, they were the central figures in a good old boys political culture that rewarded personal patronage over profes-sionalism. These men embraced the persona of the gregarious rural politician who had little use for bureaucracy and could be relied on to act decisively and to get the job done—a persona reflected in the clothing worn by county officials around election time up through the 1980s. The *Courier* consistently showed the county treasurer, attorney, and district judge dressed in suits. They were elected for their professionalism. The sheriff, county judge, and county commissioners, in contrast, dressed in jeans, boots, and cowboy hats, exuding ranching culture and its western image. They were men of the people and men of action.[14]

The good old boys system kept the line between public work and personal favor porous. County work crews graded and repaired private roads, hauled gravel and dirt to political supporters, and, on occasion, used county equipment and labor to maintain their own properties. Some treated their road and bridge money as an informal welfare fund, supporting constituents with pressing needs. County commissioners had no legal obligation to account for their spending to grand juries into the 1960s, and they used this freedom to its fullest. In spite of its problems, this political system ensured that most roads were maintained and that white landowning citizens had recourse if they were unsatisfied. The strengths of this rural commissioner system, its personalism, and its flexibility, however, made it a poor fit in a metropolitan county whose newcomers expected policy-driven, efficient government.[15]

Even when commissioners were willing, local government lacked the tools necessary to deal with growth. Montgomery County was years behind Loudoun County in its power to regulate development. The northern Virginia county had established rural zoning, subdivision regulations, and a county planning office more than a decade before large-scale suburban development arrived in the 1960s. Montgomery County, like most counties in the South, had none of these planning tools. This was not completely their fault. County government was, legally speaking, an appendage of the state. The commissioners could only exercise those powers expressly granted to them by the Texas legislature. During the early 1960s those powers were effectively limited to the power to collect taxes and maintain roads. The commissioners court faced the onrush of suburban development with a very small governmental toolbox that expanded slowly over the following two decades. They had no power to zone, to enforce building codes, or to regulate sewage disposal. Over the first two decades of development, county commissioners slowly established the basic regulatory frameworks only when the failures and abuses of unregulated development became unmistakable. Even then, enforcement remained spotty, as limited government confronted nearly unlimited growth.[16]

Throughout the period, the number of unrecorded subdivisions remained high, and the regulations were poorly enforced on those who did file plats. Rural people valued a government that allowed landowners to use their property as they saw fit. The commissioners court worked within this political world, only moving toward regulation in specific cases where a failure to act might directly cost the county taxpayers money and, even then, only when state legislation permitted it. For more than the first decade of suburban development in Montgomery County, developers enjoyed free rein. During that period, the county did nothing to regulate where they could build or where septic tanks could go. There was no building code and only limited road inspections. For developers, the county was a municipal frontier where the quality of developments was determined solely by what developers could convince Houstonians to pay for. This upfront price was, of course, only the beginning of the cost—a cost residents and the county as a whole would pay over the following decades.[17]

Even as developers made the most of their free hand, the ecological limits of the Montgomery County woods asserted themselves. Many suburban families discovered that their frontier fantasy was more realistic than they had bargained for. Their reactions to these crises reveal that Houstonians had expected to move away from the city to the beauty of the woods without losing urban services and security. As they settled into their new homes, they realized that the county government only provided a rural level of waste disposal, road repairs, and police and fire service. Even more troubling, they realized that the county had done little to protect them from the hazards of floods and inadequate septic systems. For all of their desire to be close to nature and far from the city, many became disillusioned when they realized they had settled within a rural world.

Solid waste was the most visible of these problems. Dumping was especially acute on the metropolitan fringe where services were sparse and governments weak. The dearth of landfill sites, the rising population, and the ever-expanding waste stream fomented a local garbage and litter crisis that county government was woefully unprepared to handle. Piles of broken refrigerators, car tires, household waste, and construction materials lined the county's roadsides, making a mockery of the developers' image of life in the forest. Fixing the dumping problem required money (always in short supply), a willingness among the commissioners court to provide services (something many resisted), and authority from the state to purchase landfill sites (something the legislature was slow to grant). The resulting hodgepodge program of waste disposal left the countryside just as full of trash in 1975 as it had been in 1965. During this decade, precincts 3 and 4, those areas experiencing most of the suburban growth, had no landfills. For these residents, the poorly managed dump in Conroe was as much as twenty miles away. This made roadside dumping a sore temptation. The *Courier* could still report in 1976, "Mounds of garbage, old refrigerators, broken furniture with the stuffing hanging out and dismantled plastic toys seem to grow and multiply overnight" along the county's roads.[18]

Many drivers were too busy dodging potholes and washed-out shoulders to notice discarded appliances and last month's issues of the *Houston Chronicle* hanging from the pine boughs. As the clearinghouse for all road complaints, the commissioners court endured the complaints of irate homeowners. It was common for developers to construct substandard roads, begin selling lots, and then donate these roads to the county. This left the county with the financial burden of upkeep. Using legislation passed in 1957, the commissioners court approved an ordinance in February 1961 requiring developers to submit subdivision plats for approval and to put up a performance bond to ensure their roads would meet county standards. The impact of this ordinance was limited. It did not apply to developments with private roads, leaving the bulk of the county's subdivisions to go unrecorded and unregulated. Continued road problems convinced the commissioners to update their policy in July 1965, requiring developers to maintain their own roads for a year before the county would accept them. They also moved to close the private road loophole in August 1966 and required a preliminary plat to gain approval by the newly hired county engineer beginning in April 1967.[19]

Poorly constructed subdivision roads joined the ever-lengthening backlog of needed repairs. Many complaining homeowners were surprised to learn that their roads were private and therefore it was up to them to figure out how to pay the repair bill. One of the most common complaints came from newcomers incensed at the noisy and destructive truck traffic that marred their country roads. The same rural areas whose forests, low land prices, and proximity to the city were so appealing for residences had also attracted the gravel quarries and sand pits that paved the city and its suburbs. That the surrounding landscape was being mined to develop the convenient roads that residents demanded did little to assuage them. In one especially fitting case, residents called on the commissioners court to prevent fully loaded trucks from rumbling down Sleepy Hollow Road. Another resident complained that an "outlaw gravel operation" had been using roads in his subdivision and, along with its "Outlaw Bunch" of employees, had either intimidated residents or bribed them with promises of free fill dirt in order to keep them quiet. This was the state of road construction on the metropolitan frontier, where rural people joined in the rush to develop the county and make a few bucks in the process.[20]

The lack of police protection was especially worrisome for those newcomers who had left the city out of fear. Rural law enforcement relied on social and familial constraint, a generally self-reliant citizenry, and, where necessary, intimidation and strong-arm tactics to keep the peace. Rapid population growth stretched this system beyond its breaking point. Into the mid-1970s the county had as few as four deputies patrolling at night in a county whose population was approaching one hundred thousand. Little wonder, then, that the county sheriff's office had no resources to devote to cracking down on dumping violations, stray dogs, or speeding. Across Montgomery County, response times were high and break-ins common. In one particularly galling episode, one family living on the outskirts of Conroe waited for over three hours for a deputy to show up after someone fired a volley of bullets through their bedroom wall. The county's proximity to Houston and its relatively weak law enforcement made it popular among narcotics rings and racketeering operations. Crime tarnished the county's image as a place where children were safe from urban crime. Quite the opposite was true. Montgomery County had one of the highest juvenile crime rates in the state by 1980, as boredom and limited police protection encouraged vandalism and petty theft. The level of fire protection was just as bad, forcing suburban newcomers to develop rural fire control districts to protect their homes. Barbecues and bake sales could only raise so much of the needed funds, leaving these cash-strapped volunteer units unable to cover the county's ever-expanding subdivisions—a fact that a rash of fires in the southern part of the county in 1974 made clear. County government was incapable of providing the level of services suburban newcomers expected and increasingly demanded.[21]

The most traumatic suburban crises swirled around the movement of water. Here newcomers faced the perfect storm of developer opportunism, local government's light regulatory hand, and the land's environmental limits. Developers understood how to capitalize on the county's natural image. They were both ignorant and negligent when it came to the dangers posed by the county's hydrology, soils, and climate. Each contributed to the county's significant flooding and septic tank hazards. Local soils wreaked havoc on the septic tank systems, which were a vital cost-saving measure for rural subdivisions. The soils in the southern part of the county, for instance, have a layer of sand overlying thick layers of clay. While much of the land appears at first to be well drained, once the sand is saturated, water pools on the surface. This causes frequent system failures and the leaching of sewage into drainage ditches and onto yards.[22] As long as the county remained largely rural, septic problems were a minor inconvenience. When developers appropriated this rural technology for denser development, problems ensued. Most paid little attention to these potential issues, which did not become apparent until months after families moved in. Limited resources and political will undermined the county health department's attempts to limit where such systems could be installed and to prevent the installation of additional systems where previous ones had proved to be a health hazard. Nationally, septic tank failures were only beginning to inspire regulation in the early 1960s. Even if developers had attempted to design with soils in mind, they would have found a persistent lack of available information. There was no comprehensive soil survey of the county available until the Soil Conservation Service completed one in 1972. It was a rare developer indeed who would be willing to fund his own soil study. Even with the survey in hand, interpreting soil information and planning around it took time, money, and expertise—each in short supply among the economically marginal developers who tended to rely on septic systems. As a result, septic tank subdivisions proliferated. By 1973 the county had thirty-one major subdivisions on septic tanks. The failings of these systems became one more hazard faced by newcomers. Those stuck with failing systems had to rely on an inefficient and overloaded local court system for any hope of getting restitution from developers.[23]

The county's history of flash flooding compounded septic failures and created a host of problems all its own. Here, too, developer negligence, ineffective county government, and ignorance about the county's environment placed newcomers in harm's way. Experience instilled in locals a respect for the limits on where one should build. Floodwaters had ripped through the county's bottomlands long before development arrived. "Old-timers" could point to fence posts and trees inscribed with high-water marks to support their stories of flash floods and the raging San Jacinto River. Local memory had it that the highest point in River Plantation, one of the county's more elite developments, had flooded as high as a horse's flanks in the record-setting flood of 1940. To Houstonians and transplanted northerners, it was hard to imagine that this sandy stream was capable of such feats. To them, the sawtooth palmettos and spider lilies that blanketed the county's floodplains lent a subtropical ambience to their wooded subdivisions. To those who knew the land, these plants were a warning to build elsewhere. Topography, climate, and soils combined to make much of Montgomery County flood prone. The topography is generally flat. The same soils that hampered septic systems also caused water to pool in temporary wetlands. The county's average of 46.1 inches of rain per year tends to fall in heavy downpours in spring and fall. These heavy rains could turn the San Jacinto River into a raging torrent with little warning. The hot and humid climate also encourages the rapid growth of brush, which clogs up drainage ditches, causing localized flooding. Along with the rest of the watershed, and all of southeast Texas, for that matter, seasonal flash floods were the rule. Although Montgomery County's upstream location and its relative lack of impermeable surfaces ought to have saved it from some of Houston's flooding problems, the lack of flood control planning and developer regulation ensured that some of the county's developments would have some of the most frequent flood damage in the metro area.[24]

Much of the blame for these issues rests at the feet of developers. O. J. McCullough provides a case study in the type of hydrological hubris that characterized many of these ambitious businessmen. McCullough joined the wave of speculators and developers who descended on the county in the mid-1960s. He purchased a wooded tract along the San Jacinto River east of I-45 and south of Conroe. All that the site lacked was a lake. In a moment of inspiration, McCullough decided that the San Jacinto River could meet that need. Beginning on September 16, 1965, his workmen constructed a sand dam 12 feet high, 30 feet wide, and 225 feet in length. At its base, the entire flow of the San Jacinto River, a river whose floods would rip through subdivisions, gushed through a ten-inch pipe. Near the top of the dam, McCullough had placed ten twenty-four-inch pipes as a spillway—a hopelessly inadequate precautionary move. When word of the dam reached the *Conroe Courier* and the SJRA, each threw a fit. McCullough had dammed a state-owned river without requesting a permit, consulting an engineer, or holding a public hearing. The SJRA dragged McCullough before the Texas Water Rights Commission on October 14. His lawyers defended his prerogative to develop the property as he saw fit, provided he did not harm downstream property owners. The commission ruled that the dam was "unstable, unsafe and dangerous to lives and property downstream." They gave him ten days to remove it. McCullough refused, ultimately forcing the state to take him to court. In the meantime, the river did its own work. Like a child's sandcastle at high tide, McCullough's dream washed away as the San Jacinto carved out a channel around the dam and washed the sand into the Houston Ship Channel. Such was the cavalier attitude with which many developers viewed the San Jacinto.[25]

Texas law was very clear about who could develop the state's rivers. That same body of law had nothing to say about building on floodplains before 1969. Developers took full advantage, rushing to meet market demand for suburban lots in the woods and along streams under the legal umbrella of caveat emptor. They ignored local knowledge and sound engineering principles in their rush to turn a quick profit. Even the Corps of Engineers advised potential home buyers and developers to seek out local knowledge on flooding and heed its warnings. Few did so. Suburban development was predicated on dismissing the landscape's rural history and reshaping its environment to meet market demand. Only through the environmental alchemy of suburban development could flood-prone acreage that one county commissioner labeled a "natural fishpond" be packaged and sold as Porter Heights. Some developers were simply ignorant of the dangers they were passing on to their customers. Others knowingly deceived and defrauded their customers or channeled their drainage problems on to other developments that had the misfortune of being downgrade. These practices set the stage for decades of suburban wreckage on the metropolitan fringe.[26]

As the pace of development quickened, so too did the flood damage. In 1964 a twelve-inch rain inundated homes in subdivisions across the southern and eastern parts of the county. A flood in 1967 caused enough damage to get the county designated a disaster area. The financial benefits from this designation conveniently remained in effect when two more floods visited the area in May and June 1968. June 1973 saw the evacuation of over 6,400 homes. The total damage for the 600 homes flooded in this case came to $3,976,760. This was for a flood during which the San Jacinto River was still nine feet below its 1940 record. For some subdivisions, even normal rainfall caused serious flooding. Particular south-county homes flooded as many as six times a year. The seasonal flash floods that had been a nuisance to rural residents now became localized and chronic suburban disasters.[27]

Flooding continued because of the failure of regulation and planning. The county had no ordinance protecting new home buyers from predatory developers who sold flood-prone lots until 1973. This delay was in spite of the swarms of suburban residents who descended on the commissioners court with demands for action. Why, one such group asked, were developers allowed to sell such lots when "it was common knowledge to all but the purchaser that such areas flooded during and after heavy rains"? The developer had assured them that their homes would never flood. Now they were stuck with lots that no one would buy and that they could not build on (the subdivision covenant prohibited building on piers). All the commissioners had to offer was their sympathy. They had noted flood-prone areas on county plats. It was up to purchasers to look at them. The county had no regulations preventing flood-prone subdivisions from being built or preventing people from buying homes in them.[28]

Inundated homeowners next reached out to the SJRA to save them. Unscrupulous developers and realtors had used the promise of Lake Conroe's construction to soothe buyers' fears about flooding along the San Jacinto. Flood control, after all, was part of the SJRA's state-mandated mission. Once the dam's gates closed in January 1973, complaints poured into the SJRA offices every time water lapped at the foundations of these homes. The SJRA had nothing to offer suburbanites. The Lake Conroe that emerged out of the SJRA's negotiations with Houston had no provision for flood control. The SJRA's contract with Houston prohibited it from operating the dam to prevent flooding.

To drop the lake level two feet would mean the loss of nearly half of its year's permitted supply. If a drought occurred, such a loss could seriously jeopardize both Houston's water supply and the SJRA's financial solvency. The SJRA's commitments to downstream customers made flood prevention in Montgomery County impossible. Montgomery County residents did not pay for Lake Conroe. It did not operate in their interest.[29]

Trials and tribulations confronted those who braved the metropolitan frontier. As one Spring Forest resident complained to the commissioners court, their homes had been flooded, their roads washed out and destroyed by dump trucks, and their woods buried in trash, and the local government was nowhere to be found. "We have begun to feel like a lost tribe out here," another resident explained. A 1969 report by the Houston-Galveston Area Council (HGAC), a metropolitan planning organization, summarized this swath of metropolitan frontier problems well:

> What may appear to be a quality sub-division at its beginning may degenerate into a marsh of septic tank effluent. Its streets may deteriorate. Garbage collection and disposal may become a severe problem. The lack of fire and police protection can become critical. . . . Water systems may become inadequate because of undersized original facilities. Properties may be depreciated because of nuisance-type and offensive activities conducted on adjoining and unrestricted areas. . . . Some developments . . . are inadequately provided with street and utility improvements. . . . [O]ften, there are no effective codes, ordinances or regulations covering sanitation, utilities and soundness and safety of structures. At initial low density, such developments in a semi-rural context appear to present no problems. But with added time, more people and higher densities, such developments will become blighted and liabilities to the region.

This was the darker side of metropolitan fringe development. These problems expose the contradictions inherent in the suburban appeal. Newcomers expected to move close to nature while still keeping the benefits of the city. In reality, they moved to rural areas that were unable to meet their expectations. They moved beyond the reach of city government with its taxes and perceived crime. In so doing, they placed themselves at the mercy of unregulated developers. When they attempted to hide under the wings of local government, they found a rural political system with little protection to offer. These frontiersmen pursued the look and lifestyle of the woods. They found it difficult to cope with the backwoods and sometimes hostile ecology that came with it. The local regulatory state began to catch up with development during the 1970s and 1980s, partially in response to local activism and partially because of new enabling legislation at the state level. The benefits of these improvements, however, largely went to new construction. Earlier subdivisions were left to deal with the hazards of the metropolitan fringe on their own.[30]

☙

In their works on suburban environmentalism, Adam Rome and Christopher Sellers find the beginnings of the national environmental movement in septic tank failures, flooding, and developer abuses. These failures, each argues, fomented grassroots activism (Sellers) and top-down policy changes (Rome) that shifted the focus from the logic of public health to wider concerns over chemical contamination and the rape of the natural world. In Montgomery County, regulation did come at least in part through grassroots pressure. The arguments for regulation, however, rarely moved beyond the rationale and rhetoric of preserving public health and consumer protections. This was symptomatic of a broader failure of environmentalism to take root in Montgomery County's suburban landscapes. In Houston, Earth Day, April 22, 1970, brought thousands to attend teach-ins, protests, public lectures, and other forms of grassroots empowerment. The event registered barely a ripple in Montgomery County. The only event recorded in the local newspaper was a group of Conroe High School students who took a field trip to Jefferson Chemical Company to be reassured that the factory was a good environmental citizen and that no new regulation was needed. County subdivisions produced a handful of garden clubs and civic groups concerned with beautifying area roads and a small ecology club. When students at the Montgomery Elementary School created a nature trail, they were faced with piles of litter and trash. The students devoted hours of class time from two landscaping classes to collect some thirty truckloads of trash from the area before marking out the trail. In Montgomery County, creating suburban nature was a process of landscaping or even excavation—a labor-intensive process that few were willing to take on at the county level. Most newcomers rarely did more than complain. When it came to opposing sprawl and development, most did not even go that far.[31]

This is not to say that the national environmental movement had no resonance in the county. The commissioners court passed a resolution in January 1970 committing itself to defend its "naturally beautiful land area" from the problems of "air pollution, water pollution, garbage disposal, [and] sewage disposal." Even the local chamber of commerce got on board with this, warning in the lead-up to Earth Day that the county must "control those industries and individuals which would fill our air and water with filth and create a veritable cesspool of our beautiful county." Such noble sentiments reflected fears that the county's reputation as a natural haven from Houston might suffer if it did not appear to be addressing environmental problems. In terms of activism, however, the environmental decade in Montgomery County was anything but.[32]

Why didn't suburban newcomers mobilize for the environmental cause? At least part of the answer lies in the more general political apathy among suburbanites. After reapportionment in 1970, south-county residents used their newfound political power to replace their precinct 3 commissioner and rural establishment candidate Bo Damuth with businessman George Wood in 1972. Wood ran on a platform that spoke to the concerns of south-county suburbanites. He called for modern services, good roads, effective law enforcement, local planning, accessible landfills, county parks, and improved flood control. Suburban Montgomery County did not build on this victory, however. Throughout the 1970s, newcomers continued to view local politics with a self-defeating mixture of scorn and apathy. Most invested their political energies into either the management of their development or the politics of the metropolis and the nation. In the 1974 Democratic primary election, for instance, only 11 percent of registered voters in the well-established subdivision of River Plantation bothered to show up. In 1978 only 25 percent of registered Democrats participated in that party's primary. This apathy was concentrated in the suburban areas that now made up a majority of the population. Oak Ridge North sent only 17 percent, The Woodlands 18 percent, and River Plantation 18 percent. "What is wrong with these well-educated, supposedly in-the-know, most affluent people?" local journalist Joyce Everhart complained. "Why don't they care? Don't they realize that . . . they could literally swing about any election they wanted?" Candidates continued to give suburban areas short shrift in their campaigning. Suburban voters, they learned, did not turn out for elections.[33]

Why such apathy when so many suburban residents obviously needed stronger government? Certainly part of the answer lies in the general malaise that blanketed the Watergate era. The fact that these were off-year elections certainly did not help. Yet voter apathy also had roots in the suburban dream itself. Newcomers did not move to the county to become engaged in its political and social world. They moved to free themselves from the troubles of the daily grind and political wrangling of the city. Everhart explained it well. "Most are escapists," she argued. "They move out to the suburbs to live among the trees and the birds. They are seeking their own islands in the sun. They want to be left alone. And so they are." The suburban dream blunted the suburban political mobilization that might have saved it from the hazards of life on the metropolitan fringe. These voters were quick to complain to local government when rain washed out their roads, when their homes flooded, or

when their forests filled up with trash. Yet south-county residents did not believe it was worth the effort to transform the county's still largely rural political
landscape to suit their needs. They would not do so until the 1980s, when The
Woodlands began its rise to dominance in county politics.[34]

Without this suburban political pressure, county government made only
halting steps toward regulating growth. These efforts had to overcome daunt-
ing obstacles. Local resistance to tax increases and to the revaluation of land-
holdings made securing the funds to maintain services an uphill battle. The
Texas legislature, for its part, continued to stymie county efforts to develop
land-use planning and regulation. The Texas Association of Realtors, the Texas
and Southwestern Cattle Raisers Association, and the Texas Farm Bureau each
adamantly opposed any regulation that might decrease the value of rural land
and landowners' power to do with it what they willed. At both the state and
local levels, rural landowners and developers found common cause in opposing local regulation. The one area where the state legislature did acquiesce to
increased regulation was flood control. Montgomery County passed an ordinance restricting home construction within the one-hundred-year floodplain
and thereby qualified its residents for flood insurance and federal disaster relief
under the 1973 Flood Disaster Protection Act. Limited resources and a lack of
political will, however, continued to make enforcement difficult at both the
federal and local levels. The program amounted to a federal subsidy of environmentally untenable development.[35]

In spite of these limitations, county political leaders took some steps to
cope with the unfolding chaos of development. They began requiring permits
for septic tank installation in October 1971. Yet once again, having these regulations on the books did not necessarily improve development practice. The
poorly funded and understaffed board of health faced strong political pressure
from rural landowners and developers to look the other way when violations
were discovered. Even when the board did deny a permit, it had no power to
file injunctions to prevent developers from selling lots within these noncom-
pliant developments. Legally, home purchasers, not developers, were liable for
failing septic tanks, a fact that let developers off the hook. Not unexpectedly,
ill-planned septic systems continued to proliferate across the county.[36] May
1973 brought another ray of hope to Montgomery County's suburban frontier families when the Texas legislature passed a strong consumer protection
law that empowered the attorney general's office to prosecute developers for
false claims made about drainage and septic tanks. Before this new law, consumers had to file suit on their own and prove false representation, an intent
to deceive, and injury. This new law made the attorney general's office an
active consumer advocate and ended the principle of caveat emptor in Texas

real estate. The impact of this new law was immediate. The attorney general's Houston office received 1,490 consumer complaints about development and land sales between October 1973 and May 1974 alone. The office's prosecutions successfully collected damages from developers.[37]

It was only with the development of the North Country subdivision east of Conroe in 1974 that public pressure forced the county commissioners to address the issue. The developer was in the process of installing six hundred septic systems within a densely packed subdivision even though the county health department had denied him a permit. With the issue so prominently in the county spotlight, the commissioners court passed more intensive regulations and empowered the health department to use court injunctions against illegal septic tanks. Enforcement would remain a significant problem, but the passage marked a turning point in the county's regulation of the worst suburban abuses of this rural waste system. The county's regulatory system gradually extended its powers over developments across the countryside. All told, local and state government made halting progress toward solving the most flagrant developer abuses.[38]

&

Those who had purchased homes during the 1960s found little consolation in these halting steps toward regulation. Rather than working with local government, many metropolitan frontier families carved their own hyperlocal governments out of the materials at hand. They chose to reform their developments rather than their county or state. The most prominent of these state structures was the service district, originally designed for use in rural areas. Developers and residents adapted drainage districts, water supply districts, and rural fire prevention districts for their own purposes. The municipal utility district (MUD), created in 1971, became the most powerful of these special districts. MUDs could provide water, drainage, sewage treatment, and, from 1978 on, fire protection; they also had the power to tax and take out bonds. The number of districts in the county ballooned to nearly fifty by 1973, with a combined debt of $421 million, an astronomical sum given that many were approved in elections involving fewer than a dozen voters. For the developer, these districts offered control over the costs and extent of suburban services. For suburban residents, MUDs provided what residents needed: the assurance that their tax money would go directly to pay for the MUD's services. While never as democratic as their proponents claimed, MUDs empowered a coterie of politically engaged residents to manage their development's infrastructure. This propelled the fragmentation of municipal services that was common across the nation. Amateur management, limited resources, and small districts contributed to these districts providing inefficient services and teetering debt loads. This was the cost of local control and limited county services.[39]

Incorporation added increased regulatory powers and protection from annexation to the standard MUD capabilities. With the city of Houston pursuing an aggressive program of annexation, extending its extraterritorial jurisdiction (ETJ) into Montgomery County in 1965, incorporation was no small matter. Inclusion within either Houston's city limits or its ETJ brought with it the city's oversight and regulations but not necessarily city services. The thought of having their homes sucked back into the very city they had fled was not one most residents could stomach. Incorporation solved this problem. By forming their own city, residents could regulate construction, provide police and trash removal, and maintain roads, all for themselves. Incorporation was as much about building a town as it was about rejecting the city. Caught next to an expanding Houston and confronted with the failures and inefficiencies of county government and their own service districts, close to a dozen of the county's subdivisions incorporated during the late 1960s and 1970s. Incorporation seemed poised to make their suburban dreams come true. Yet residents soon found that these new municipalities faced the same issues as MUDS: they were perennially underfunded, inefficient, and amateur-led. Those fortunate enough to have commercial properties within their boundaries balanced their books. Those dependent entirely on residential taxes often became overburdened with debt. Just as importantly, incorporation brought political conflict and compromise into communities that had originally offered escape from such things. Incorporation brought towns into the countryside.[40]

Oak Ridge North, a development in south-central Montgomery County, was one of these towns. The name encapsulated its appeal to Houstonians: homes nestled in the forest at a higher elevation than the city and in the northern outskirts of the metropolis. Oak Ridge changed hands multiple times as various developers built out its ten sections between 1964 and the early 1980s. The first developer sold one-third- to one-acre "country-sized lots" on the appeal of wooded nature, class and racial segregation, low taxes, and privacy. A steady stream of white professionals bought into this bedroom community. Once there, they confronted the perils of life on the metropolitan fringe. As future town councilman John Planchard explained in jest, "There were Indians out here when I moved in." As had so many developments, Oak Ridge North made an impossible promise. Its advertisements boasted that home buyers would enjoy "all the benefits of city and country living and Montgomery County Government." In other words, they would have city services, country living, social segregation, and rural taxes. Fulfilling this promise would require a great deal of new residents. Within only a few months after opening in 1964, parts of the development flooded during a heavy rainstorm. This became a recurring problem. The development also faced damaged roads, roaming dogs, inadequate police and fire protection, and the continuing failures of the developer to provide promised amenities.[41]

Finding little help from the county or developers, residents turned inward, marshaling their own resources. The community's population of engineers, businessmen, accountants, and lawyers provided a deep well of expertise, education, and engagement. These homeowners organized a local civic club, managed the two MUDs and the freshwater supply district, and performed the grassroots community service that kept the development running. The looming threat of annexation by Houston provided the catalyst the civic club needed to call for incorporation in 1974. The political bickering that followed revealed a sharp divide between the development's northern and southern sections. As Oak Ridge built out, new developers improved the building standards and increasingly molded this rural recreational subdivision into a commuter suburb. Those who moved into sections 4 to 10 tended to be more white collar and more conversant in the workings of state power. Sections 1 to 3 had fewer amenities. Their residents jealously defended their rural lifestyles and opposed expanded local government and the taxes that would support it. Those in the northern sections feared that Houston would take their power of self-determination and thereby limit their ability as a community to improve their quality of life and property values. The southern sections were unwilling to place themselves under the control of a town, even if not doing so might mean annexation by Houston. The vote pitted a rural subdivision against a suburb. With the help of some northern defectors, the south won 325 to 205.[42]

Oak Ridge North residents on both sides of the divide pressed on with the tools they had at their disposal. Flooding later that year torpedoed developer-sponsored bond issues that would have buttressed Oak Ridge North's drainage, water, and sewer systems. Resident complaints got the attention of the state attorney general's office, and a lawsuit against Oak Ridge developer Dean Couch became the first case handled by the Houston office under the 1973 consumer protection law. A settlement in April 1974 forced Couch to admit guilt and thereby opened the door to citizen lawsuits. John Burgers, head of a south Oak Ridge group that sued Couch, explained, "To be honest, we feel like a bunch of minutemen. We plan to use a lot of talent, effort and energy. We have a lot more time than money." The failures of suburban development could both unite and divide residents.[43]

Oak Ridge North residents tried incorporation again in 1979 as Houston's ETJ expanded to include sections 1 to 3. Abandoning these southern sections to their fate, the remainder of the subdivision voted 318 to 230 to incorporate on January 20, 1979. After the May elections, civic leaders set about building a suburban town. The first year was a bonanza of hundreds of pages of ordinances and laws. They addressed flood hazards. They called for and got voter approval for a 1 percent sales tax to raise funds. They passed a noise ordinance, an animal ordinance, and a building code with a detailed permitting process. With the creation of a drainage district in January 1980, the city's takeover of the Oak Ridge North MUD, and the creation of an Oak Ridge North police department a few years later, residents were well on their way to establishing their city as an efficient suburban enclave within a county still enmeshed in rural East Texas. For Oak Ridge North, incorporation, supported by civic activism, effectively addressed the perils of life on the metropolitan fringe.[44]

Yet there were limits to what incorporation and grassroots activism could accomplish. In some cases, neither could redeem the failures of developers and home buyers to respect the natural limits imposed by these piney woods. Along Montgomery County's suburban frontier, no group of residents could tell a tale of more woe than those whose dreams of life in the forest brought them to Whispering Oaks. This rural subdivision nestled within a low-lying woodland south of the San Jacinto River. Longtime county residents would not have even put a chicken coop on some of the land, its danger of flooding was so great. Yet Houstonians snatched up the scenic wooded lots. For those hesitant about the dangers of flooding, the developer allegedly explained that the SJRA and the Corps of Engineers had fixed the river's flooding problems—a blatant falsehood. With this assurance, customers signed a release form recognizing the potential flood hazards and began construction. Poor site design, a lack of drainage structures, heavy vegetation, flat topography, and the proximity of the river all made Whispering Oaks especially vulnerable to floods. Less than two years after the houses started going up in 1972, the eastern section of the development had already flooded four times. It would continue to do so with numbing regularity. Seventy percent of the homes in the development were in the path of a twenty-five-year flood, and some were even in the floodway, a fact that earned Whispering Oaks the nickname Gurgling Oaks. One resident who maintained his sense of humor asked a reporter, "Do you know anyone who would like to buy a nice water-front lot with a boat launch?" In spite of its obvious problems, the county could do nothing to prevent the developer from continuing to sell lots in the troubled development to unsuspecting home buyers.[45]

This was only part of the problem. Frequent floods wreaked havoc on the development's poorly designed water and septic systems, leaving algae in the streets and sewage in the drainage ditches. Residents appealed to the county for assistance to no effect. They then decided to establish a private water district.

As in Oak Ridge North, they assembled a lineup of motivated professionals to pilot the development through the legal hurdles and administrative barriers. The Texas Water Quality Board (TWQB) became Whispering Oaks' savior. It promised to purchase the development's water bonds if it, in turn, incorporated to insure it had the taxing power to pay for any improvements. Residents enthusiastically agreed, voting 106 to 5 to incorporate on September 29, 1973. Months of frustration followed as the TWQB, the county commissioners, HGAC, and the SJRA bickered about the town's place within regional sewage plans. Finally, after over a year of waiting, Whispering Oaks got a $210,000 loan from the TWQB to build a small sewage treatment plant. With the purchase a year before of a 1928 fire truck, Whispering Oaks had set off on the road to being an incorporated community. Difficulties, however, continued to mount. Seven months later the community was no closer to having its sewer issues fixed. In April 1976 the developer forfeited his road bonds, leaving the village with washed-out roads and little money to fix them. The San Jacinto flooded most of the development again that June. Residents struggled on until extensive flooding hit the entire metropolitan area in June 1979, causing $650 million in damage. These floods finally convinced the commissioners court to crack down on developers who ignored floodplain and septic regulations. It was too late, however, for Whispering Oaks.[46]

Incorporation failed to solve Whispering Oaks' water problems. The developer had placed these residents in an untenable environmental position. No economic investment or new state powers could mitigate that fact. Whispering Oaks' only hope came from the newly formed Federal Emergency Management Administration (FEMA), which took on the development as a pilot project for its newly minted Constructive Total Loss Program. Rather than paying flood insurance claims, FEMA offered to pay fifty-one of the seventy-eight homeowners a total of $1.4 million to relocate. FEMA subsidized their retreat from the nature they had paid so much to live near. Landowners deeded the two hundred empty lots to the county and filed to have the roads closed. The county allowed the land to grow back into forest. FEMA would repeat this process in small developments up and down the San Jacinto River, wherever poor subdivision regulation and the dream of being close to nature had lured developers and residents to the water's edge.[47]

Inadequate planning, weak and ineffective regulations, environmental hubris, and deception characterized Montgomery County's metropolitan development. The construction of The Woodlands represented the antitheses of each of these. George Mitchell, a Houston oilman, constructed this "new town" on seventeen thousand acres of swampy forests along the county's southwestern border. His project far surpassed earlier developments in size, the types of amenities, and the quality of housing it offered. Its planners retained and even intensified the natural appeals used by earlier developers while at the same time incorporating a greater respect for natural limits into the design. In this way The Woodlands represented both a national model of development and the fulfillment of the promise of suburban life in Montgomery County. Mitchell's intensive planning and the extensive resources his company invested in the project freed The Woodlands from the constraints imposed by the county's weak rural government and found a way to work with its often unruly environment. The Woodlands refashioned the county's rural landscapes into a wooded suburban enclave in a way that later developments would imitate but never successfully recreate.

George Mitchell originally envisioned The Woodlands as a means to transform the way Americans built cities. The "new town" would recreate the efficiencies, the commercial and industrial tax base, and the employment opportunities of an urban downtown, eventually including condominiums, luxury hotels, high-rise office buildings, and a shopping mall. Its residential areas, in turn, would recreate suburban life in wooded nature. Mitchell's hopes for racial and class integration saw only limited success. The Woodlands' sophisticated environmental planning and natural drainage system, in contrast, gave the new town a national reputation even before it opened on October 19, 1974. Mitchell's company invested millions of dollars in fully knowing nature, even as the company developed the woods, fauna, and streams as amenities. As George Mitchell put it, "What people really want is the rural lifestyle and to be part of the big city, and I think The Woodlands is an answer in that direction." In this, The Woodlands offered the same threefold promise that past developments had offered—forests, lakes, and recreation—but it did so within the rhetorical framework of a now-dominant environmentalism. Where other developments had offered residents a chance to enjoy nature, The Woodlands offered something more: an opportunity to live in harmony with nature. Here newcomers could "find a home in a rolling forestland without destroying the forest" and without having their homes destroyed by that forest. Mitchell's planners freed residents from environmental guilt and allowed them to fully enjoy the benefits and amenities of a thoroughly planned life in the woods of Montgomery County, Texas.[48]

In order to make legible the ecology and environmental limits of the site, Mitchell hired nationally known landscape architect Ian McHarg of the firm Wallace, McHarg, Roberts and Todd (WMRT). McHarg's 1969 magnum opus *Design with Nature* called for development that protected environmentally sensitive wetlands, aquifer recharge zones, and farmland by pushing homes onto less sensitive land. With Mitchell's extensive resources at their command,

McHarg and his team set about analyzing and mapping every facet of the site's ecology, from soil and hydrology to vegetation and topography. They then overlaid all of these data onto a master map that was to guide development. His planning method sought nothing less than to understand the total environment of the site. In the process, McHarg made The Woodlands the most intensely studied suburban landscape on the continent.[49]

The crux of McHarg's plan was its treatment of the site's drainage. Locals, upon hearing of Mitchell's plans, had shaken their heads and wondered when developers would learn that some places were too flood prone to be worth building on. McHarg offered an innovative solution to this problem. By incorporating topography and hydrology into the design, McHarg allowed Mitchell to save an estimated $68 million on drainage while preserving and enhancing the wooded landscape and its nonhuman inhabitants as a valuable suburban amenity. Mitchell enthusiastically approved the proposal. Skip Christie, a Woodlands employee, best summed up the genius of The Woodlands' planning when he recalled that they had "landscaped a forest and irrigated a swamp." The Woodlands maintained the existing contours of the landscape, leaving the floodplains and lowlands with more permeable soils undeveloped and shifting development to higher ground and soils that were relatively impermeable already. Flood control and forest preservation went hand in hand, for by leaving the site undrained, The Woodlands preserved the high water table that many of the site's large trees depended on. McHarg's plan adroitly joined a commitment to protecting large areas of woodland from development with a developer's commitment to packaging the woods to be sold to prospective home buyers. As McHarg would later put it, "Nothing beats the combination of righteousness and profit."[50]

Yet in spite of these innovations, McHarg and his team worked within the assumption common to all development in Montgomery County, that "the residential and recreational value inherent in the forested environment" was "its prime resource." Where earlier generations profited from the forest by cutting it down, The Woodlands perfected the art of profiting off the preservation of trees. In one encounter George Mitchell made this logic very explicit. While touring the property in a jeep, Max Newlin, a Montgomery County native and Mitchell's chief forester, encouraged Mitchell to allow him to cut down some of the larger trees on the land as a way to raise capital for the project. Seeing a large pine, Newlin stopped the jeep and pointed to the tree and told Mitchell that that tree alone would be worth $50 as timber. Mitchell stepped out of the car, looked at the tree, and informed Newlin that such a tree would add over $1,000 to the value of a housing lot. Mitchell refused to allow any unnecessary timber harvests on the site. These trees anchored The Woodlands' golf courses, boating, hiking, tennis, biking, and swimming. In a period of national concern over the unrelenting bulldozing of forests and farmland, The Woodlands promised "a forest that is going to remain that way forever . . . [where] [n]o building will ever intrude." These same forests also enhanced the project's exclusivity. The woods restricted line of sight and protected homes from casual glances and passersby. As a former member of The Woodlands' staff put it, this was the kind of place where "if you don't know where you are, you shouldn't be here." The Woodlands was unpolluted, quiet, and preserved—a place to relax and enjoy nature to its fullest without the environmental guilt that came with traditional suburban development.[51]

In its planning, The Woodlands was world class. Its designers divided the project into a series of well-funded MUDs and subsidized a branch office of the county's sheriff department within the development. In an effort to ensure no one hijacked his vision, Mitchell convinced Houston to extend its ETJ to cover The Woodlands to prevent incorporation. This ensured that residents looked to Mitchell Development for solutions to their problems. Company representatives, in turn, were the ones who met with the commissioners court, interceding between their customers (now county residents) and local government. In the decades since its construction, some have criticized The Woodlands for the limits of its environmental planning. Such criticisms are fair, but they neglect The Woodlands' place within the larger context of suburban growth in Montgomery County. They do not appreciate just how successful The Woodlands was in comparison with its neighbors. Yet when one compares The Woodlands to developments like Oak Ridge North and Whispering Oaks, there is a sense in which something was lost. Its privileged upbringing freed residents from the need to develop the civic participation forged by necessity from the tenuous suburban experiences of residents in smaller developments. To echo Frederick Jackson Turner, the political culture of these more marginal developments was forged on the metropolitan frontier. The Woodlands replaced that frontier with a planned utopia, a "new town." Residents took over its management and worked to make it their own, but it was largely built for them, not by them.[52]

The Woodlands promised suburban life in nature with the planning, infrastructure, and leadership required to make a success of a development located on a flood-prone swath of East Texas piney woods and bottomland. Where other developments faced significant, occasionally catastrophic setbacks as they refashioned these rural landscapes into suburbs, The Woodlands fulfilled the perceived promises of environmentalism, yet it fulfilled them without the grassroots struggle and popular mobilization that so often characterized the movement. It also fulfilled them within a localized enclave. For a premium home price, new residents could rest assured that the developer had made peace with nature for them. A resident living in The Woodlands and working in Houston could spend his or her entire life without ever journeying into the more rural areas of the county or to Conroe, which, for all its growth, still retained the character of a Texas small town. Many in The Woodlands could even imagine that their homes really had been carved out of primeval nature that had never been farmed, cut, or developed.

Every once in a while, however, something came along to shake up this collective amnesia. Workers cutting a new drainage ditch east of The Woodlands near Oak Ridge North in 1980 noticed tar-like waste leaking into their newly cut channel. Research in the county records provided no answer to where it might be coming from. Only when officials began interviewing nearby rural residents did they learn that the site had been used by a contract hauler who had disposed of thousands of barrels of corrosive waste from local chemical companies at the site. The county health department had forced him to shut down and cover the site in 1967, but they left no paper trail. Now here it was. Even though many of the visual markers of rural life were gone, the county's history, environment, and social and political world persisted even as developments came to dominate the built and imagined landscape. The rural persisted amid the suburban.[53]

CHAPTER 5

Enshrining the Countryside

By the late 1960s Dulles Airport, the Potomac Interceptor, and the planned housing development of Sterling Park had transformed Eastern Loudoun into a series of bedroom communities for Washington. On the front porches of crossroads stores, behind the iron gates of the Leesburg courthouse, and in the pages of the local newspaper, locals grumbled about the rapid changes overtaking the county. It was not simply the new people or the traffic that frustrated locals. "It is a bureaucratic invasion," local resident Merlin Johnson proclaimed in a letter to the *Loudoun Times-Mirror*, "as inevitable [and] devastating [as] a glacier. It is backed by the one invincible conqueror of our time—the Tax Collector. Soon, along with federal bureaus, we can expect to have civilization spewed all about our lovely landscape—schools, dedicated to the suppression of learning, homes replaced by boxes, the roar of traffic, the poisons of exhaust gases, maiming and murder by auto, juvenile crime waves, alcoholism, signboards, honky-tonks, gum wrappers, ever rising taxes, divorces, the pace that kills, boredom, anxiety, ulcers and meddling clubwomen." In the face of such an onslaught, he feared, Loudoun's "obsolete rural folk" were powerless.[1]

What makes Johnson's bilious spewing of southern rural conservatism noteworthy is not his comprehensive attack on the acids of modernity. Rather, it is the defense of agrarian Loudoun and its beauty that he interwove within that conservatism. "We have child-like natures," he explained. "Our delights are in such silly pleasures as the ghostly blue of the mountains, the lush rolling green of the fields, a lungfill [*sic*] of fresh air, a weedless garden, a goldfinch on the grapevine on the lawn, a moonlight lake over the pasture, the unexpected view from a hill top." These things were under threat from "a masterful people intoxicated by the joy of destroying other people's rights." Here was an unreconstructed agrarian conservative from Virginia recounting a rapturous catalog of natural delights that could just as easily have come from the writings of Aldo Leopold or Rachel Carson.[2]

Historians have located a taproot of environmentalism among socially progressive, middle-class, suburban white families angered over the destruction of nearby forests and creeks and the pollution of their air and water.[3] While certainly not wrong, this focus obscures people like Merlin Johnson who do not easily fit within the ideological boundaries of suburban environmentalism.[4] In Loudoun County, sprawl stirred up resistance, yet the cacophony of activism that followed was loosely organized around preservation rather than environmentalism. Residents inherited from an earlier generation of gentlemen farmers and clubwomen both a gentrified landscape and an ideological justification for protecting it. The central tenet of this preservation culture was a commitment to defend the countryside—its aesthetic qualities, its history, and its sense of place. This is not to say that the popularization of ecology and looming fears of toxic waste and overpopulation had no effect on local activists. Rather, the legacy of early preservation activism channeled environmentalist stirrings into the defense of agrarian landscapes. The ecological value of rural land in Loudoun County added another set of justifications for a preservation commitment already made. The environmental decade provided activists with new terminology and a grassroots appeal, but it did not fundamentally shift the movement's focus or goals. Where much of environmentalism's power came from its emphasis on the chemical and nuclear pollution that people could not see, Loudoun activists continued to combat the sprawl, billboards, unplanned development, and roadside trash that demarcated a cluttered, disordered landscape—a landscape marred by visual pollution. Activists grafted environmentalism onto existing preservation roots. Doing so allowed these groups to retain their strength among rural conservatives and blue-blooded socialites even as they reached out to suburban newcomers. Their fight engaged people like Johnson who resented suburbanization as a federal and an urban takeover of their county as much as it did suburban newcomers who wanted to protect the neighboring woodlot from the bulldozer.[5]

A focus on preservation culture also resists the tendency among environmental historians to divorce historical preservation from environmental preservation and to cede the study of the former to public historians. In Loudoun the two were inseparable. Grassroots opposition to suburban expansion seamlessly interwove the defense of historical buildings and homesteads with the defense of open space. Both were, in turn, expressions of an underlying commitment to defending landscapes whose historical homes, green pastures, stone walls, and rolling topography enshrined deep-seated cultural values within a particular place: Western Loudoun.[6] These landscapes offered residents permanence, belonging, and community. Loudoun preservationists defended this world and its *placeness*, for lack of a better word, against what they saw as an expanding frontier of crass commercialism, uniformity, transience. They struggled to preserve Loudoun from *placelessness*: "a labyrinth of endless similarities," in the words of one contemporary scholar. In so doing they grasped hold of the overarching narrative that defined the contemporary historical preservation movement and combined it with the religious language of sacred and profane, of prophecy and judgment that characterized much of the period's environmentalism.[7]

There was, of course, a bit of hypocrisy in Western Loudoun taking up the critique of suburban development as a reflection of Americans' frontier mentality. Many of these preservationists had themselves left the city and come to the countryside in search of a new life—a refuge from the crabgrass frontier. Their arrival continued to shape this agricultural hinterland into a hotbed of rural gentrification. American environmental activists have long fended off accusations that they represent the interests of the nation's privileged classes. In Western Loudoun this critique hits rather close to the mark. The Western Loudoun preservationists defended was as socially exclusive and status conscious as any elite suburb.[8] Loudoun's preservation movement retained and even celebrated the class-encoded aesthetic, social values, and prejudices of the blue-blooded Virginians, foxhunters, retired military brass, and federal bureaucrats who created it. Refinement pervaded every aspect of the local preservation movement, from the defense of open space to the creation of historic districts to the cleaning up of roadside litter. For these preservationists, defending Western Loudoun was as much a moral imperative as preventing the desecration of a Renaissance fresco or a Turner seascape. Western Loudoun was not only beautiful; it was priceless. While these activists were never as elitist as their accusers claimed, a privileged and occasionally aristocratic spirit pervaded local opposition to sprawl.[9]

This chapter begins by examining the transformation of historical preservation from a hobby of those seeking an alternative to suburban homeownership to a movement that laid claim to large swaths of the countryside. This preservation activism collided with suburban sprawl in the county's continuing battles over development. It was against this backdrop that the Piedmont Environmental Council (PEC) and Keep Loudoun Beautiful (KLB) organized to protect the Loudoun countryside. The PEC was born among the horse farms and plantation homes of Western Loudoun and became a powerful advocate for environmental planning across northern and central Virginia. KLB began as an offshoot of local garden clubs. Its war on trash incorporated the defense of the county's ecology from pollution into the long-standing defense of the countryside from commercialism and clutter. These commitments would make KLB a state leader in container deposit laws. Both groups defended the beauty and permanence of Loudoun's landscapes against modern suburban life. Each demonstrates the continuity that characterized local preservation in an environmental era.

ↄ৯

The national popularity of historical preservation exploded in the 1970s as urban professionals sought escape from modern consumer life. In revitalizing old houses on the metropolitan fringe, newcomers grafted themselves onto the deep historical roots and respected heritage of Loudoun's extensive collection of abandoned farmhouses and dying villages. In these lichen-encrusted stones and rough-hewn timbers, newcomers found a place to dwell. As with the environmental critique formulated by nature-seeking suburbanites, this historical lifestyle implicitly opposed modern suburbia. Historical preservation promised something that suburbia could not offer: a sense of place, of permanence, and of belonging.[10] In Loudoun County John Lewis became the voice of this disparate movement. Lewis was a native Virginian whose father had worked at the United States Department of Agriculture in Washington during World War II. Fears of possible food shortages and enemy attacks drove the family to the countryside, where they purchased an abandoned 140-acre farm north of Leesburg. There Lewis spent his young adult years bringing the farm back into production and integrating himself into the local community. After serving briefly during the Korean War, he began purchasing, restoring, and then selling historical properties. The quality of his work quickly gained him a reputation among Washingtonians looking for fashionable homes in the countryside. By 1970 Lewis had secured a job as the northern Virginia representative of the Virginia Historic Landmarks Commission. While in that position, he documented and researched over seven hundred historical homes in the county and spearheaded multiple preservation causes. Lewis combined a love of rural freedom and a deep distrust of modern life with a brand of political activism that pushed for strong, government-enforced growth controls. His studies of Loudoun's homes and villages reveal an architect's sharp eye and taste for aesthetic unity that often led him to acerbic critiques of modern development in the form of either highway construction or subdivisions. A short selection from Lewis's study of the Loudoun town of Hillsboro is emblematic of his work:

> Hopefully in the future Hillsboro will be spared the ravages and destruction of so called transportation "improvement," and can continue to maintain the pleasant unspoiled rural character for generations to come to enjoy, as it has been passed down to us. There is no question that the historic and highly sensitive environmental qualities of the area should be preserved and respected. Unfortunately it is the nature of certain people with limited ability, aided by reams of senseless regulations,

to "improve" such places that have existed without their interference for one hundred years or more. Thus [the area] shall face from now on constant threats to its obliteration without a continual vigil of all its concerned citizens.

This need to preserve the "quality" of Loudoun's communities is a continued refrain in his notebooks. Protecting historic homes from development was, at the same time, both a fight against the desecration of the beautiful and a fight to protect a valuable amenity: Loudoun's history.[11]

Civic leaders in Loudoun were quick to realize just how valuable history could be. During the 1960s Leesburg mayor Frank Raflo led a coalition of local politicians, property owners, and preservationists to develop that town's historical look to draw tourists and increase property values. They convinced the town council to adopt brick sidewalks, iron lampposts, buried utilities, sign controls, and the town planning tools needed to craft and protect this image. Their efforts culminated in the creation of the Leesburg Historic District in 1970 and a more concerted effort to lure suburban and urban tourists to the quaint town. As Raflo explained, "You can build all the pseudo-Colonial stuff you want but you can't build a 200-year-old shopping center. And that's what we think Leesburg's main street can be."[12]

The Preservation Society of Loudoun County (PSLC) became the most important advocate for historical preservation at the county level. Evelyn Johnson and Mary Alice Wertz began organizing in 1973 in response to the destruction of trees in Leesburg and the continued threats of a dam in Loudoun. On February 14, 1974, they joined with other concerned citizens to create an organization to "preserve the natural and cultural heritage of Loudoun County" as a way to protect "Loudoun's high quality of life." The society joined national environmental groups in opposing extractive industry, in this case uranium mining, and promoting government limits on the development of wetlands and mountainsides. Their most prominent activities, however, were related to historical preservation and protecting the county's built environment. The PSLC worked on beautification projects and opposed unplanned development. Immediately after organizing, the group traveled to Charleston, South Carolina, to learn the latest in historical preservation techniques. Upon their return they began offering workshops and yearly awards to promote private historical preservation. Each year the group traveled to Richmond to visit the city's heritage sites and to lobby for increased state government support for their goals.[13]

These local preservationists armed themselves through local history research and genealogy. New residents spent hours in genealogical libraries not to trace their own heritage, which would have emphasized their status as outsiders, but to demonstrate the historic credentials of their newly purchased homes.

Western Loudouners' claims to belonging were only as strong as the depth of their home's historical pedigree. Like the Thoroughbred horses many were also raising at this time, the pedigree of one's home, the stories that went with it, and the care with which one restored it were markers of status and belonging. History became an object to possess, a badge of honor that set authentic Western Loudoun apart from the Anywhere, U.S.A., that was Eastern Loudoun. As with environmental preservation, local history research sanctified the landscape. Environmentalists fought development by populating undeveloped land with endangered species and threatened ecosystems, while Loudoun preservationists settled the countryside with ghosts of the past, endangered stories, and threatened architecture. When during this period local historian Eugene Scheel wandered the county collecting the place-names and forgotten histories that made up the county's cultural and historical geography, he was doing more than recording quaint lore for posterity. This was a political act, a statement that these places were not fields ripe for development but instead historical communities.[14]

Such activities extended the logic of preservation from particular properties to historic landscapes. Through the efforts of preservationists, many of Loudoun's villages passed over the series of hurdles to gain county recognition as historic districts. This special zoning designation, created by the county in 1971 as a response to preservation activism, provided increased architectural controls and development protections and brought with it recognition by the Virginia Historic Landmarks Commission. The county led the state in the number and acreage of such districts, as well as in the number of structures on the state's historic register—no mean feat in a state with so much of its identity invested in the past.[15] Goose Creek Historic and Cultural Conservation District was the most ambitious of these projects. It sprawled over ten thousand mostly rural acres owned by over two hundred landowners. This district, the county's eighth, exemplified the preservationist values of Western Loudoun. The roads were unimproved, the stone houses and frame barns still stood.[16] John Lewis's petition for Goose Creek's historic zoning is telling as much for what it says about preservationists' fears and rejection of the symbols of modern rural life as for the area's historical bona fides:

> This is an area which at this time in our history has no stores or gasoline stations, with the exception of the modest country store. . . . There are no trailers or trailer parks; there are no drive-in eateries; there are no movie houses, junkyards, billboards, commercial or industrial operations. There are only about 25 newer homes in the area, most of which have been built within the past 10 years, the major portion blending in with the overall rural scene. So far there are no scattered subdivisions, except those recently proposed. . . . [T]here are no regional shopping

centers, super highways, government installations or facilities. The preponderant character of the area is rural; the major uses of the land follow historic and traditional agrarian patterns.[17]

Here Lewis captures the class-encoded vision of rural life he deemed worth protecting. Goose Creek was a rural area without the markings of modern rural life: trailer parks, junkyards, industry, and scattered development. Preserving Goose Creek's rural countryside and historic homes was distinct from, and in many ways antithetical to, the preservation of a living rural community. By the early 1980s a large number of these farms and homes had been purchased by Washington commuters, retirees, and weekend restorationists who had moved to the countryside. Their money and engagement made the district possible.

Goose Creek, and all of historic Loudoun, for that matter, was a refuge, a rural escape from the acids of modern suburbia and modern rural life. Yet this escape from suburbia was itself a reaffirmation of the suburban ideal and its capacity to restore and refresh those whom urban life had alienated from the countryside. By the 1970s, though, to paraphrase historian Becky Nicolaides, hell had moved to the suburbs. The national media's critique of suburbia had refashioned the housing development, rather than the inner city, as ground zero for humanity's alienation.[18] The popular environmentalism of the period offered to ameliorate this alienation through restored harmony with nature and a rejection of consumerism. Loudoun's preservation movement took a parallel but distinct path, offering to ameliorate alienation through landscapes of pastoral wholeness and permanence. Loudoun's preservationists felt no deep need to save the earth or the nation from the ravages of pollution and exploitation. They already had their vision of beauty, health, and permanence. They mobilized to protect and restore privileged rural landscapes from the careless neglect and aesthetic ruination that marked modern rural and suburban life. Historic zoning was one of these tools, ensuring that the land would retain its pastoral beauty while persisting in private ownership.

When suburban development knocked on their doorstep, these preservationists mobilized much of the fight against sprawl. Here the structure of county government played an important role. Suburban development in Montgomery County, Texas, with a few notable exceptions, continued to be the province of wildcat developers who subjected county leaders and residents to the death by a thousand cuts as single homes and small developments proliferated, swamping county officials and flooding the landscape with poorly planned developments. In Loudoun relatively strong zoning and planning policies limited such development. This left large-scale corporate developers in the forefront, turning local politics into a high-stakes zero-sum game where the board of supervisors' approval or denial of one development could single-handedly transform hundreds of acres and bring thousands of residents to the county. This had been the case for Sterling Park in 1962, the county's first large-scale development constructed in partnership with U.S. Steel. It would continue as Boise-Cascade and Levitt and Sons each tried their hand at developing Loudoun during the 1970s.[19]

The *Washington Post* reported on January 24, 1969, that Levitt and Sons, the famed builder of Levittowns across the nation, planned to develop 1,250 acres along the Potomac River in Eastern Loudoun. Company representatives claimed they were "intrigued by the beauty of the Loudoun countryside," and they hoped "to act in such a way as to relate to the history of the county."[20] Yet the company confronted a board of supervisors transformed since the approval of Sterling Park in 1962. The intervening decade saw the county's population increase 52 percent. Over the same period, the county budget increased 250 percent, and the per-capita debt tripled.[21] New supervisors rode opposition to suburban development into office. All told, five of the six supervisors either retired or lost reelection in 1967. Each had been on the board for over a decade. The message was clear: Loudoun residents demanded forceful action to deal with new growth and to keep taxes low.[22] The Levittown name that journalists had heralded as the savior of a nation facing an acute housing crisis after World War II had, by the eve of the first Earth Day, become a symbol of the sprawl, conformity, consumerism, and environmental arrogance of suburbia. News of Levitt's application galvanized Loudoun's disparate preservation activists in their opposition to a development that, in the words of the county's planning officer, contained "an amorphous mix" of low-density housing, "which sprawls the whole length of the central portion of the tract." Feeling the weight of their constituents' calls to halt the county's growth, the supervisors voted in August 1970 to freeze all rezoning applications. After a series of additional hearings and discussions with the developer, they voted on February 2, 1971, to reject Levitt and Sons' proposal. The company challenged the decision in the state courts and waited for the wheels of the justice system to turn.[23]

The threat of Levittown proved a powerful motivating force, stirring one well-connected Leesburg couple to action. Agnes Grant Harrison and B. Powell Harrison became tireless defenders of the county's Piedmont landscapes and historical homes and fierce opponents of the degradation, shoddiness, and tawdriness of suburban development. Agnes became a crusader for beautification through her involvement in the Leesburg Garden Club and KLB. Powell had worked to preserve Leesburg's historic downtown, collaborated with the National Trust for Historic Preservation in its work on the local Oatlands Plantation, and become one of the founders of the PEC. This couple did much to

B. Powell Harrison.
Photograph vc_0003_2358-01, Winslow Williams Collection (vc 0003),
Rust Archive, Thomas Balch Library, Leesburg, Va.

shape Loudoun's preservation movement. Both Harrisons were blue-blooded
southern elites. Powell Harrison's family roots in the county went back to the
1700s. After graduating from the Virginia Military Institute and serving as a
lieutenant colonel in World War II he returned to Leesburg, sold insurance,
and embroiled himself in Democratic politics. Powell's upbringing had in-
grained in him the racial and class paternalism of the interwar Virginia gentry,
and he remained committed to the traditions of the Virginia gentry throughout his life. Agnes, who grew up in Burlington, North Carolina, shared this

love of hierarchy and deference. Both understood their social activism through the lens of paternalism. Neither Agnes nor Powell was opposed to economic growth per se. Each promoted industrial development and improved infrastructure where they believed they would bring prosperity without damaging the area's character. The Levitt plan failed this test. As Powell explained, William Levitt had boasted that "he was going to build a Levittown down here that would absolutely put to shame the ones he had built up in New York. And the more he talked about it, the more everybody around here got absolutely horrified. . . . [E]verybody you talked to was consumed with, 'My God, do we want a damn shantytown with 50,000 people down here?' What's it going to do to this county?" "All hell broke loose," he remembered. With the new county supervisors coming into office and Levitt now locked in a court battle with the board of supervisors, Harrison searched for a way to prevent the total suburbanization of Loudoun County. His solution would have implications for Loudoun's growth politics for decades.[24]

Loudoun County was certainly not unique in confronting sprawl. Conflicts over the speed and shape of suburban growth had become a national issue by the early 1960s. Urban planners, conservation groups, and government agencies at every level struggled to cope with runaway development. Warnings about the destruction of open space fomented a media frenzy, with journalists and popular authors transmuting personal experiences of bulldozed landscapes and new subdivisions into a national crisis. William Whyte's jeremiad on the pages of *Life* magazine in 1959 warned Americans that the American countryside, a place synonymous with "streams, brooks, woods and forests," was in peril. Margo Tupper, a Fairfax County, Virginia, housewife, lamented the loss of her children's wooded playgrounds in the dreaded advance of housing developments like her own. Such exposés brought sprawl to the front of the nation's consciousness and convinced many Americans that development was a threat to metropolitan fringe landscapes. In response, the Johnson administration hosted a national conference on natural beauty and preservation in May 1965 to discuss policy solutions to the crisis. Depending on whom you read, the open-space movement was either a crucial moment in shifting the national conservation focus from forests, rivers, and agriculture to metropolitan sprawl and ultimately pollution, or an elitist dead end that failed to mobilize mass environmental activism the way pollution concerns would soon after. Open-space activism certainly had deep veins of elitism. It was also, for many, a way station on the path to environmentalism. What both these interpretations miss is that for places like Loudoun County, open-space preservation *was* the movement. Pollution concerns, when they emerged in the early 1970s, played a subservient role within this earlier framework. These metropolitan fringe preservationists adapted environmentalist language to the goals of open-space preservation.[25]

The state of Virginia made its first moves toward open-space preservation on March 31, 1964, when the General Assembly created the Virginia Outdoor Recreation Study Commission. Members of this commission represented the state at the White House conference in 1965, which became a key moment in clarifying the commission's recommendations. Its November 1965 report called for legislation creating a scenic highway system, strengthening zoning laws, encouraging historic preservation, and supporting open-space preservation. Each of the proposals passed over the next year. The resulting policies reflected the state's particular blend of fiscal conservatism and preservation culture focused on aesthetics. Richmond supported private landowners as they voluntarily preserved and protected their land and thereby protected the state's aesthetic and environmental resources. As with so much in Virginia's history, it was preservation for the common good by the better sort—preservation via noblesse oblige.[26]

These policies and political assumptions remained in force in 1972, when, with further development looming, Powell Harrison conceived of a seemingly unorthodox yet, in hindsight, entirely predictable idea. Dissatisfied with the range of growth-control tools the state had provided, he decided to fly the county supervisors to England to study that country's land-use controls and farmland preservation programs. Loudoun residents had long embellished their countryside's similarities with the English shires. Now they would make a pilgrimage to their cultural hearth to learn how to save their landscapes from the city. Harrison first suggested this trip while eating lunch with Arthur Arundel, the wealthy owner of the *Loudoun Times-Mirror*. The next day Arundel put up $5,000 to help pay for it. Harrison made a few phone calls and had the rest of the $25,000 needed by that night. He convinced the director of the National Association of Counties and the executive director of the National Trust for Historic Preservation, who was also a fellow Leesburg resident, to tag along. Both organizations acted as official sponsors. Robert Stripe, a University of North Carolina law professor who had spent a year studying land-use law in England, agreed to take part and connected Harrison with Graham Ashworth, the chairman of the northwest region of England's Civic Trust and future president of the Royal Town Planning Institute. County supervisors from both Loudoun and neighboring Fauquier County, their spouses, planning officials, and five journalists—forty-two people in all—boarded a plane in January 1972 and set off to study preservation in the birthplace of the Anglo-American pastoral.[27]

Once there, the Virginians toured historic country homes, drove across the rolling hillsides, and listened as British planners outlined their policies. Rural England, they learned, had been protected from urban encroachment by a landmark piece of parliamentary legislation: the Town and Country Planning Act of 1947 and its subsequent revisions. These laws were a response to a widespread belief, as historian Jeremy Burchardt explains, that the "loss of rural land [through development was] damaging not only to agriculture, but at a more fundamental level to national identity itself." In practice, the act effectively nationalized the development value of rural land, made all such land tax exempt, and established strict land-use planning. Developers who gained approval to subdivide and build were required to pay a 40 percent tax on the initial development value of the land to offset the increased service costs. County planners and the supervisors saw in the English model a solution to their most pressing governmental problems: paying for services and providing tax relief for farmers. At the same time, touring these iconic landscapes provided the county supervisors with living proof that urban growth could coexist with picturesque agricultural landscapes rich in culture and beauty. All that was needed was the right policies.[28]

Unfortunately, such policies faced insurmountable obstacles in Loudoun. The English system restricted the property rights of rural landowners and gave planning agencies extensive authority over developers. Attempting either of these moves in a Virginia county would have brought howls of protest from Richmond. The second barrier was financial. The British system compensated rural landowners for the depreciation of rural land that came with the loss of development rights and provided substantial tax breaks. The state effectively paid landowners not to develop their land. Plagued with rising service costs, Loudoun did not have the money to do either of these things. Finally, counties did not have the legal authority to enact this type of land-use regulation. Virginia subjected its counties to the Dillon Rule, a stifling legal principle that prevented local jurisdictions from exercising any powers not expressly permitted by the state legislature. Adopting the British system in Loudoun was a political, financial, and legal impossibility. Undeterred, preservationists returned to Virginia and began to cobble together a local approximation of England's national land policies. They used aesthetic, fiscal, and environmental justifications to attempt to convince local voters that the preservation of private agricultural land through local policy provided a public good. It was a tough sell.[29]

Within two months after the supervisors returned, on March 22, 1972, circuit court judge Carleton Penn upheld their rejection of Levitt's rezoning application. County officials, he ruled, could consider the economic effect of subdivisions as part of their zoning criteria. Fresh off this victory, with a popular mandate from voters to limit growth and with the vision of the English countryside to inspire them, Loudoun officials moved decisively to set up governmental machinery to slow growth and protect open space. They oversaw a comprehensive revision of the county zoning map and the zoning ordinance. They set up ten-acre-minimum zoning west of Leesburg to help preserve open spaces and established the historic district zoning that provided special development controls and architectural oversight to places like Goose Creek. With their rezoning moratorium still in effect, Loudoun supervisors next passed Article 12, a planning tool that placed the county at the cutting edge of slow growth. The policy followed the English model by requiring developers to pay for the bulk of capital facility costs associated with new development. Developers and local landowners were incensed and raised cries of socialism. Purcellville's mayor grumbled that "some of the county officials have spent too much time in England and not enough here in America."[30]

Levitt representatives chose to work with the county rather than risk being unable to develop their property. The company withdrew its Virginia Supreme Court appeal in early May 1972, partially out of fear that if the Virginia Supreme Court upheld Loudoun's position, it might set precedent that would transform growth politics nationwide. Rather than risk this, Levitt filed a rezoning application under the new rules, agreeing to pay the county $866.92 per house, $1.9 million total, in order to offset the cost of schools, roads, and trash services. Other developers also refiled, expecting to negotiate their way out of most of the costs threatened by Article 12. Discussions with Levitt continued through the end of 1973 and into 1974. In December 1973 the county went a step further in its zoning controls, claiming the right to block subdivisions deemed by the supervisors to be premature because of anything from lack of road access to insufficient classroom space.[31] The courts struck this down as an overextension of county power and a violation of the state's Dillon Rule. At this point, Loudoun's experiments in British growth control began to unravel. By mid-March 1974 the state legislature had passed a bill, largely in response to neighboring Fairfax County's persistent refusals to hear and approve rezoning applications, that required counties to respond within a year after applications were filed. Forced to act, Loudoun supervisors voted 7–0 against Levitt's plan on July 2, 1974, finally ending the company's chances to build on its land. In a landmark Virginia Supreme Court decision in January 1975, the court ruled that development in keeping with county plans could not be delayed because the supervisors deemed it premature. This decision in neighboring Fairfax County ended Loudoun's experiment with Article 12 and severely restricted a county's ability to limit growth. The supervisors' failure to enact meaningful growth controls exposed the stark legal limits that state government placed on the county's political power. Land-use reform following the British example was simply beyond the legal reach of county governments. Conservative, pro-business, and prolandowner state politics hemmed in the county's attempt to preserve its landscapes through local government policy.[32]

The PEC would prove the most enduring fruit of the trip to England, establishing itself as a leading voice in Loudoun land-use policy. The organization's institutional roots went back to 1969. George C. McGhee, a retired diplomat and wealthy foxhunter living outside Middleburg, was the first to propose a regional conservation and planning organization for the Virginia Piedmont. Mc-Ghee did so while serving as a member of the Virginia Economic Development and Conservation Commission. Beginning in January of that year, McGhee began sending letters to prominent Western Loudoun landowners, including Paul Mellon and Arthur Arundel, as well as to state planning professionals and academics. Governor Linwood Holton gave his support to the project in February.[33] The first organizational meeting was May 28, 1970, at the City Tavern Club in Washington, D.C. Close to a dozen men showed up, representing a who's who of the Virginia Piedmont, including John Warner, Powell Harrison, Arundel, and Mellon. The men in the room selected forty founding members and pledged $30,000 per year to get the group off the ground. The initial membership included conservationists, farmers and gentlemen farmers, landscape architects, planners, and academics. For reasons that remain unclear, the organization floundered for two years before Powell Harrison took the reins and relaunched the PEC at the first planning conference, held at Oatlands Plantation on August 4–5, 1972.[34] The event solidified the connections between Loudoun and England, as Harrison brought in Graham Ashworth, the British planner and preservationist who had shown Loudoun supervisors around the English countryside six months earlier. Here Ashworth lectured to a crowd of preservationists from across the Piedmont about the benefits of English planning. The event generated enthusiasm for the PEC, which incorporated on December 22, 1972.[35] These preservationists organized the PEC to defend a nine-county region stretching from Charlottesville to Leesburg. In doing so, they placed Loudoun County squarely within the cultural, historical, and environmental unit of the Piedmont and implicitly challenged the county's inclusion within metropolitan Washington, D.C. Loudoun may have had economic and infrastructural ties to the city, but it was culturally, socially, and environmentally part of the Piedmont. The same did not hold for Fairfax County, which preservationists quickly dismissed as being too developed to save, its Piedmont character having been swallowed up by suburbia. Loudoun became PEC's advance salient in the war against sprawl. If Loudoun fell, then the rest of the Piedmont was in jeopardy. From its headquarters in Warrenton, in neighboring Fauquier County, the PEC funneled funds, personnel, and policy studies to the county's preservationists and spoke for them in Richmond.[36]

Over the coming decades, Harrison would make the PEC the most important planning organization in the region and one of the most active in the state. It advocated for historical preservation, open space, and land-use planning and opposed polluting industry and mining. It did so with the stated purpose "to preserve the traditional character and visual order of the countryside, towns, and villages of the northern Piedmont region of Virginia—while providing for orderly economic progress which is sensitive to conservation of its land, water, air and other natural resources, as our legacy to generations to come." Its "general objective" was "maintaining and enhancing the pastoral landscape." The PEC was the project of the well connected. It was conceived within the state government, and its financial support came from rural gentry. In terms of method, its representatives dealt in political influence rather than popular protest, in dispassionate planning studies rather than impassioned obstructionism. When George McGhee first proposed the PEC, he did so as the Piedmont Conservation League. The founders only integrated the word *environmental* into their title after Arthur Arundel suggested that doing so would allow them to ride the coattails of the national environmental movement, which had the ear of politicians in Washington and Richmond. Charges of elitism and snobbishness were inevitable for an organization that expected its first members to commit $1,000 to the cause. In a 1972 letter to Graham Ashworth, Harrison bragged that the PEC's board of directors included diplomats, high-ranking federal officials, and prestigious academics. As PEC's country-club pedigree became a favorite target of developers using class antagonism to undermine preservation, Harrison became more defensive. In battles with outside corporate developers, he later argued, the PEC was the voice of the people. When pressed, Harrison admitted, "My answer to [the charge of elitism] is that I don't want to be a member of any organization unless it's elite. These lousy organizations are no good; when you want to do something, you want to get the best. And you get the best, and you go after it. And if rich people got money, so be it." Most of the success the PEC had against large-scale developers who fielded skilled attorneys and large budgets came from its ability to foot its own substantial legal bills and fund policy research.[37]

In its ideology, the PEC followed its British cousins in prioritizing aesthetics and sprawl over ecology and pollution. They had only passing interest in the warnings of Rachel Carson and Paul Ehrlich. The victim, in the PEC's rhetoric, was not the suburban nature of the floodplain and the vacant lot. Nor was it the unspoiled wilderness of the Sierra Club. It was the agrarian landscapes that Loudoun garden club women Vinton Pickens and Edith Sands had defended from the onslaught of commercial billboards and early subdivisions in the 1940s.[38] It was Loudoun's countryside that was imperiled. Speaking before a state committee on land-use policy on December 2, 1972, Harrison channeled the national rhetoric of the period, warning of "the environmental decay which is spreading across Virginia." As his testimony continued, however, he made it clear exactly what he understood this danger to be: "Without proper controls there soon would be filling stations at every cross roads, commercial development along all major highways blocking the view of the landscape beyond, and rows of houses along all of the back roads." Tapping into deeper fears over the waning power of Virginia's rural elites, Harrison warned that the state was descending into "a desultory chaos." Rural Virginia faced the "violence and the overwhelming force" of urbanization. "Like the main effort of a conquering army," he continued, "it strikes suddenly and massively and destroys all before it; beauty, cleanliness, the old culture which has been built up over generations, visual order, and most of [the] things which are essential to a quality life in a progressive civilization." Harrison's list is as telling in what it omits as in what it includes. In comparison with the national environmental movement, PEC's mission—"to preserve the character of the historic countryside of Virginia's Piedmont, which requires the preserving of its quaint and historic towns, and the maintenance of an economically healthy farming community"—seems stolid next to the environmental movement's warnings of overpopulation, chemical pollution, and the destruction of humanity. Yet this was the rallying cry of local preservationists. These commitments made the PEC a tireless defender of Loudoun's landscapes and an active force in promoting the restoration of the county's historical villages and homesteads.[39]

Farmland preservation became the PEC's focus as members extended the logic of preservation from historic homes to the historic countryside. The England trip clearly demonstrated to PEC leaders that preventing development required reducing the pressure on farmers and other rural landowners to sell out. This meant addressing the problem of rising property taxes. These taxes, which funded the overwhelming majority of local services, had ballooned anywhere from 200 to 800 percent depending on the case. Taxes on an Eastern Loudoun farm near Ashburn, for instance, rose from $418 to $3,540 between 1963 and 1972. The figures for a Leesburg area farm over the same period were $1,181 and $3,501, respectively. This was in spite of farmers receiving little increase in services. A Purcellville-area farmwife, for instance, complained in the *Loudoun Times-Mirror*: "So many people move to Loudoun for its 'country atmosphere, easy living, and slower pace,' but no sooner do they unpack than they start wanting more police protection (mainly for the problems they brought with them); better, larger, fancier schools, public transportation; and publicly funded recreation and then they want to tax to death the very people who developed the county, who have been here for years and want to stay for a few years more seeking some kind of satisfaction and moderate living from agriculture." Farmers subsidized suburban growth and, in exchange, received rising values of their land, a fact that left many feeling ill used by newcomers and a county government that seemed committed to drive them to sell out.[40]

The state government offered a solution to this problem as part of the 1966 Open-Space Land Act. Under this law, any landowner could donate a conservation easement on his land to a nonprofit or state governmental agency. This easement donated the development value of the land to a third party and legally bound the landowner to keep the land in open space. In return the landowner received both an immediate federal and state income tax deduction for the gift and a reduced yearly property tax liability because of the land's decreased value. This solution meshed well with Virginia's preservationist culture, as it depended on and rewarded the patronage of elite rural landowners who could afford to retain large undeveloped landholdings in economically unsustainable agricultural production. Western Loudoun foxhunters used this tool extensively beginning in 1968. By 1980 twenty thousand acres within the Virginia Piedmont were under easement. For farmers whose retirement depended on securing a steady stream of income on their land, however, such donations were never a viable solution. Donating a large percentage of the unrealized value of their land to limit tax liability simply did not make economic sense. Even as they played the victim, most farmers expected to cash in on their most valuable investment—their acreage.[41]

This left preservationists searching for an alternative. Here land-use taxation (LUT) offered a potential solution. LUT had been gaining popularity in other states facing metropolitan growth because it provided all the tax benefits of conservation easements without requiring any permanent reduction in the development value of the land. LUT works through assessment, determining the taxable value of farmland based on its productive (agricultural) value rather than its best-use value (potential value if developed). Maryland became the first state to enact LUT legislation in 1956, and by 1970 forty-one states had passed some kind of LUT law. Counties, however, were slow to embrace the measure because it required them to voluntarily forgo tax revenue that they would then have to make up by raising taxes on suburban voters, a choice fraught with political peril.[42] Loudoun supervisors, especially those from western districts, began looking at LUT as early as 1965. They could not act, however, until after 1971, when Virginia governor Linwood Holton signed the state's enabling legislation. Under the law, landowners in participating counties who had at least five acres and a gross income of $500 a year for five years qualified to have their tax calculated based on agricultural use. If land-owners chose to develop their land, they would have to pay back taxes for the past five years equal to the difference between their assessed taxes and the LUT rate plus interest.[43]

The law was ostensibly designed to protect farmers. Exactly who counted as a farmer, however, was an open question. The law did not differentiate be-tween market-oriented farmers, gentlemen farmers, owners of farmettes, and speculators who temporarily held land in agricultural production. As the law made its way through Richmond, many warned that it would be a boon to wealthy landholders and speculators. Agricultural economists pointed out that the minimum acreage and income levels were ridiculously low in an industry where profitable farms encompassed hundreds of acres. Similar warnings ac-companied Loudoun's embrace of LUT. The *Loudoun Times-Mirror* prophesied that tax breaks would go to "the wealthy land manipulator who caused many of the local tax problems to begin with" and who would "sit back, play farmer, and enjoy land use taxation benefits." Who counted as a "genuine working farmer" was a question that preservationists and landowners were reticent to address. Preservationists wanted the county to throw money at rural landown-ers in the hope that some of it would land in the pockets of those committed to preserving pastoral landscapes. Powell Harrison and his preservationist allies praised LUT for restoring to farmers the freedom to remain in agriculture. He testified in Richmond that "the Piedmont farmer is overworked, underpaid, overtaxed and not appreciated for the vital services he provides." Exactly what those services were had changed a great deal from the agrarian producerism of earlier decades. When facing the imminent development of Dulles Airport a decade earlier, one Eastern Loudoun dairy farmer had warned, "If I closed down, it would mean the loss of thousands of gallons of milk to the Washing-ton area." In a suburbanizing county during a period of agricultural surplus, such arguments carried little weight. Preservationists argued that farmers' so-cial value had little to do with commodity production. Farming kept taxes low and produced the amenity of open space and the cultural and environmental benefits that came with it merely by keeping land in production. Under this logic it did not matter for preservationists who maintained the land in open space or what economic benefits they gained from it. What mattered was the preservation itself.[44]

With so much money on the line, farmers and developers lined up in sup-port of the LUT, reinforcing the rhetoric of agricultural relief and preservation as a public good. After five hours of public hearings, the Loudoun supervisors voted on September 27, 1972, to join the program. The final vote split down the middle of the county, with Western Loudoun supervisors supporting this tax break and Eastern Loudoun supervisors opposing what they saw as a rural subsidy. The county became one of only four jurisdictions in the state to sign on in the program's first year. Its passage unleashed a flood of applications from rural landowners, with 288 filing in the first weeks after its passage. As expected, the county's largest corporate landholders—including the Northern Virginia Development Company and IBM—were some of the first to sign up. Even with the state legislature tightening the requirements in 1973, the county had to find a way to make up $518,000 in lost revenue from LUT. It did so through a tax increase in 1973. The program continued to grow over the decade, with over nine hundred landowners signed up by 1976. That figure would reach fifteen hundred by 1980.[45]

The effect of the LUT was to subsidize speculators as much as farmers, a fact that even Powell Harrison, LUT's most active booster, admitted. Speculators could buy agricultural land, maintain it in agricultural production for five years while waiting for the land to appreciate, and then pay back taxes and develop it. In such cases, the county sacrificed current tax revenue to effectively rent open space. For those in Loudoun who hoped to continue to farm on the same scale that they had in the 1950s, LUT was a poor savior. Farmer Edwin Potts remembered,

> The sad part of [the growth in the county] is all these people moving out here are working in Washington . . . and they buy 3 acres or 10 acres, and they call that land a farm. Back when they put the farm use tax laws into effect to save the farms . . . they've got so many loopholes built into that law. . . . So they put four or five horses on [their land] and spend some money in veterinary fees and buy some feed for these horses and they qualify for land use. They're the people that are running the farmers out of business, and they're the people that are costing the county so much revenue.[46]

LUT freed farmers from the compulsion to sell, to use Harrison's language, yet it also gave them the freedom to wait for their right price and provided an increased incentive for newcomers to buy up rural acreage. The law could not address the systemic economic difficulties farmers confronted. The fact was that most Loudoun farmers would sell out anyway during the farm crisis and development boom of the early 1980s. Farmland would pass to the hands of those who were willing to farm with money rather than for money.[47]

Loudoun farmers renegotiated their economic position within a changing countryside. Metropolitan development eroded agriculture's economic and social foundations even as it provided economic opportunity to landowners. Programs like LUT relieved some of the pressures that pushed these families to abandon agricultural production. Given their general commitment to environmental sustainability and preservation, journalists, policy analysts, and historians have largely celebrated these efforts to preserve the countryside and downplayed the economic and social transformations that refashioned these rural areas into countryside.[48] Yet the county's attempts to preserve open space could never preserve commodity agriculture. They could only preserve the countryside. This limitation was built into the very nature of open-space preservation. In England rural planning reaffirmed deeply held romantic ideals about rural life that no longer fit the realities of modern agriculture. As Burchardt argues, this legislation rested on an impossible dream, that "the countryside could be radically modernized [for agricultural production] and yet remain an unchanging refuge from modernity at the same time." Rural tourism and landscape preservation obscured the "radical forces of modernization at work beneath the relatively unchanging visual appearance of the countryside." In England the aim was not the protection of agriculture so much as it was the preservation of a countryside for urban enjoyment. Loudoun preservationists had already turned down this path in the 1940s and 1950s. Their pilgrimages to England reaffirmed these assumptions. Tourist dollars were the financial foundation that made open-space preservation economically viable. Loudoun may not have had Amish farmers for tourists to gawk at, but its rural landscapes and historical buildings could provide a similar romantic destination for metropolitan consumers willing to pay for the aesthetic and cultural resources of the countryside. In spite of the PEC's implicit claims to the contrary, preservation was an act of development. Preservationists built these tensions into the PEC. In saving the county's agricultural landscapes as countryside, preservationists blanketed the realities of industrializing and pesticide-dependent agricultural production under a layer of romantic agrarianism. Romantic agrarian myths provided a powerful cultural image—a way of understanding landscapes that both motivated and sustained local preservationists' activity. Farmland became open space, a term that collapsed productive and recreational land, public and private, forest and field into a single category worthy of preservation. Open space recharged aquifers and prevented erosion, protected the county's pocketbook through tourist promotion and limited service demands, and protected the county's cultural landscape and aesthetics by reaffirming its pastoral image. Yet agriculture had been more than open space. It had also been the backbone of a rural culture and economy. This was what did not survive metropolitan expansion.[49]

❦

The PEC conducted its most important work outside the public spotlight. KLB, in contrast, organized a highly visible grassroots movement beginning in the early 1970s to confront what the *Loudoun Times Mirror* identified as "a steadily mounting layer of trash creeping across this county, butchering its landscape, polluting its waterways and poisoning its earth." Yet in spite of this difference in strategies, KLB joined the PEC in combining contemporary environmentalist rhetoric with a long-standing commitment to preserving the beauty of the countryside. KLB represented the same turn outward—toward the countryside—that historical preservation and the PEC had made. Litter stained and sullied the countryside. It degraded the landscape. It lowered property values. It ruined pastoral scenery. That it also polluted and poisoned the earth provided yet one more reason that it had to go. Scattered bottles, decaying mattresses, and construction debris were a persistent reminder that urban consumerist America had crept into the county. In cleaning up litter, then, KLB restored Loudoun to its former agrarian beauty even as it also participated in the broader environmentalist moment. KLB also crossed the divide between rural and suburban, replacing it with a divide between the vulgar and their trash, be they the rural poor or suburban newcomers, and those tasteful enough to clean it up.

The roots of this movement lay within Loudoun's garden clubs, which were part of a national antibillboard movement that protected pastoral scenery—usually seen from the window of an automobile—as a means of social uplift. These tea-drinking ladies, both blue-blooded Virginians and newcomers, plotted the destruction of the roadside billboard. The county's farmers and laborers had always understood the countryside to be a working landscape whose value was closely tied to urban markets. For farmers, billboards were just another way to make a living off the land. The antibillboard cause held little appeal for them. This was a movement led by those whom prosperity had freed to bind the value of the countryside to its visual purity.[50]

This local crusade began with two women who had few qualms about taking the law into their own hands. Edith Kennedy Sands, the wife of foxhunter Daniel Sands, and Eugenia Fairfax, who had moved into the Oak Hill mansion with her husband in the 1890s, formed the garden club's County Conservation Committee in October 1930 with the express purpose of preserving the country "as Nature wrought it." These two women and their half dozen compatriots waged a guerrilla campaign against placards and billboards. Late at night they would have their chauffeurs drive them across the county. Once they had spotted their prey, the chauffeurs would wait in the cars while the women ripped out, tore up, and hacked the offending signs to pieces. There was little doubt who committed these acts of righteous vandalism. At the committee's luncheons, each place setting included a small hatchet to aid members in their efforts. Edith Sands became a state leader in the cause, taking on the presidency of the Associated Clubs of Virginia for Roadside Development. Under her leadership, the group lobbied for and eventually won passage of the Virginia Outdoor Advertising Act of 1939, which put modest restrictions on roadside signs. With this victory achieved, the County Conservation Committee disbanded, its members nursing their fervent hatred of billboards from within the county's garden clubs. Some of these women would spend much of the 1940s pushing the board of supervisors to make the county a state leader in rural zoning, planning, and subdivision ordinances.[51]

Later preservation groups would look back on Vinton Pickens and her garden club colleagues as "indomitable environmentalist[s]."[52] Such labels, however, are anachronistic and distort the local preservation movement of the 1940s. For these women of taste, the fight against billboards and later for rural zoning was part of a larger commitment to protecting the countryside from the stain of commercialism. Roadside advertisements obstructed these women's consumption of the agrarian landscape. Billboards and zoning were about more than the individual's appreciation of rural beauty. The issues spoke to the county's identity. As one historian of the antibillboard movement explained, removing billboards was a way to preserve "veneers of gentry civility."[53] The county's garden clubs defined, defended, and etched into local laws a particular vision of Loudoun County that privileged rural aesthetics over economic development and landscapes of consumption rather than commodity production. These people already enjoyed the benefits of the modern industrial economy. In Loudoun they sought to shield themselves from the visual reminders of that economy. These women invoked the class-encoded moral rhetoric of disorder and decay to claim the authority to shape the county's landscapes. Their activism carved deep ideological channels into which the popular environmental activism of the 1970s flowed.[54]

Solid waste and litter problems were endemic to the metropolitan fringe and the nation as a whole. Local communities, municipalities, and states grappled with a garbage crisis during the period, making the rising tide of solid waste one of the most ubiquitous environmental issues of the day. Americans emerged from World War II ready and eager to consume their way to prosperity. Market segmentation, planned obsolescence, and Keynesian economic policies filled American kitchens and living rooms with the latest products from GE and RCA and thereby filled the nation's dumps, roadsides, fields, and forests with last year's latest products. American waste production increased from 88.1 million tons in 1960 to 121.1 million in 1970 to 151.6 million in 1980, a rate well above population growth.[55] The most dramatic increase came from beverage containers because an industry-wide adoption of nonreturnable bottles and cans foisted this new disposal problem on local American communities. Between 1959 and 1972 the quantity of beer and soft drinks consumed increased 33 percent per capita. Over the same period, the number of containers consumed skyrocketed by 221 percent. The typical beer bottle made thirty to forty cycles in the 1950s. By the 1970s used bottles and cans made one trip, from the store to the garbage or the roadside, tossed wherever was most convenient.[56]

The garbage crisis was an especially acute problem for metropolitan fringe areas for three reasons. First, scores of littering motorists drove along country roads, the nation's busiest rural byways and the closest open space to urban areas. At the same time, metropolitan fringe counties had weak enforcement structures and few available funds to directly confront litter. Finally, these counties found themselves playing host to a flood of garbage from both inner suburbs and their own new developments. Relatively low land prices and their proximity to these communities made these counties prime locations for private waste disposal businesses whose management ranged from unscrupulous to exploitative. KLB members counted seventy-five illegal roadside dumps across the county in 1970.[57]

In spite of these issues, nonhazardous solid waste has largely taken a back seat to air and water pollution in studies of environmental politics.[58] Where air and water pollution brought unprecedented threats to ecology and human health, litter primarily threatened visual health. Such activism has therefore seemed too prosaic to deserve special attention.[59] In Loudoun County, however, trash cleanups were the most popular form of environmental activism. The county had no chemical plants, no smog beyond what came from burning garbage, and few issues with septic tanks leaking detergents and sewage into groundwater and streams. Thus when popular environmentalism taught Loudoun residents to speak in the language of pollution, they took up their fight to preserve the countryside from solid waste pollution.[60]

These actions were part of a national movement against litter that nurtured distinctly conservative politics. The national nonprofit Keep America Beautiful bears some of the blame for this. Funded by container producers and beverage companies, the organization became a symbol of corporate deflection of environmental reform. Keep America Beautiful, as historian Heather Rogers describes it, channeled the stirrings of environmentalism away from industry reforms and toward "the eyesore of litter and . . . the notorious 'litterbug.'" In Loudoun, at least, this is too conspiratorial. The fight against trash united Loudoun's more socially active suburbanites with established preservationists in the defense of the county's landscapes. The litter motivated their activism rather than distracting from it. Their methods revived the billboard battles of the 1940s as much as they embraced the environmentalism of the 1970s. They picked up trash to restore the countryside. If they happened to save the planet, so much the better.[61]

Mrs. J. Earle Weatherly, litter committee chairman of the Purcellville Garden Club, began organizing KLB in November 1965 as a way to consolidate the county's beautification efforts. The organization launched the following year. KLB's board reflected the continued influence of Loudoun's upper crust within the county's preservation activism. Only one board member, Sybil Wanner, was from Eastern Loudoun, and she and her husband were residents in the established subdivision of Broad Run Farms. The remaining board members included three prominent men from Leesburg (one a retired general) and Mary Godfrey, the wife of the national radio personality Arthur Godfrey. This was in addition to Agnes Harrison and Mrs. Earle Weatherly, both of whom were ladies of high reputation. The group's membership and participation quickly expanded beyond these social circles. When the popular excitement swirling around the first Earth Day arrived and Governor Holton called for Virginians to clean up their state, KLB was already making headway. Agnes Harrison, an active Leesburg Garden Club member, took the lead. A meeting at the Oatlands carriage house the week before Earth Day brought forty people to discuss the roadside litter problem. Another held two weeks later brought seventy-five to Leesburg to discuss the county's landfill problems, which many believed to be at the core of the litter problem. From that point, the organization grew rapidly.[62]

KLB mobilized the broadest coalition of any of the county's preservation groups. It engaged society ladies and suburban county residents with suburbanites who feared the despoiling of their newly adopted landscapes. It even attracted a few working farmers for whom litter meant injured cattle and hours of lost labor. The KLB's yearly cleanup brought together local 4-H clubs, Boy Scouts, civic groups, churches, and the Izaak Walton League. In its second year, the event yielded 587 cubic yards of trash from the county's roadsides. By the early 1980s, KLB's four hundred members maintained forty area leaders to coordinate the thousands of people who participated. KLB members relished their newfound role as local litter watchdog. These concerned citizens educated the county's youth and fought for local recycling, a bottle deposit law, and the closing of the county's poorly run dumps.[63]

The surge of popular interest in ecology surrounding Earth Day increased KLB's popularity by reinterpreting anger at the despoiling of the county's agrarian landscapes through the environmentalist categories of pollution and waste. Yet beauty remained the central goal. The *Loudoun Times Mirror* explained the local environmental spirit this way: "[KLB] in Loudoun is born of the final disgust with the appearance of the roads which wind their way through

Agnes Harrison (*second from left*) receiving an award from KLB leadership.
Photograph vc_0034_0097, Keep Loudoun Beautiful, 1969– (M 052),
Rust Archive, Thomas Balch Library, Leesburg, Va.

this county. Along some of them, there seem to be more beer cans and other assorted debris than there are blades of grass. . . . [T]he reason literally thousands of Loudoun residents are working now to clean the county up is because they are concerned with its appearance, not only to themselves, but to the tourists who come here because they think it beautiful." Agnes Harrison was especially instructive on the way the new and the old mixed within KLB. When asked why she joined the movement, Harrison recalled that her first involvement came when she caught local workmen throwing beer cans on her lawn in Leesburg and called the sheriff to put a stop to it. This is certainly far from the type of radicalizing experience that inspired green crusaders. Yet like many during the period, she connected her commitment to cleaning up her corner of the world with images of "spaceship earth" sent back by the first Apollo missions. Environmentalism gave global significance to Harrison and her fellow garden club members' war against ugliness. As head of KLB, Harrison called for county residents "to get Loudoun clean and to keep Loudoun clean." This cleanliness now included sanitation, beautification, *and* environmental purity. Even as she headed this new cleanup crusade, Harrison articulated a broader vision for preservation: "highway planning and zoning, the removal of billboards and automobile graveyards, the cleaning up of our public ways, the planting of trees, and . . . air pollution control." The new ecological vision and

Keep Loudoun Beautiful cleaning up trash along Loudoun roadsides. Much of the labor involved came from paid workers from the Loudoun County Youth Corps.
Photograph from scrapbook, 1976 Keep Loudoun Beautiful, 1969– (M 052),
Rust Archive, Thomas Balch Library, Leesburg, Va.

the popular fervor that came with it reaffirmed the culture of preservation's defense of the aesthetic purity and agrarian character of Loudoun's privileged landscapes.[64]

Tidying the landscape ultimately propelled KLB into state politics. As members cleaned up the county's roads, they quickly discovered that close to 90 percent of the county's roadside litter came from disposable bottles and cans. In response, the group's leadership joined a growing national movement for deposit laws. Oregon's law became the first in the nation, going into effect in October 1972. Jim Brownell, a conservative farmer and Republican county supervisor, proposed a similar local deposit law for Loudoun in January 1971. KLB rallied popular support, and on May 17, 1971, the supervisors voted 5–0 to become the first political entity in the state to ban the sale of nonreturnable soft drink and malt beverage containers. An estimated twelve hundred states, towns, cities, and counties across the nation had proposed some sort of bottle bill by 1976, yet Loudoun was one of only five counties in the nation to have one on the books by that point.[65] As with the county's growth regulations, the container law drew powerful opposition from well-financed industry lobbyists and ultimately fell victim to the Dillon Rule. Yet locally, the ordinance represented the high point of grassroots preservation activism.[66] All told, the group cleaned up more than sixty unauthorized dumps during its first decade. Through its local lobbying efforts and popular campaigns, its leadership forged a local movement that crossed the suburban/rural divide. It focused popular attention on the most obvious stains on the landscape and took strides toward remedying them. KLB's leadership allied their organization with the county's slow-growth preservation coalition. Yet, as with the PEC, KLB's activism retained its preservationist roots—roots that ensured that the organization would emphasize landscapes over environment, beauty over health, and clutter over pollution.[67]

ℰℐ

The number of local preservationist and conservationist groups ballooned during the 1970s as Loudoun's towns became historic districts and its creeks and streams became state scenic rivers. By 2007 there were thirty-nine such groups in the county. These were primarily staffed and led not by Eastern Loudoun suburbanites but by newcomers to Western Loudoun.[68] These newcomers included Eleanor Adams. Both Adams and her husband had attended elite universities, and they moved to a farmhouse in Sterling in 1963 when Mr. Adams got a job at the CIA headquarters in Langley. When development got too close in 1968, the couple picked up and moved to a 215-acre farm off a dirt road north of the historic village of Waterford. There they ran some cattle, gardened, kept horses, and became involved in the local community. Originally from a small Alabama town, Eleanor Adams became enamored with both the agrarian beauty and the cultured sophistication of Western Loudoun. When she saw these things under threat from development, she devoted an increasing amount of time to their protection. The catalog of her activities is extensive. She spent time on the boards of the local soil conservation office, the Waterford Foundation, and Loudoun's local PEC committee; she was part of a group of landowners who successfully fought to reroute a natural gas pipeline that was slated to go through her farm; and she worked with the League of Women Voters and a series of county committees to develop policy solutions to the decline of agriculture in the county. For Adams and many other newcomers, preserving agrarian Loudoun—their adopted home—became a consuming passion.[69]

As Merlin Johnson closed his letter to the editor that opened this chapter, he proposed a far-fetched solution to Loudoun's growth problems. "Other primitive peoples, such as the Indians are protected as instructive relics of prehistoric periods," he argued. "Why can't we turn Loudoun County over to the government as a museum? Surely it would be most inspirational for the bureaucrats to come out and study us. They would leave with a deep gratitude for the advance of civilization which has freed them from the cruel necessity of providing for themselves. By thus serving our masters, we could hope for survival." In one sense, Johnson completely misread the government bureaucrats, many of whom would make Loudoun their home over the following decades. Most did not come to be reminded of the joys of modern conveniences. Instead, they came to live among the same agrarian landscapes that Johnson had praised, but without the labor that went with the agrarian life. Yet in another sense, Johnson's words were prophetic. Agrarian Loudoun survived by becoming Washington's backyard: a tourist destination and a place for commuters and gentlemen farmers to reenact their own vision of historic agrarian life. Protecting Western Loudoun, however, was not the work of the federal bureaucracies that Johnson despised. It was, rather, the work of a diverse group of preservationists who saw something worth protecting in the countryside.[70]

The PSLC, PEC, and KLB preserved their countryside. Yet their very successes only added to the county's reputation as Washington's garden spot: an area where Washingtonians could enjoy "the charm and relaxed beauty of a history-studded rolling countryside." Outside consultants had, from the mid-1960s, called on Loudoun's leadership to follow the example of Colonial Williamsburg, Lexington, Virginia, and Charleston, South Carolina, in promoting historical tourism as a county industry. One of the most important lessons from the supervisors' trip to England was that historical and farmland preservation would only work if buttressed with tourist money. Hunt Country, rolling pastures, and historical villages were all major tourist destinations for Washingtonians. By 1978 one out of every five retail dollars spent in the county was travel related, and the county was eighth in the state in tourist income. Even as preservationists enshrined the countryside, tourism promoters opened these shrines to pilgrims. Convincing them to return to their homes afterward often proved a difficult task.[71]

By the 1980s this preserved countryside had itself become central to selling suburban development in Loudoun. Loudoun became what *Washington Post* journalist Joel Garreau would rather prosaically term "nice." Nice is country clubs, scenic vistas, boxwood-framed historic homes, and horse farms. Nice includes all the markers of class- and race-segregated, manicured landscapes. Loudoun County's image included all of these. Loudoun's public relations literature integrated this Western Loudoun image into its advertisements. It portrayed the county as "uncrowded and unspoiled" and as "a land of quiet roads with stone fences and rolling fields and woods" where a "tranquil country environment, rich in history and in beautiful surroundings," awaited newcomers. Yet at the same time that it celebrated the "rustic and unspoiled" countryside, it also emphasized the county's large lots of former farmland ready for development.[72]

Where subdivisions in Montgomery County, Texas, embraced an image of wooded leisure, Loudoun developers took up a combination of pastoral and historical images for their projects. History was not simply what had happened. It was a quality, a style, an amenity. This is what allowed Loudoun tourist pamphlets to print the otherwise nonsensical statement, "The history of centrally located Loudoun is surpassed only by its beauty."[73] Suburbia has been sardonically described as a place where developers cut down the trees and name the roads after them. In Loudoun developers have more commonly named suburban streets and model homes after historical figures and plantation mansions.[74] Historical preservation increased property values and added to the county's reputation as a refuge from suburbia. At the same time, this added prestige attracted developers who were eager to cash in on the county's landscapes. The experience of the aptly named Countryside development during the early 1980s is particularly instructive on this point. The developers named its sections after iconic Loudoun plantation homes, embodying their goal of "honoring the past, relishing the present, building the future."[75] They preserved an old barn silo as part of their new shopping center and named the Home Owners' Association after the colonial era Proprietary of the Northern Neck of Virginia. For Barbara Haller, a resident and newcomer, this thin veneer of historicity provided the sense of empowerment and belonging she craved. "Now," she explained in her short history of the development, "as I roam through Countryside, I am constantly reminded of historical events and of the people who have created Loudoun's incredible past. I no longer feel estranged from local history. Rather, I am very much a part of it."[76] It is easy to smirk at the shallowness of such historical preservation. Yet the motivations driving this home purchase were the same as those propelling preservationists. Twentieth-century Loudoun was a place where, for the right price, mobile modern people could graft themselves onto historical roots, transplanting themselves onto and into pastoral landscapes. Of course, these landscapes could never fully satisfy the expectations placed upon them. Yet even as they searched for a home, these preservationists developed this metropolitan fringe county.

A Tale of Two Villages

Virginia: A Guide to the Old Dominion, published in 1940 by the Works Progress Administration, offered Washingtonians scripted rambles through the Virginia countryside. Those embarking on Tour 13 westward from the capital read of one promising detour. Turning right at Clark's Gap some forty miles from Washington and venturing north on dirt roads across the countryside, travelers would stumble upon Waterford, "the oldest settlement in Loudoun County, dozing between low hills that roll down to meadows along a lazy creek." Here "old houses—white frame or red brick—are set along lanelike streets" beside a stone mill. Waterford was a quaint hamlet off the beaten path to the Blue Ridge Mountains and Winchester.[1] Photographs taken as part of the National Park Service's Historic American Buildings Survey captured the village as intrepid motorists would have seen it. Waterford was in its dotage. The old houses were crumbling; the old mill had closed. It was a rural backwater past its prime.[2]

Past its prime, but not without hope. The first stirrings of Waterford's restoration had begun in 1931, when Edward and Leroy Chamberlin, inspired by the Rockefellers' efforts to restore Colonial Williamsburg, hired local laborers and artisans to repair a handful of properties they had purchased. The Chamberlins were uniquely positioned to accomplish this. The marriage of their father, a Union cavalry officer from New York, to a Waterford Quaker made the brothers an embodiment of sectional reconciliation. Edward's marriage to a wealthy heiress in turn provided the necessary funds. Over the next decade the brothers purchased and restored some two dozen properties and installed the town's first community septic system and cistern. These efforts stalled with Edward's death in February 1940.[3]

A few years later, Paul and Polly Rogers bought their piece of the Virginia countryside on a whim. During the summers, while their kids were away at camp, the couple would drive out from the city to their former tenant house. There they camped out in the yard, cooking over an open fire and looking up at the stars. On one of their many afternoon excursions into the countryside, the couple happened upon Waterford. There, Polly Rogers later intoned, "I lost my heart." She was smitten with the town's crumbling stone houses, rolling

Waterford, ca. 1938.
Photo Town of Waterford (General Views), Waterford, Loudoun County, VA, Historic American Buildings Survey, Va., 54-WATFO, 1–2, Prints and Photographs Division, Library of Congress, Washington, D.C., 1938.

pastoral scenery, and winding country lanes. "Waterford haunted me," she remembered. "It was like finding an abandoned child. You wanted to take it home, love it and try to save it from complete disintegration."[4]

In September 1943 four couples, including the Rogerses, met with Vera Chamberlin, Edward's widow, and Edward "Ned" Chamberlin Jr. to organize restoration efforts. With the blessing and continued involvement of the Chamberlins, the group formed the Waterford Foundation.[5] Its stated goal was to "re-create the town of Waterford as it existed in previous times with its varying crafts and activities, and to restore as many buildings as possible in the town of Waterford in like manner in which they were originally constructed." The group selected Allen B. McDaniel, a prominent Washington architect, as their president. McDaniel had restored the former Waterford Quaker meeting-house. He was brimming with ideas for his next project.[6] For these residents, Waterford was the "deserted village" out of the romantic past, ripe for rebirth.[7]

The foundation purchased and restored town properties, beginning with the mill. Some of these it kept to house its expanding operations. Others it resold. Locals shook their heads in bewilderment as foundation members returned each evening from their city jobs to pour their time and money into Waterford ruins.[8] A restored Waterford promised these Washingtonians a sense of place, of permanence, of belonging. As one visitor explained, its "lackadaisical charm" came from its "haphazardness." The romance of restoration drove the town's revitalization.[9]

The Waterford Foundation celebrated this restoration through its yearly homes tour and craft exhibit. While in Sorrento, Italy, during World War II, McDaniel had been fascinated by the potential for folk festivals to preserve local traditions and employ the industrious poor. He led the foundation in reinvigorating Waterford's weaving, blacksmithing, boot making, and other early nineteenth-century trades by marketing them to postindustrial consumers.[10] He believed these sales would uplift residents; provide a fire department, recreational facilities, and health care; and thereby revitalize Waterford.[11]

The foundation held the inaugural fair in 1944. Close to a hundred local producers exhibited their quilts, rugs, hot pads, pots, pans, jars, and artwork. Six hundred people perused these goods, buying choice items to adorn their suburban mantels. A *Good Housekeeping* article celebrated the fair for drawing American consumers "to behold the handiwork of a resourceful and rejuvenated people, to buy their wares like hungry locusts." The article went on to profile some of the vendors. A widowed polio victim braided rugs to pay her daughter's way through college. An African American broom maker and basket weaver earned enough money to remodel his home. An eighty-five-year-old glove maker exclaimed, "I declare it's a tonic being useful. . . . I feel buzzy as a young bumblebee."[12] The fair provided the "constructive and profitable employment" that McDaniel had hoped to bring to the residents.[13] Within a few years the segregated event would draw tens of thousands to tour the old houses, steep themselves in the town's history, and purchase crafts. Visitors driving from across the Washington metro area caused gridlock on the town's dirt roads, giving Waterford a yearly rush hour that rivaled what many faced on their weekday commutes.[14]

The fair brought national attention to this small Piedmont village. In the process, it established Waterford as a metropolitan tourist destination of the sort the Works Progress Administration authors could have scarcely imagined. As in Amish country a few hundred miles to the north, Waterford's craftsmanship reinforced the quaintness of the county's rural landscapes, naturalizing labor and making the countryside itself an object of urban consumption.[15] The prosperity the fair brought these locals was genuine. It was not, however, sustainable. By the 1970s the fair's popularity had slowly reoriented the event from a means of local uplift to a celebration of the village's historical preservation. With the fair drumming up interest, artists, authors, retirees, and commuters spent increasingly lavish amounts of money to buy into the local housing market. In the process they remade Waterford into one of the most exclusive residential enclaves in metropolitan D.C.[16] Gentrification priced local

Visitors at the Waterford fair.

artisans out of the town. At the same time, the fair's well-established market lured national craftsmen to the fair. The restored Waterford was a place where craftsmanship was demonstrated, appreciated, and purchased rather than rescued, cultivated, and practiced.

In reward for the foundation's efforts, the secretary of the interior declared Waterford to be a national historic landmark in April 1970.[17] By 1972 the foundation owned close to a dozen buildings, including the old mill, the Methodist church, the old Waterford school, and the town's general store. Its members dedicated themselves to interpreting the town's history for a national audience.[18] This increased the pressure for the foundation to remain vigilant in protecting this aesthetically fragile village from what one member termed "sloppy and unsightly" metropolitan sprawl.[19] The resulting gentrification predictably stoked resentment among locals. Polly Rogers recounted, only partially in jest, that "the CIA is not more suspect of evil and underhanded doings than was the Waterford Foundation in the eyes of the citizenry."[20] Longtime residents not only chafed at the loss of local control but also grew frustrated with the appropriation of the minutest details of the village's past. The foundation tastefully labeled the built landscape with plaques and guidebooks, consecrating it for historical consumption. These visual markers of historic Waterford coexisted with the road signs and realtor advertisements—visual reminders that the town's preservation depended on the automobile and the housing market as much as it did on memories of the past. While visually incongruous, all three types of signs interpreted the landscape for visitors, making Waterford legible to metropolis visitors.[21]

Just as galling to many rural people, some preservationists defended inconveniences as a badge of historical authenticity. One newcomer snidely commented that if the locals had been left to themselves, they would "have [a] 7-Eleven on the corner . . . [with] 10 pickup trucks in the front." Such symbols of rural life represented the commercialism that newcomers had left behind. Waterford had no restaurants and only one small store. Foundation members resisted both the highway department's attempts to build a bypass around the town and the county sanitation authority's attempts to provide water and sewage treatment—both moves that would have encouraged exurban development.[22]

Those driving north along State Highway 662 from Clarke's Gap toward Waterford in the twenty-first century will find a countryside just as lush as it was in 1940. Where dairy cows had roamed, five-to-ten-acre farmettes and three-to-four-thousand-square-foot homes now dominate. After passing through a creek-side forest, visitors are greeted by a bright and polished Waterford. The decaying ruins of yesteryear have been reborn as refined village homes set among country gardens. Upon entering Waterford, visitors feel like they are discovering a lost village that has somehow avoided the pitfalls of modern society.

ፀ⁊

African Americans founded Tamina (pronounced "Tammany"), Texas, along the Missouri Pacific Railroad line in southern Montgomery County in 1871. This rural community offered recently freed slaves the chance to own land on the margins of white oversight and control. It also offered moonshine and other illicit entertainments to lumber and railroad workers. Tamina was poor. Even with the arrival of electricity in 1962, Tamina's infrastructure and housing stock were woefully inadequate. The community's 154 homes shared five wells and stored their water in drums. For sewage, most homes relied on outdoor privies. Less than a mile from the ever-growing, prosperous enclave The Woodlands, Tamina testified to the persistence of structural inequality and rural poverty in the midst of metropolitan development.[23]

Had the community been nestled off a backcountry road in the northeastern part of the county, Tamina might have struggled on unnoticed. Positioned

Aerial view of modern Tamina adjacent to a subdivision
in southern Montgomery County.
Courtesy of Marti Corn.

as it was among the county's booming southern developments, however, fixing Tamina became a county priority. In the early 1970s officials at the newly
formed health department worked with the local county commissioner and
their congressman to secure a Farmers Home Administration loan to install
basic water and sewer services for the community and thereby limit its potential threat to public health. The effort was only partially successful, buying a
small water system that served part of the community. A lack of trust between
Tamina leaders and the county government, itself a historic legacy of decades
of racism, prevented the construction of a sewer system.[24]

Over the following decades, the county established building standards and
permitting processes to protect residents from substandard development. The
first generation of subdivisions, whose failures drove these reforms, each hammered out its own local water, sewer, and road systems. Tamina, however,
never generated the civic momentum or secured the political leverage to follow
suit. The community's political and economic marginalization meant residents
endured some of the worst consequences of development. Area drainage systems sent water from housing developments onto residents' lawns and through
the town's cemetery on its way to the San Jacinto River. The main roads
through the community carried persistent truck traffic as eighteen-wheelers
roared night and day in and out of a nearby quarry, delivering building mate-

rials to pave new roads and build new houses. Tamina's land literally served as the foundations of metropolitan growth.

Into the 2000s the community displayed the characteristic signs of blight: overgrown lawns, sagging homes, decaying infrastructure, and pervasive litter. The community's residents continued to lack trash service, fire hydrants, sewer lines, and, for some, indoor plumbing. Wells and leaking cesspools had to suffice. Continued mistrust undermined renewed efforts to address these issues. Having been marginalized and locked out of local political power and the economic benefits of development for decades, community members were understandably suspicious of nearby Oak Ridge North's offer to tie the community into its water and sewer systems. What, after all, would prevent developers from buying out and building up parts of Tamina once it had been improved? Tamina residents chose to protect their underserved rural community from attempts by all levels of government and by neighboring towns to address their infrastructure needs. Its community pride has been a double-edged sword: protecting its identity and local control even as it has stymied solutions to its most pressing quality-of-life issues. Its story is one of persistent suspicion and apathy, as well as one of environmental injustice and structural racism. Rather than risk development by outsiders, Tamina residents have chosen to remain an underserved rural community in the midst of a metropolitan county.[25]

The community, a symbol of the many failings of developing Montgomery County, endures within a mile of The Woodlands, a world-class, environmentally friendly, planned community of over one hundred thousand upper-middle-class residents. Tamina's choice to remain outside modern development might not be open to it much longer. Twenty-first-century Tamina represents one of the last underdeveloped areas of land in south-central Montgomery County. As such, it has attracted attention from both nearby towns hungry for tax revenue and from developers looking for a new project. As local water board member Kenny Pierson argued, "Everybody wants to cash in on Tamina. They claim they want to help and next thing you know all the benefits are going to them."[26]

℘

Waterford and Tamina: these villages represent the tensions and possibilities that came with metropolitan growth in the twentieth century. Waterford's historic commuter paradise encapsulates all that metropolitan money, expertise, and local political power could accomplish. Tamina's rural poverty and decay, in turn, exposes the chronic burden of class and racial inequalities, entrenched governmental neglect, and the suspicion and mistrust that these nurtured. Each community persists in tension with neighboring suburbs, clearly distinct from their planned lots and culs-de-sac. Each represents the persistence of the rural on the metropolitan fringe. Waterford postures as if progress has by-passed it even as it welcomes metropolitan home buyers and tourists. Tamina struggles to cope with the reality that it has been passed by—at least for now. Waterford is a model of preservation among sprawl. Tamina reminds us that preservation and stagnation are very different things.

For all this, what is most striking to me in visiting Tamina today is the horses. For all the community's struggles, a number of residents continue to assert their place in the county's equestrian culture. Here in the shadow of The Woodlands, African American southerners proudly lay claim to the countryside and its exurban lifestyle. Tamina remains both an underserved metropolitan community and a place of rural recreation. As such, it represents the complexity of the metropolitan fringe and the convergence between Western Loudoun and Montgomery County around countryside recreation. It is a place where rural South and metropolitan Sunbelt carve out a tenuous coexistence, where eddies of rural life persist amid metropolitan growth, and where each has profoundly reshaped the other.[27]

Our historical understanding of the metropolitan fringe has allowed the bulldozer to completely overshadow the horse as the dominant symbol of development—the bulldozer rumbling over the landscape, clearing away nature to make way for housing developments. Suburban housewife Margo Tupper lamented in her 1966 antisprawl diatribe *No Place to Play*, "These huge earth-eating machines raped the woods, filled up the creek, buried the wildflowers and frightened away the rabbits and birds. . . . In less than a month the first of two hundred look-alike, closely-set small houses rose to take the place of our beautiful forest." The bulldozer loomed as a symbol of developers' unbridled destruction of nature and the ineffectiveness of regulation to stop it. It also catalyzed environmental activism. Yet from the perspective of the metropolitan fringe, this dichotomy between unbulldozed open space and postbulldozed sprawl is misleading. Activists and policy makers were right to point out the costs of bulldozing: silted streams, increased runoff, damaged wetlands, and paved fields. This image obscures the fact that the bulldozer, along with the chainsaw and the dump truck, was already busy in the countryside before suburban development, reshaping rural landscapes in a myriad of ways. Bulldozers cleared and graded highways to connect these areas to the metropolis. They cleared runways for jet airports. They graded farmland to remove gullies and reduce erosion. They dug stock ponds, recreational lakes, and reservoirs to store water, prevent flooding, and recharge aquifers. They bulldozed vines, undergrowth, and competing tree species to make way for commercial timber stands. Bulldozers thundered over abandoned tenant cabins and decrepit

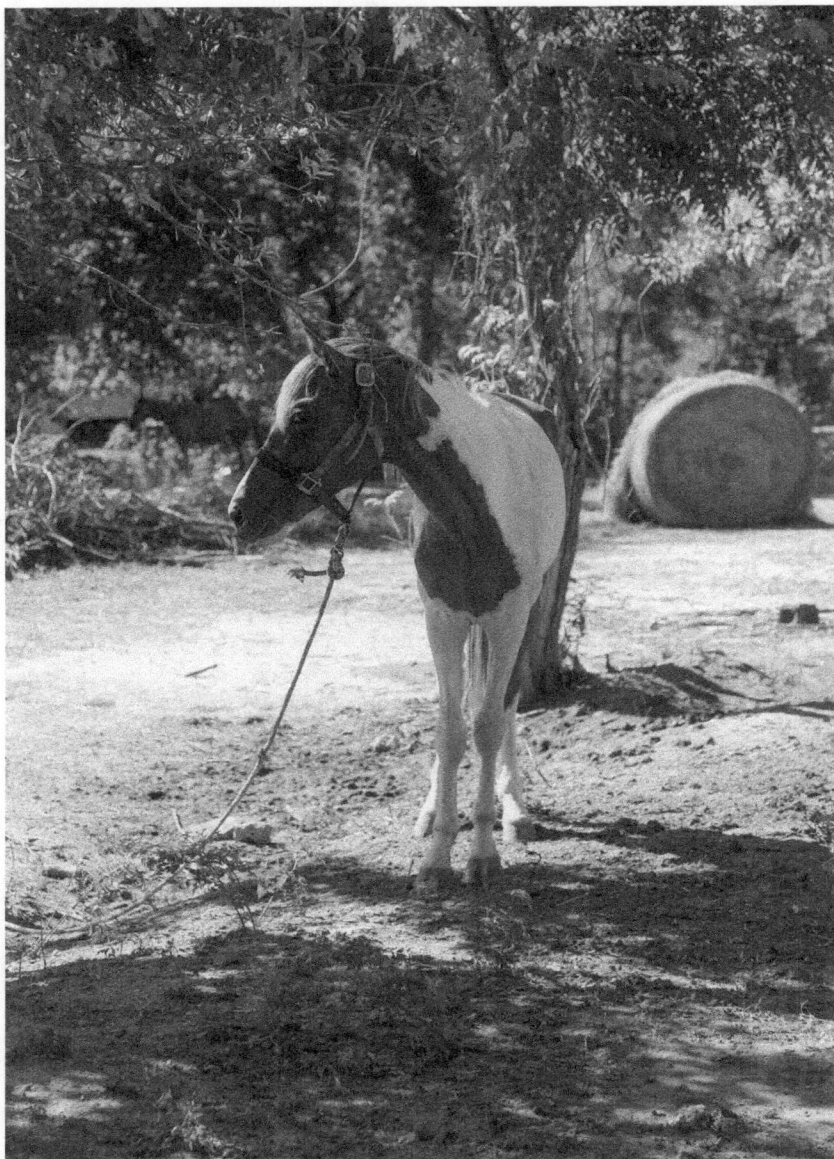

Backyard horse in Tamina, Texas.
Courtesy of Marti Corn.

A bulldozer at work in the East Texas forest.
TGF 22 (October 1964): 4. Photo courtesy of *Texas Parks & Wildlife Magazine*.

barns as farmers consolidated their holdings and abandoned cotton tenancy. Bulldozers cleared the way for Cold War installations and military bases. Bulldozers graded and sculpted land in preparation for development.[28]

In metropolitan fringe subdivisions, developers often worked to limit the destruction of trees and therefore wildlife, both of which were central to their sales strategies. In the case of The Woodlands, the bulldozer manicured the woods to carve out suburban homes in the forest. In areas where the bulldozer reshaped farm fields into parkways and culs-de-sac, it often did so on land that earlier bulldozers and tractors had already cleared for improved hay or row crops or timber stands. Looking farther back, centuries before the bulldozer, farmers girdled, burned, and plowed forests to make way for their brand of development: agriculture. In Loudoun County up to 90 percent of land was cleared for agriculture during the late eighteenth and early nineteenth centuries, creating the very countryside that preservationists protected from development.

All of this is another way of restating the obvious, that metropolitan rural America has a distinct history. Suburban development may have drawn national attention to the countryside, but it was not the only transformation at work. Girdling, plowing, burning, clearing, planting, grading, paving—these had been the way of things in rural America for decades. Metropolitan subdivisions were only the latest form of development. The closer one looks at rural America, the harder it is to find a stable world for development to destroy. This is not to downplay the reality of development's costs. Sprawl provided an effective rallying point for national environmentalism. It also served as a midwife for microgovernments, which funneled civic engagement into local community needs, and for preservation movements. These acted as much as a force of transformation and gentrification as a force of continuity and environmental protection. These movements were not malformed or stillborn environmentalism. Rather, they were branches of local activism that demonstrate the diversity of ways through which people confronted the very real problems of development.

These activists worked within counties that retained much of their rural character during the first decades of development. Rural people both resisted and adapted to metropolitan transformations without being obliterated. Their social relations and political networks were ultimately weakened and marginalized by these changes, but never as quickly or as completely as either suburbanites or their historians assumed. Rising property values, generational turnover in rural land, shifting agricultural economics, the cultural celebration of historic landscapes, and favorable tax policies formed the metropolitan fringe as a distinct social and cultural world, one characterized by relatively dense rural settlement, outdoor recreation, and private space. Many from city, suburb, and country joined together in the celebration of a lifestyle based on access to countryside and forest and crafted in opposition to the city. The metropolitan fringe promised life in the countryside—whiteness vested in the land. As a result, agricultural economics on the metropolitan fringe became increasingly bound to agricultural leisure and celebrations of a rural lifestyle. The metropolitan fringe was, at times, a battleground between city and countryside. Yet rural counties were neither the victims of urban imperialism nor the stubborn thorn in the urban booster's side. The power of both city and countryside was contingent upon national and state politics and policy, the actions of particular individuals, and, often, the natural world. The metropolitan fringe was a place where these decisions were forged, as well as where they played out.

ACKNOWLEDGMENTS

This book would not have been possible without the generosity of local historians, archivists, and longtime residents of Loudoun and Montgomery Counties. In Loudoun, Mary Fishback and Elizabeth Preston at the Thomas Balch Library patiently retrieved and contextualized boxes of archival material. Bronwen Souders gave me free rein within the Waterford Foundation records and patiently commented on numerous drafts. The staff at the Loudoun Heritage Farm Museum provided me with a wealth of oral history material. A fellowship from the National Sporting Library and Museum in Middleburg provided me a two-week crash course in all things equestrian. Charles Poland Jr., James Hershman, Eleanor Adams, Peggy Maio, and Bill Harrison each generously oriented me within the county's past.

Travel grants from the Rice University history department and the East Texas Historical Society made my reverse commute along I-45 from Houston into Montgomery County possible. Jodi Chaney at the San Jacinto River Authority was a model of hospitality. The staff at Oak Ridge North and the Montgomery County court and district court were each welcoming. Ike Barrett, Gary Calfee, Wendell Daniel, David Hendricks, and Dorothy Reece were particularly generous in sharing their memories.

I received helpful feedback and encouragement on conference papers given at the Agricultural History Society; the Southern Forum on Agricultural, Rural, and Environmental History; the Virginia Forum; and the Southern Historical Association. Tom Okie provided keen insight on the manuscript. The graduate program at Rice University was a model academic community. Ben Wright, Sam Abramson, and Blaine Hamilton were always willing to argue about titles, challenge my broader conclusions, and stare at maps with me. Uzma Quraishi, Allison Madar, and Jim Wainwright helped me keep my sanity throughout the writing process. The *Journal of Southern History* office was a welcoming place to think or escape, depending on the day. Bethany Johnson shared her own personal insight on life in The Woodlands. Randal Hall's understated comments and keen eye saved me from countless errors of interpretation and style. As an advisor John Boles was a model of patience, encouragement, insight, and, above all, good sense.

Thanks are also due to Mark Graham, Jason Edwards, David Dillard, Skip

Hyser, Gabrielle Lanier, and Steve Reich, who have taught me that an academic career is a record of debts that one cannot repay. The only honorable response is to pass such debts on to the next generation.

At the University of Georgia Press, Mick Gusinde-Duffy, Jon Davies, and Mary Hill, along with the anonymous readers, provided excellent guidance in squeezing a sprawling dissertation between these covers. As for series editor Jim Giesen, what a guy.

Friends and family have long granted me the freedom to leave my writing at school, for which I am grateful. Clayton Huthwaite reminded me of the beauty of the written word. My parents have been ever loving and supportive. My thanks to Edmund, Samuel, and Cora for greeting me with jubilation each day when I return from school. Finally, Shannon, I stand by my promise: I'll never make you read it.

NOTES

Introduction. A More Rural Metropolitan History

1. Arthur Daley, "Sports of the Times," *NYT*, August 17, 1958; *CC*, July 10, 1958 (quotation). The most extensive coverage is in Joe David Brown, "A Tall Texan Tale," *Sports Illustrated*, August 18, 1958; and Gay Talese, "Roy Harris: A Rootin', Tootin' Fighter from Cut 'n Shoot," *NYT*, July 11, 1958.

2. Milton Gross, *New York Post*, reprinted in *CC*, July 27, 1958.

3. "Patterson's Title Bout against Harris Tonight Is Expected to Draw 12,000," *NYT*, August 18, 1958; Robin Navarro Montgomery, *Cut 'N Shoot, Texas: The Roy Harris Story* (Austin: Eakin Press, 1984), 175–78; and Bob St. John, "Road Back to Cut and Shoot," *Texas Parade*, October 1964, 8–13.

4. Kenneth J. Jackson, *Crabgrass Frontier: The Suburbanization of the United States* (New York: Oxford University Press, 1985); Dolores Hayden, *Building Suburbia: Green Fields and Urban Growth, 1820–2000* (New York: Vintage Books, 2003); Kevin M. Kruse, *White Flight: Atlanta and the Making of Modern Conservatism* (Princeton, N.J.: Princeton University Press, 2005); Michael D. Lassiter, *The Silent Majority: Suburban Politics in the Sunbelt South* (Princeton, N.J.: Princeton University Press, 2006); Lizabeth Cohen, *A Consumers' Republic: The Politics of Mass Consumption in Postwar America* (New York: Vintage, 2003); David M. P. Freund, *Colored Property: State Policy and White Racial Politics in Suburban America* (Chicago: University of Chicago Press, 2010); and Christopher W. Wells, *Car Country: An Environmental History* (Seattle: University of Washington Press, 2013).

5. Andrew Wiese, *Places of Their Own: African American Suburbanization in the Twentieth Century* (Chicago: University of Chicago Press, 2004); Becky Nicolaides, *My Blue Heaven: Life and Politics in the Working-Class Suburbs of Los Angeles* (Chicago: University of Chicago Press, 2002); and Kevin M. Kruse and Thomas J. Sugrue, eds., *The New Suburban History* (Chicago: University of Chicago Press, 2006).

6. R. Douglas Hurt, ed., *The Rural South since World War II* (Baton Rouge: Louisiana State University Press, 1998), for instance, hardly mentions metropolitan areas. Anthropologist Peggy F. Barlett follows a similar path in her *American Dreams, Rural Realities* (Chapel Hill: University of North Carolina Press, 1993). This trend may be an unfortunate by-product of the strength of oral history within rural historiography. As Melissa Walker points out in *Southern Farmers and Their Stories*, interviewees use their stories to construct "communities of memory" that praise the virtues of the past and serve as a means of coping with rural change. A reliance on such sources, for all their richness, can lock the historical gaze onto the period between the New Deal and the 1960s, when much of the nation left the land. Such a chronology leaves the post–World War II rural South relegated to the epilogue, as aftermath rather than narrative. Melissa Walker, *Southern Farmers and Their Stories: Memory and Meaning in Oral History* (Lexington: University Press of Kentucky,

2006), 4–7. Mark Schultz's *The Rural Face of White Supremacy: Beyond Jim Crow* (Urbana: University of Illinois Press, 2005) is a notable exception on this point.

7. David Vaught, "State of the Art—Rural History, or Why Is There No Rural History of California?," *Agricultural History* 74, no. 4 (2000): 759–74; Claire Strom, *Making Catfish Bait out of Government Boys: The Fight against Cattle Ticks and the Transformation of the Yeoman South* (Athens: University of Georgia Press, 2010); Kendra Smith-Howard, *Pure and Modern Milk: An Environmental History since 1900* (New York: Oxford University Press, 2014); and Gabriel N. Rosenberg, *The 4-H Harvest: Sexuality and the State in Rural America* (Philadelphia: University of Pennsylvania Press, 2015).

8. Harlan Paul Douglass, *The Suburban Trend* (New York: Century, 1925); John Herbers, *The New Heartland: America's Flight beyond the Suburbs and How It Is Changing Our Future* (New York: Times Books, 1986); and Frederick H. Buttel, "The Political Economy of Part-Time Farming," *GeoJournal* 6, no. 4 (1982): 296–97.

9. James L. Wunsch, "The Suburban Cliché," *Journal of Social History* 28, no. 3 (1995): 647 (first quotation); Andrew Needham and Allen Dieterich-Ward, "Beyond the Metropolis: Metropolitan Growth and Regional Transformation in Postwar America," *Journal of Urban History* 35, no. 7 (2009): 944 (second quotation), 947 (third quotation). See also Raymond A. Mohl, "City and Region: The Missing Dimension in U.S. Urban History," *Journal of Urban History* 25, no. 1 (1998): 3–21.

10. Needham and Dieterich-Ward, "Beyond the Metropolis," 960.

11. Robert Fishman, *Bourgeois Utopias: The Rise and Fall of Suburbia* (New York: Basic Books, 1987); Robert E. Lang and Jennifer B. LeFurgy, *Boomburbs: The Rise of America's Accidental Cities* (Washington, D.C.: Brookings Institution Press, 2007); and Hayden, *Building Suburbia*.

12. Ebenezer Howard, *Garden Cities of To-Morrow*, ed. Frederic J. Osborn (Cambridge, Mass.: MIT Press, 1965); Andre Sorensen, "Subcenters and Satellite Cities: Tokyo's 20th Century Experience of Planned Polycentrism," *International Planning Studies* 6, no. 1 (2001): 9–32; Joel Garreau, *Edge Cities: Life on the New Frontier* (New York: Doubleday, 1991); Robert E. Lang, *Edgeless Cities: Exploring the Elusive Metropolis* (Washington, D.C.: Brookings Institution Press, 2003); Hayden, *Building Suburbia*; Pierce Lewis, "The Urban Invasion of Rural America: The Emergence of the Galactic City," in *The Changing American Countryside: Rural People and Places*, ed. Emery N. Castle (Lawrence: University Press of Kansas, 1995).

13. Hayden, *Building Suburbia*; Robert D. Lewis, ed., *Manufacturing Suburbs: Building Work and Home on the Metropolitan Fringe* (Philadelphia: Temple University Press, 2004); Wiese, *Places of Their Own*; Nicolaides, *My Blue Heaven*.

14. Paul J. P. Sandul, *California Dreaming: Boosterism, Memory, and Rural Suburbs in the Golden State* (Morgantown: West Virginia University Press, 2014); Cary McWilliams, *California: The Great Exception* (New York: Current Books, 1949); Hayden, *Building Suburbia*; and John R. Stilgoe, *Borderland: Origins of the American Suburb, 1820–1939* (New Haven, Conn.: Yale University Press, 1988); Carl Abbott, *How Cities Won the West: Four Centuries of Urban Change in Western North America* (Albuquerque: University of New Mexico Press, 2008); Joe Goddard, *Being American on the Edge: Penurbia and the Metropolitan Mind, 1945–2010* (New York: Palgrave Macmillan, 2012); Becky M. Nicolaides, "'Where the Working Man Is Welcomed': Working Class Suburbs in Los Angeles, 1900–1940," *Pacific Historical Review* 68, no. 4 (1999): 531; Lincoln Bramwell, *Wilderburbs: Communities on Nature's Edge* (Seattle: University of Washington Press, 2014).

15. Here I am building on the work of Jon C. Teaford, *Post-suburbia: Government and*

Politics in the Edge Cities (Baltimore, Md.: Johns Hopkins University Press, 1997) and *The Metropolitan Revolution: The Rise of Post-urban America* (New York: Columbia University Press, 2006).

16. Anne Whitson Spirn, *The Language of Landscape* (New Haven, Conn.: Yale University Press, 1998), 17; Denis Cosgrove, *Social Formation and Symbolic Landscape* (Madison: University of Wisconsin Press, 1984); and Peirce F. Lewis, "Axioms for Reading the Landscape: Some Guides to the American Scene," in *The Interpretation of Ordinary Landscapes: Geographical Essays*, ed. D. W. Meinig (New York: Oxford University Press, 1979), 11–32. Raymond Williams associated the concept of the landscape exclusively with bourgeois idealizations of rural space in which those with the luxury of not having to work the land admired its aesthetic qualities. I follow more recent geographers in emphasizing the way landscape functions as a site of social and cultural conflict. See Raymond Williams, *The Country and the City* (New York: Oxford University Press, 1973), 120–26; Simon Schama, *Landscape and Memory* (New York: Alfred A. Knopf, 1995); Laura Pulido, "Rethinking Environmental Racism: White Privilege and Urban Development in Southern California," *Annals of the Association of American Geographers* 90, no. 1 (2000): 12–40; Laura R. Barraclough, *Making the San Fernando Valley: Rural Landscapes, Urban Development, and White Privilege* (Athens: University of Georgia Press, 2011); Richard H. Schein, ed., *Landscape and Race in the United States* (New York: Routledge, 2006); and James S. Duncan and Nancy G. Duncan, *Landscapes of Privilege: The Politics of the Aesthetic in an American Suburb* (New York: Routledge, 2004).

17. On rural politics within the metropolitan fringe, see Lisa McGirr, *Suburban Warriors: The Origins of the New American Right* (Princeton, N.J.: Princeton University Press, 2001), 29–30; and Douglas Smith, "Into the Political Thicket: Reapportionment and the Rise of Suburban Power," in *The Myth of Southern Exceptionalism*, ed. Matthew D. Lassiter and Joseph Crespino (New York: Oxford University Press, 2010).

18. William Cronon, *Nature's Metropolis: Chicago and the Great West* (New York: W. W. Norton, 1991); Robert D. Lewis, *Chicago Made: Factory Networks in the Industrial Metropolis* (Chicago: University of Chicago Press, 2008); Allen Dieterich-Ward, *Beyond Rust: Metropolitan Pittsburgh and the Fate of Industrial America* (Philadelphia: University of Pennsylvania Press, 2015); and Andrew Needham, *Power Lines: Phoenix and the Making of the Modern Southwest* (Princeton, N.J.: Princeton University Press, 2014).

19. Gray Brechin, *Imperial San Francisco: Urban Power, Earthly Ruin* (Berkeley: University of California Press, 1999); David Stradling, *Making Mountains: New York City and the Catskills* (Seattle: University of Washington Press, 2007); Craig E. Colten, *Southern Waters: The Limits to Abundance* (Baton Rouge: Louisiana State University Press, 2014); David Soll, *Empire of Water: An Environmental and Political History of the New York City Water Supply* (Ithaca, N.Y.: Cornell University Press, 2013).

20. Williams, *The Country and the City*, 125; Goddard, *Being American on the Edge*, 2 (quotation); Stradling, *Making Mountains*, 12–13; Peter J. Schmitt, *Back to Nature: The Arcadian Myth in Urban America* (New York: Oxford University Press, 1969).

21. Distinctiveness need not become exceptionalism to be historically significant. Edward L. Ayers, "What We Talk About When We Talk About the South," in *All Over the Map: Rethinking American Regions*, ed. Edward L. Ayers et al. (Baltimore, Md.: Johns Hopkins University Press, 1996), 62–82; and C. Vann Woodward, "The Search for Southern Identity," in *The Burden of Southern History* (Baton Rouge: Louisiana State University Press, 1968), 3–26.

22. Lassiter, *The Silent Majority*; Kruse, *White Flight*; Joseph Crespino, *Strom Thurmond's*

America (New York: Hill and Wang, 2014); and Lassiter and Crespino, *The Myth of Southern Exceptionalism.*

23. Orville Vernon Berton, "The South as 'Other,' the Southerner as 'Stranger,'" *Journal of Southern History* 79, no. 1 (2013): 7–50.

24. While there are major differences in the way these historians understand the motivation for and process of environmental mobilization, each agrees that the experience of suburban development was central. Adam Rome, *The Bulldozer in the Countryside: Suburban Sprawl and the Rise of American Environmentalism* (New York: Cambridge University Press, 2001); Christopher C. Sellers, *Crabgrass Crucible: Suburban Nature and the Rise of Environmentalism in Twentieth-Century America* (Chapel Hill: University of North Carolina Press, 2012); and Samuel P. Hays, *Beauty, Health, and Permanence: Environmental Politics in the United States, 1955–1985* (New York: Cambridge University Press, 1987), 90–92.

25. Tom Daniels, *When City and Country Collide: Managing Growth in the Metropolitan Fringe* (Washington, D.C.: Island Press, 1999); and F. Kaid Benfield, Matthew D. Raimi, and Donald D. T. Chen, *Once There Were Greenfields: How Urban Sprawl Is Undermining America's Environment, Economy and Social Fabric* (Washington, D.C.: Natural Resources Defense Council and the Surface Transportation Policy Project, 1999).

26. Rural landscapes were, in other words, hybrid landscapes. By hybridity, environmental historians mean the way human actions and technologies are inextricably combined with the natural world to the point where no part of "nature" can be understood apart from human history. Paul S. Sutter, "The World with Us: The State of American Environmental History," *Journal of American History* 100, no. 1 (2013): 96–99.

27. Rome, *Bulldozer in the Countryside*, illustrations 9–12.

28. David G. McComb, *Houston: A History*, rev. ed. (Austin: University of Texas Press, 1981); Joe R. Feagin, *Free Enterprise City: Houston in Political-Economic Perspective* (New Brunswick, N.J.: Rutgers University Press, 1988); Barry J. Kaplan, "Houston: The Golden Buckle of the Sunbelt," in *Sunbelt Cities: Politics and Growth since World War II*, ed. Richard M. Bernard and Bradley R. Rice (Austin: University of Texas Press, 1983).

29. U.S. Census of Population, 1970, vol. 1, *Supp. Report PC(S1)-7*, table 32 (1972); U.S. Census of Population, 1980, vol. 1, General Population Characteristics, Virginia, table 14 (1980) and General Population Characteristics, Texas, table 14 (1980).

30. Thomas Froncek, ed., *The City of Washington: An Illustrated History* (New York: Alfred A. Knopf, 1977), 357; and David L. Lewis, *District of Columbia: A Bicentennial History* (New York: W. W. Norton & Co., 1976), 175, 193.

31. Richard L. Forstall, ed., *Population of States and Counties of the United States: 1790–1990* (Washington, D.C.: GPO, March 1996), 3:158, 166; Montgomery County's land area (1,042 square miles) was more than double Loudoun's (515 square miles). For this reason, population density is a more effective measure of population growth. Area figures from "State and County Quick Facts," U.S. Census Bureau, quickfacts.census.gov/qfd/states/48/48339.html and quickfacts.census.gov/qfd/states/51/51107.html, accessed March 27, 2014.

Chapter 1. Clearing the Backwoods

1. This paragraph is an amalgamation of foxhunting practices as they generally occurred in the region. Thad Sitton, *Gray Ghosts and Red Rangers: American Hilltop Fox Chasing* (Austin: University of Texas Press, 2010).

2. "Night Hunting," *TGF* 4, no. 4 (1946): 4–5, 30–32 (quotation). On local foxhunting,

see History Book Committee, Montgomery County Historical Society, *Montgomery County History* (Winston-Salem, N.C.: Hunter Publishing Company, 1980), 231–32, 272.

3. T. J. Peel, "Old Lip," *TGF* 2, no. 4 (1944): 6, 15–16, 18.

4. By "commons" I mean a legally or extralegally supported claim to the use and management of a resource by members of a particular community. Commons systems are dependent upon interlocking systems of local custom and law that protect rights of access and appropriation. The resources in question here included the harvest of game, the grazing of cattle, the foraging of hogs, and recreation. Merchantable timber was more tightly controlled. Derek Wall, *The Commons in History: Culture, Conflict, and Ecology* (Cambridge, Mass.: MIT Press, 2014). On timber harvests and the commons, see Katherine Newfont, *Blue Ridge Commons: Environmental Activism and Forest History in Western North Carolina* (Athens: University of Georgia Press, 2012).

5. Timber statistics from *CC*, December 19, 1956. On timber management and access demands, see Jack Temple Kirby, *Mockingbird Song: Ecological Landscapes of the South* (Chapel Hill: University of North Carolina Press, 2006), 113–200; Albert E. Cowdrey, *This Land, This South: An Environmental History* (Lexington: University Press of Kentucky, 1983); Thomas D. Clark, *The Greening of the South: The Recovery of Land and Forest* (Lexington: University Press of Kentucky, 1984); and Mason C. Carer, Robert C. Kellison, and R. Scott Wallinger, *Forestry in the U.S. South: A History* (Baton Rouge: Louisiana State University Press, 2015).

6. Sellers's work focuses on the natural world suburbanites purchased, experienced, and defended within and immediately surrounding their developments. This "suburban nature," he argues, nurtured the ecological thinking of some suburbanites. From the perspective of rural history, however, this suburban nature was as much imported as it was appropriated from metropolitan fringe landscapes. It was nature delivered by flatbed truck. This chapter, in contrast, explores the process of taming and reshaping rural nature into suburban nature. Both approaches draw on the pioneering work of Harlan Paul Douglass, *The Suburban Trend* (New York: Century, 1925). See also Christopher C. Sellers, *Crabgrass Crucible: Suburban Nature and the Rise of Environmentalism in Twentieth-Century America* (Chapel Hill: University of North Carolina Press, 2012), 41 (quotation), 24–35.

7. Leon Charles Hallman, "A Geographic Study of Montgomery County, Texas" (M.A. thesis, Southern Methodist University, 1965), 7–18; William Harley Gandy, "A History of Montgomery County, Texas" (M.A. thesis, University of Houston, 1952), 7; and Robert S. Maxwell and Robert D. Baker, *Sawdust Empire: The Texas Lumber Industry, 1830–1940* (College Station: Texas A&M University Press, 1983), 4–5. For general histories, see Robin Navarro Montgomery, *The History of Montgomery County* (Austin: Jenkins Publishing Co., 1975); History Book Committee, *Montgomery County History*; Melinda Reeves Cagle, ed., *History of Montgomery County, Texas—Volume II* (Baltimore, Md.: Otter Bay Books, 2012).

8. Christopher Long, "Montgomery County," in *Handbook of Texas Online*, http://www.tshaonline.org/handbook/online/articles/hcm17, accessed March 21, 2014.

9. Maxwell and Baker, *Sawdust Empire*; Ruth A. Allen, *East Texas Lumber Workers: An Economic and Social Picture, 1870–1950* (Austin: University of Texas Press, 1961), 19–34; and Robert S. Maxwell and James W. Martin, *A Short History of Forest Conservation in Texas, 1880–1940*, Bulletin 20 (Nacogdoches: School of Forestry, Stephen F. Austin State University, January 1970).

10. Gandy, "A History of Montgomery County," 99–102; *CC*, June 2, 1957; Mary Alice Hunt, *Ruts to the Miracle City* (Conroe, Tex.: Self-published, 1975), 112–16.

11. They were also number 1 on this list in 1870 and 1880. Allen, *East Texas Lumber Workers*, 29.

12. Montgomery and Walker County Soil and Water Conservation District, "District Program and Work Plan, 1969," Walker County SWCD Records, Huntsville, Tex.; Coleman Newman, "A Rootin', Tootin' Texas Rooter," *TGF* 1, no. 3 (1943): 7, 14. Some more prosperous farmers used the range. See Celeste (Gayle) Graves, ed., *Magnolia Memories* (Conroe, Tex.: Genealogy Department, Montgomery County Library, 1993), 401–2; History Book Committee, *Montgomery County History*, 201; Terry G. Jordan, *Trails to Texas: Southern Roots of Western Cattle Ranching* (Lincoln: University of Nebraska Press, 1981), 103–24.

13. Claire Strom, *Making Catfish Bait out of Government Boys: The Fight against Cattle Ticks and the Transformation of the Yeoman South* (Athens: University of Georgia Press, 2010); and Henry Mostyn, "Grover Cleveland Mostyn," in Graves, *Magnolia Memories*, 503. Like *Montgomery County History*, the *Magnolia Memories* book is a compilation of short family histories written by various authors.

14. Ike Barrett, interview by the author, November 11, 2010, Dobbin, Tex.; and David T. Schultz, interview by the author, August 13, 2012, Chateau Woods, Tex.; History Book Committee, *Montgomery County History*, 231–32.

15. Brooks Blevins, *Cattle in the Cotton Fields: A History of Cattle Raising in Alabama* (Tuscaloosa: University of Alabama Press, 1998), 23–24, 49–55; J. Crawford King, "The Closing of the Southern Range: An Exploratory Study," *Journal of Southern History* 48, no. 1 (1982); and Shawn Everett Kantor, *Politics and Property Rights: The Closing of the Open Range in the Postbellum South* (Chicago: University of Chicago Press, 1998).

16. Thad Sitton, *Backwoodsmen: Stockmen and Hunters along a Big Thicket River Valley* (Norman: University of Oklahoma Press, 1995), 239–40, 244–46; William T. Chambers, "Pine Woods Region of Southeastern Texas," *Economic Geography* 10, no. 3 (1934): 302–18; and John W. Cooper, "Forest Riches," *TGF* 19, no. 3 (1961): 22–23, 29.

17. Bernadette Pruitt, *The Other Great Migration: The Movement of Rural African Americans to Houston, 1900–1941* (College Station: Texas A&M University Press, 2013); R. L. Skrabanek and Gladys K. Bowles, *Migration of the Texas Farm Population*, TAES Bulletin 847 (College Station: Texas A&M University, February 1957); U.S. Census of Agriculture, vol. 1, pt. 37, county table 1, 1945.

18. Jack Temple Kirby, *Rural Worlds Lost: The Rural South, 1920–1960* (Baton Rouge: Louisiana State University Press, 1986); Paul Conkin, *A Revolution Down on the Farm: The Transformation of American Agriculture since 1929* (Lexington: University Press of Kentucky, 2008); and Gilbert C. Fite, *Cotton Fields No More: Southern Agriculture, 1865–1980* (Lexington: University Press of Kentucky, 1984).

19. Cagle, *History of Montgomery County*, 58; Carer, Kellison, and Wallinger, *Forestry in the U.S. South*; and William Boyd, *The Slain Wood: Papermaking and Its Environmental Consequences in the American South* (Baltimore, Md.: Johns Hopkins University Press, 2015); *CC*, December 19, 1956.

20. Richard F. Weingroff, "President Dwight D. Eisenhower and the Federal Role in Highway Safety," Federal Highway Administration, U.S. Department of Transportation, 2003, www.fhwa.dot.gov/infrastructure/safety.pdf, accessed March 27, 2014.

21. *CC*, August 16, 1951.

22. "Proclamation," January 12, 1952, CCR; *CC*, November 20, 1952; *CC*, December 25, 1952. On the legal requirements for stock law voting in Texas, see *Vernon's Annotated Revised Civil Statutes of the State of Texas*, 1948, Title 121, chaps. 5–6.

23. *CC,* July 9, 1953 (first quotation); *CC,* September 17, 1953 (second quotation); *CC,* July 30, 1953; *CC,* September 24, 1953.

24. *CC,* September 17, 1953 (quotation); and William N. Foster to R. G. Calfee, Guy H. Hooper, and J. H. Calfee, September 11, 1953, printed in *CC,* September 17, 1953. Most of the more capital-intensive producers had already fenced their land by this time and therefore had little economic stake in the matter. Gary Calfee, email correspondence with the author, January 10, 2011.

25. The *Courier* claimed that there were close to sixty-five hundred county residents who would have been eligible for the stock law election. *CC,* September 24, 1953.

26. *CC,* October 8, 1953.

27. *CC,* June 14, 1956.

28. *CC,* June 14, 1956; *CC,* August 16, 1956; and *CC,* October 11, 1956.

29. *CC,* October 24, 1956 (first, second, and third quotations); *CC,* December 13, 1956 (fourth quotation).

30. *CC,* September 6, 1956 (first quotation); *CC,* December 13, 1956 (second quotation).

31. Petition, February, 1953, CCR.

32. J. C. Davis Jr. to George W. Norris, October 24, 1956, November 1956, CCR.

33. Resolutions, March 1, 1955, in folder March 1955, CCR.

34. *CC,* June 14, 1956.

35. The year 1956 was the height of the drought. *CC,* October 31, 1956; and *CC,* October 17, 1956.

36. *CC,* August 23, 1956; "Notice to the People of Montgomery County," pamphlet, ca. 1956, Gary Calfee personal collection, Willis, Tex. (quotation).

37. For claims of intimidation, see *CC,* December 13, 1956; and *CC,* December 16, 1956. Gary Calfee, who was a child at the time of the election, cast doubt on these claims. Gary Calfee, interview by the author, July 19, 2012, Willis, Tex.

38. "Proclamation of Election Results," December 1956, CCR; and "Stock Law Passes by Large Majority in County." This turnout was around half of the *Courier*'s 1953 estimate of sixty-five hundred possible freehold voters in the county.

39. *CC,* January 3, 1957; and *CC,* January 8, 1957.

40. In August of that year, Montgomery County had half of the eighty-six fires in its fire district, of which fourteen (33 percent) were confirmed as incendiary. The previous August, the district had only two fires. *CC,* September 13, 1956.

41. Texas Motor Vehicle Traffic Accidents 1953–59, data generated by Texas Department of Public Safety, September 15, 2017.

42. History Book Committee, *Montgomery County History,* 431; U.S. Census of Agriculture, vol. 1, pt. 37, county table 8, 1959, and 7.1, 1954. Because of their mobility the census tended to undercount the number of cattle and hogs on the open range. The decline of each was likely even more dramatic.

43. History Book Committee, *Montgomery County History,* 527–28.

44. The county's first recorded deeding of a subdivision road came in June 1957, six months after the closing of the range. Resolution, June 10, 1957, CCR.

45. Sitton, *Backwoodsmen;* Steven Hahn, "Hunting, Fishing, and Foraging: Common Rights and Class Relations in the Postbellum South," *Radical History Review* 26 (1982); and Kirby, *Mockingbird Song,* 113–55. For a local example, see *CC,* September 22, 1965; and Robin Navarro Montgomery, *Cut 'N Shoot, Texas: The Roy Harris Story* (Austin: Eakin Press, 1984).

46. *CC*, August 23, 1956 (first quotation); "Notice to the People of Montgomery County" (second and third quotations); and *CC*, September 17, 1953.

47. Thad Sitton and James H. Conrad, *Nameless Towns: Texas Sawmill Communities, 1880–1942* (Austin: University of Texas Press, 1998), 164–73; *CC*, March 27, 1975 (first quotation); Graves, *Magnolia Memories*, 469; *Principal Game Birds and Mammals of Texas: Their Distribution and Management* (Austin: Texas Game, Fish, and Oyster Commission, 1945), 3 (second quotation). It was common practice across the rural South to use dynamite, electric shocks, or chemicals such as rotenone to disable or kill fish. *CC*, June 30, 1965.

48. John F. Reiger, *American Sportsmen and the Origins of Conservation*, 3rd ed. (Corvallis: Oregon State University Press, 2000); Louis S. Warren, *The Hunter's Game: Poachers and Conservationists in Twentieth-Century America* (New Haven, Conn.: Yale University Press, 1997); Karl Jacoby, *Crimes against Nature: Squatters, Poachers, Thieves, and the Hidden History of American Conservation* (Berkeley: University of California Press, 2001); and Robin W. Doughty, *Wildlife and Man in Texas: Environmental Change and Conservation* (College Station: Texas A&M University Press, 1983).

49. Ivan W. Schmedemann, A. B. Wooten, and W. D. Franklin, *Outdoor Recreation . . . Potential in East Texas*, TAES Bulletin 1013 (College Station: Texas A&M University, July 1964). In 1965 245,000 of the county's 697,000 acres (35 percent) were in commercial forest holdings of 1,000 acres or larger. The national forest added another 48,000 acres. Hallman, "A Geographic Study," 88.

50. *Principal Game Birds*, 15–17; and *CC*, August 22, 1965.

51. Hart Stilwell, "Just How Good Were 'the Good Old Days' of 'Free' Deer Hunting?," *TGF* 10, no. 1 (1956): 10; *Principal Game Birds*, 91–104.

52. Barrett interview, 2010. Hunting deer in the county had been illegal since 1935. See Acts 1935, 44th R.S., chap. 4, Special Laws of Texas; Acts 1945, 49th R.S., chap. 134, GSLT.

53. Phil D. Goodrum, "Bushy Tails," *TGF* 4, no. 3 (1946): 6–7, 19.

54. *CC*, January 17, 1965.

55. Gary Calfee interview, 2012.

56. Bo Calfee was never prosecuted. "Calfee a Hometown Boy Who Made Good," *HP*, January 6, 1974 (quotation); *CC*, November 3, 1965.

57. *CC*, July 2, 1953.

58. *CC*, March 11, 1954.

59. Texas v. David W. Mack, February 11, 1955, Criminal Docket No. 9331, Ninth District Court, Montgomery County Courthouse, Conroe, Tex.

60. *CC*, August 2, 1956.

61. *CC*, March 6, 1958.

62. *CC*, November 8, 1958; and *CC*, December 4, 1957.

63. Acts 1959, 56th R.S., chap. 121, GSLT.

64. Schmedemann, Wooten, and Franklin, *Outdoor Recreation*, 2; and "District Program and Work Plan, 1969," 23.

65. *CC*, February 7, 1961.

66. The 1937 passage of the Federal Aid to Wildlife Restoration Act, which offered federal matching funds to game restocking programs, proved the initial catalyst for deer restocking programs in Texas and across the nation. Daniel W. Lay, "Brief Chronology of Wildlife in Texas," *TGF* 3, no. 4 (1945): 9, 13; A. J. Nicholson, "Game Restoration in Texas," *TGF* 4, no. 9 (1946): 4–5, 20–21.

67. "Piney Woods Region Restoring Wildlife," *TGF* 18, no. 4 (1960): 39.

68. The postwar housing boom had driven up the national demand for saw timber. As demand slacked in the early 1960s, local production outstripped demand by more than 30 percent. *CC*, December 16, 1964; *CC*, January 22, 1964; and William B. Alderman, "Enterprise among the Pines," *Texas Parade* 23, no. 1 (1962): 10–13.

69. *CC*, September 25, 1963; *CC*, February 23, 1964; *CC*, October 31, 1961.

70. *CC*, May 21, 1961.

71. *CC*, February 9, 1964. State conservation leaders founded this organization in 1956 as an umbrella for Texas sportsmen groups. Townsend Miller, "Texas Outdoor Clubs Unite," *TGF* 14, no. 2 (1956): 9, 30. The County Program Building Committee, affiliated with the local agricultural extension office, also made recreation one of its rural development goals in 1964. Montgomery County Program Building Committee, *Your County Program: Long-Range Program of the Montgomery County Program Building Committee* (Montgomery County, Tex.: Self-published, 1964), 34–42, Dolph Briscoe Center for American History, University of Texas at Austin.

72. It was illegal to use dogs for hunting deer in Montgomery County from 1937. Acts 1937, 45th 2nd C.S., chap. 47, GSLT; and "District Program and Work Plan, 1969," 23. Hunters using dogs would frequently get around the law by "collar switching," or claiming to be hunting raccoons, coyote, foxes, or other less regulated game. James Scott, interview by the author, August 17, 2012, New Waverly, Tex.

73. Richard N. Denney, "The Impact of Uncontrolled Dogs on Wildlife and Livestock," in *Balancing Environmental and Economic Goals: Transactions of the Thirty-Ninth North American Wildlife and Natural Resources Conference* (Washington, D.C.: Wildlife Management Institute, 1974), 257–91; Matthew Edzart Gompper, ed., *Free-Ranging Dogs and Wildlife Conservation* (New York: Oxford University Press, 2013); John W. Laundre, Lucina Hernandez, and Kelly B. Altendorf, "Wolves, Elk, and Bison: Reestablishing the 'Landscape of Fear' in Yellowstone National Park, U.S.A.," *Canadian Journal of Zoology* 79, no. 8 (2001): 1401–9.

74. *Principal Game Birds*, 96–97; "Unrestrained Pets Can Deplete Game," *TGF* 15, no. 6 (1957): 28; Montgomery County Program Building Committee, *Your County Program*, 36; and *CC*, June 7, 1960. On deer and foxhunting, see Sitton, *Gray Ghosts*, 174–76.

75. The National Forest Service struggled to balance the competing demands of sportsmen, timber companies, metropolitan recreation seekers, and backwoodsmen, as each laid claim to the federally managed woods. *Final Environmental Impact Statement and Land Management Plan, Sam Houston National Forest, Texas*, Southern Region, National Forest Service (Atlanta: USDA, 1978).

76. *CC*, February 2, 1964; *CC*, February 16, 1964.

77. *CC*, March 4, 1964 (quotations).

78. *CC*, February 23, 1964 (quotation).

79. *CC*, October 22, 1957.

80. Deer generally respond to bright lights by blankly staring. The reflections from their eyes make them easy targets. This practice was dangerous, as it was difficult to distinguish deer from other animals or even humans at night. Sportsmen condemned it as cowardly and dangerous. *CC*, December 2, 1960 (quotation); *CC*, December 14, 1960; *CC*, June 9, 1965.

81. *CC*, January 22, 1964; *CC*, February 19, 1964; *CC*, May 9, 1965; *CC*, February 14, 1965 (quotation).

82. Of these, only fourteen were eventually dismissed—a relatively small percentage in a county whose underfunded justice system habitually dismissed cases.

83. The statistics in this section and the section that follows were taken from the county court criminal docket books for 1960–70, 1975, and 1980 and from the criminal docket books from justice of the peace, precinct 1, for 1960, 1964–65, 1970, 1975, and 1980. JP records were only complete for precinct 1. In the county court records before 1970, game violations were filed by the date disposed rather than the date filed, and so it is impossible to know if all of them for 1960, 1964, and 1965 turned up in the surviving books. Because of this, the county court records can only give a general sense of trends in game law enforcement in the county. Stream pollution and trespassing were only counted in these statistics if the game warden filed the charge.

84. *CC*, November 3, 1965.

85. Precinct 1 was more agriculturally developed than other precincts and therefore probably had fewer game violations (reported and unreported). The dearth of surviving records makes it impossible to determine conclusively that Bo Calfee's apparent refusal to enforce game violations proved the rule rather than the exception. The fact that Kincannon took so many cases to the county court rather than the JP's offices is the strongest evidence that he believed them to be unreliable when it came to game laws.

86. Montgomery County Program Building Committee, *Your County Program*, 30; "District Program and Work Plan, 1969," 22.

87. *CC*, November 9, 1966; *CC*, June 17, 1964.

88. Local Realtor Larry Jacobs described the Mitchell tract as "a deer hunter's paradise." Larry Jacobs, interview by the author, August 17, 2012, Montgomery, Tex. On leases, see Carer, Kellison, and Wallinger, *Forestry in the U.S. South*, 271–72. Any hunter caught breaking game laws on these properties would generally forfeit his lease. *CC*, November 7, 1965.

89. *CC*, November 10, 1965 (first quotation); *CC*, January 17, 1965 (second quotation).

90. *CC*, January 5, 1958; *CC*, November 9, 1966.

91. "District Program and Work Plan, 1969," 23.

92. Scott interview.

93. Gary Kroll, "An Environmental History of Roadkill: Road Ecology and the Making of the Permeable Highway," *Environmental History* 20, no. 1 (2015): 4–28.

94. When asked about the impact of these local efforts to develop game resources in the county, Morris Straughn, county extension agent during the period, replied that it was only "a minimal success." In terms of gross economic output, this is true. Hunting leases were never more than a secondary economic activity. The change for the county's woods, however, was substantial. For longtime residents in the area, the increased deer population was frequently one of the first changes mentioned in oral interviews. Morris Straughn, interview by the author, July 31, 2012, Conroe, Tex.; Barrett interview, 2010; and Bill Bergefield, interview by the author, July 19, 2012, Conroe, Tex.; Montgomery-Walker SWCD, "An Appraisal of Potential for Outdoor Recreational Developments in Montgomery County, Texas," 1967, Walker County SWCD, 11.

95. "District Program and Work Plan, 1969," 24.

96. The Tri-County Association included Montgomery, Walker, and Liberty Counties. There is no mention of the organization in the *Conroe Courier* after 1966. The *Courier's* increasingly suburban audience had little interest in such things, and so it is possible that the group did persist into the 1970s in spite of its disappearance from the newspaper. *CC*, April 15, 1964; *CC*, June 21, 1964; *CC*, March 30, 1966; Sitton, *Gray Ghosts*, 139–55. Equestrian foxhunts currently occur in Montgomery County, but their roots go back only to the 1990s, and they claim no connection to the county's hilltop tradition.

97. *CC*, October 22, 1976. This was part of a national surge in the popularity of CB radios in the 1970s. Shane Hamilton, *Trucking Country: The Road to America's Wal-Mart Economy* (Princeton, N.J.: Princeton University Press, 2008), 200.

98. *CC*, December 3, 1972.

99. *CC*, June 30, 1965; and *CC*, June 27, 1965.

100. *CC*, June 29, 1968; and *CC*, October 27, 1965.

101. *CC*, December 19, 1956.

102. *CC*, September 29, 1979; Joseph W. Kutchin, *How Mitchell Energy & Development Corp. Got Its Start and How It Grew: An Oral History and Narrative Overview* (The Woodlands, Tex.: Mitchell Energy & Development Corp., 1998), 53–55.

103. When adult hunters did stray into the suburban woods, residents generally complained. Criminal Docket Nos. 3043A and 3044A, November 1, 1970, book 100, Justice of the Peace, Precinct 2, Conroe, Tex.

104. This rise in stray and feral pet populations coincided with a national shift in the perception of these animals. Where public health officials had pushed for dog control as a means to control rabies, new advocates emphasized issues of animal welfare and concerns over the earth's ability to sustain large pet populations. Iris Nowell, *The Dog Crisis* (New York: St. Martin's Press, 1978) is emblematic of this trend. Alan M. Beck, *The Ecology of Stray Dogs: A Study in Free-Ranging Urban Animals* (Baltimore, Md.: York Press, 1973); *CC*, February 17, 1965. For an alternate interpretation of suburban dogs that emphasizes dogs' role as part of the natural world, see Sellers, *Crabgrass Crucible*, 82–86.

105. *CC*, March 3, 1968; and *CC*, February 28, 1968.

106. *CC*, June 6, 1976; *CC*, December 11, 1979; *CC*, May 28, 1978; and *CC*, March 5, 1973.

107. *CC*, February 9, 1972; and *CC*, March 2, 1973.

108. CC, December 11, 1979 (quotation); *CC*, May 2, 1980; February 1976 and June 1977, CCR; and CCM, 28:484–94. For many subdivisions, relief came through the passage of town leash laws after incorporation. Ordinance 014-79, folder Ordinances, box Ordinances and City Council Minutes, November 19, and December 4, 1979, folder 1979, box City Council Minutes, both in ORN; *WV*, March 1, 1978.

109. Kutchin, *How Mitchell Energy*, 28; George P. Mitchell, interview, 204–6, and Jim McAlister, interview, 172, both in Kutchin, *How Mitchell Energy*.

110. The Woodlands Corporation would continue to add to this acreage over the next two decades. The Woodlands eventually covered over twenty-seven thousand acres. Roger Galatas and Jim Barlow, *The Woodlands: The Inside Story of Creating a Better Hometown* (Washington, D.C.: Urban Land Institute, 2004), 21–29; George T. Morgan and John O. King, *The Woodlands: New Community Development, 1964–1983* (College Station: Texas A&M University Press, 1987), 26–27; and G. David Bumgardner, interview, 53–61, B. F. "Bud" Clark, interview, 73, Charles Lively, interview, 157–61, and Jim McAlister, interview, 173, all in Kutchin, *How Mitchell Energy*.

111. Myrtle Davidson Malone, ed., *The Woodlands: New Town in the Forest* (The Woodlands, Tex.: Pioneer Publications, Inc., 1985), 17; WMRT, "Woodlands New Community: An Ecological Inventory," The Woodlands Development Corporation, 1973, 47–48; and *Final Environmental Statement on The Woodlands Proposed New Community Montgomery County, Texas* (Washington, D.C.: U.S. Department of Housing and Urban Development, 1972), 13. On hunting, see Morgan and King, *The Woodlands*, 26; and G. David Bumgardner, interview, in Kutchin, *How Mitchell Energy*, 55; *CC*, February 15, 1951. On livestock, see Graves, *Magnolia Memories*, 401–2.

112. Developers referred to this type of harvest as a "real estate cut": it kept the timbered landscape intact while raising funds to balance the developer's books. Mitchell received $5 million for this harvest. Mitchell interview, 10, and Jim McAlister, interview, both in Kutchin, *How Mitchell Energy*, 171.

113. WMRT provided an extensive commentary on the forest types and their characteristics within The Woodlands site. WMRT, "Woodlands New Community: An Ecological Inventory," 38–48. For an aerial image of The Woodlands predevelopment, see Morgan and King, *The Woodlands*, 54.

114. Dudley Lynch, "The Woodlands Gets Down to Business," *Texas Parade* 37, no. 3 (1976): 38 (second, fourth, and fifth quotations), 37 (first quotation), 44 (third quotation).

115. Raccoons, skunks, foxes, opossums, and armadillos were also common in The Woodlands, but because of both their nocturnal habits and their greater capacity for disruptive behavior, their appeal to suburbanites was limited. Larger predators, such as the bobcat, the cougar, the red wolf, and the black bear, some of which had been sighted in the southern part of the county into the 1960s, had no place in this suburban woods. Such large predators would pose a threat to both outdoor pets and the sense of security of suburban residents. Coyotes, raptors, and some dogs were the apex predators of The Woodlands' forests. For bear and panther sightings, see *CC*, January 9, 1966.

116. Jorjanna Price, "Woodlands Planned for 150,000 People in 20 Years," *HP*, December 21, 1972; and "The Woodlands," *HP*, October 6, 1974 (quotation).

117. WMRT, "Woodlands New Community: An Ecological Inventory," 59–61.

118. Russell Claus develops this point further in his 1994 critique of The Woodlands' environmental planning: "The Woodlands, Texas: A Retrospective Critique of the Principles and Implementation of an Ecologically Planned Development" (M.S. thesis, Massachusetts Institute of Technology, 1994), 116–32.

119. Mitchell interview, in Kutchin, *How Mitchell Energy*, 231; *WV*, May 18, 1977; *WV*, August 10, 1977; *WV*, May 10, 1978.

120. *WV*, May 10, 1978; *WV*, August 22, 1979; *WV*, April 5, 1978; *WV*, November 8, 1978; *WV*, March 14, 1979.

Chapter 2. Cultivating the Fringe

1. Steven Stoll, *Larding the Lean Earth: Soil and Society in Nineteenth-Century America* (New York: Hill and Wang, 2002).

2. Patrick A. Deck and Henry Heaton, *An Economic and Social Survey of Loudoun County* (Charlottesville: University of Virginia, 1926), 42, 50–51, 57–58, 92, 120–21. Some of this prosperity reached African American farmers, who owned 5 percent of the county's farms. Charles P. Poland, Jr., *From Frontier to Suburbia: Loudoun County, Virginia, One of America's Fastest Growing Counties* (Westminster: Heritage Books, 1976, 2005), 323–25.

3. Henry Worchester Smith, "Bedford Glascock," folder History of Foxhunting in Virginia and Local Families, and "Crompton Smith at Featherbed Farm," both in box Foxhunting in Virginia, MC 0041, NSLM; and "Guernsey Breeders of Virginia Assemble at D.C. Sands' Estate," *Fauquier Democrat*, August 12, 1939.

4. In 1945 the county had 235 dairy farms, 180 poultry farms, 496 livestock farms, 218 general farms, and 669 subsistence farms along with a few dozen forest product farms and orchards. Poland, *From Frontier to Suburbia*, 337.

5. On dairy farms in Virginia, see G. Terry Sharrer, *A Kind of Fate: Agricultural Change*

in Virginia, 1861–1920 (Ames: Iowa State University Press, 2000), 163–72; Katherine L. Brown and Nancy T. Sorrells, *Virginia's Cattle Story: The First Four Centuries* (Staunton: Lot's Wife Publishing, 2004), 188–213; and William H. Harrison, Carol S. McComb, and George A. Miller, *The Story of Loudoun's Dairy Industry* (Purcellville: Mr. Print, 2006); Jack Temple Kirby, *Westmoreland Davis: Virginia Planter-Politician, 1859–1942* (Charlottesville: University of Virginia Press, 1968); Poland, *From Frontier to Suburbia*, 322n53; "Virginia State Milk Commission," *Virginia and the Virginia County* 4, no. 12 (1950): 16, 29; Harrison, McComb, and Miller, *Story of Loudoun's Dairy Industry*, 11, 18–19, 25; Sharrer, *A Kind of Fate*, 134, 147, 163.

6. Mary Brown, interview, 2003, folder 3, box 1, TBLOHP; "Jesse Hughes, Dairy Farmer," *WP*, September 2, 1964; "J. S. Smith Dies: Farmer, Civic Leader," *WP*, April 15, 1956; "Arlington Druggist Buys Dairy Farm," *WP*, July 23, 1944; Mrs. James Symington, interview by Allison Weiss, June 5, 2002, Leesburg, Va., LFOHC; and Thomas E. Taylor, interview by Vivian Chouha, February 20, 1991, Lincoln, Va., folder 26, box 3, LCOHP.

7. Poultry operators faced declining margins and stiff competition from the Shenandoah Valley and Delmarva. Orchards faced similar pressures from growers in the Pacific Northwest. Edwin Potts, interview by Allison Weiss, April 10, 2002, Round Hill, Va., LFOHC; William Harrison, interview by the author, July 18, 2013, Leesburg, Va.

8. Harrison, McComb, and Miller, *Story of Loudoun's Dairy Industry*, 33–34; Kendra Smith-Howard, *Pure and Modern Milk: An Environmental History since 1900* (New York: Oxford University Press, 2014), 85–94; and Harry A. Herman, *Improving Cattle by the Millions: NAAB and the Development and Worldwide Application of Artificial Insemination* (Columbia: University of Missouri Press, 1981), 7, 320–21; Poland, *From Frontier to Suburbia*, 354–56; "Let's Look at Loudoun," 1949, folder 80, Ephemera, TBL.

9. On inner and outer ring milk production, see Smith-Howard, *Pure and Modern Milk*, 107–15; and Shane Hamilton, *Trucking Country: The Road to America's Wal-Mart Economy* (Princeton, N.J.: Princeton University Press, 2008), 24–34, 163–86; Harrison, McComb, and Miller, *Story of Loudoun's Dairy Industry*, 3; R. G. Connelly, "Dairying in the Old Dominion," *Virginia and the Virginia County* 4, no. 12 (1950): 12, 30–32. Value of products sold is from Virginia Agricultural Census, 1954, comparing Loudoun's $4.168 million with second-place Rockingham's $2.307 million. Fairfax County had dropped to $1.868 million by this point. See Nan Netherton, Donald Sweig, Janice Artemel, Patricia Hickin, and Patrick Reed, *Fairfax County, Virginia: A History* (Fairfax: Fairfax County Board of Supervisors, 1978), 545–67.

10. Kendra Marr, "Loudoun's Defiant Dairy Outpost," *WP*, February 23, 2008, http://www.washingtonpost.com/wp-dyn/content/article/2008/02/22/AR2008022202775.html, accessed February 26, 2014.

11. Curtis and Betty Laycock, interview by Allison Weiss, Loudoun County, Va., May 14, 2002, LFOHC. Of the thirteen interviews done by the Loudoun Heritage Farm Museum that discuss suburban development, five explicitly name Dulles Airport as the primary catalyst of agricultural change. Bob Grubb, interview by Allison Weiss, September 5, 2002, Hillsboro, Va., LFOHC; Mac and Jim Brownell, interview by Allison Weiss, May 15, 2002, Purcellville, Va., LFOHC; Edwin Potts interview; Harrison interview.

12. *LTM*, July 10, 1958; Frank Raflo, *Within the Iron Gates: Loudoun Stories Remembered* (Dulles: TechniGraphix, 1998), 211–13; and William P. Frazer, interview by Eugene Scheel, December 18, 1991, Waterford, Va., folder 24, box 1, LCOHP.

13. On labor, see March 2, 1960, and January 10, 1962, folder 1, and November 6, 1963,

folder 2, box 5, Catoctin Farmers' Club Records, TBL; Brownell interview; E. Potts interview; Henry Stowers, interview by Allison Weiss, December 14, 2001, Loudoun County, Va., LFOHC; Curtis Poland, interview by Allison Weiss, February 12, 2002, Loudoun County, Va., LFOHC; and Taylor interview; Ronald Edwin Buffington, "Labor Study on Virginia Dairy Farms Employing Full Time Workers" (M.S. thesis, Virginia Polytechnic Institute, June 1967).

14. Harrison interview; Ralph E. Heimlich, "Agriculture and Urban Areas in Perspective," in *The American Land: 1987 Yearbook of Agriculture* (Washington, D.C.: GPO, 1987), 141–47.

15. Laycock interview; Grubb interview; James and Maxine Hamilton, interview by Allision Weiss, Hillsboro, Va., April 22, 2002, LFOHC; Kirk Kardashian, *Milk Money: Cash, Cows, and the Death of the American Dairy Farm* (Durham, N.C.: University of New Hampshire Press, 2012).

16. Hamilton, *Trucking Country*, 163–86; Jess Gilbert and Kevin Wehr, "Dairy Industrialization in the First Place: Urbanization, Immigration, and Political Economy in Los Angeles County, 1920–1979," *Rural Sociology* 68, no. 4 (2003): 467–90.

17. Poland, *From Frontier to Suburbia*, 345–50; Gerald B. White and R. G. Kline, *Grade-A Dairy Farm Growth in Virginia*, Research Division Bulletin 102 (Blacksburg: Virginia Polytechnic Institute and State University, June 1975).

18. Most famous was the bull Round Oak Rag Apple Elevation. Less than a decade after his sale in 1966, an industry publication labeled him the "world's most sought after bull." Through artificial insemination, he would sire some 104,434 children. Harrison, McComb, and Miller, *Story of Loudoun's Dairy Industry*, 44, 64; and Richard Denier, "The Impact of Elevation in Europe," *Holstein Friesian World*, April 10, 1978.

19. Harrison, McComb, and Miller, *Story of Loudoun's Dairy Industry*, 15, 21, 88–89.

20. Brownell interview; and Sarah Huntington and Gale Waldron, eds., *In Their Own Words: Recollections of an Earlier Loudoun* (Lincoln: Meeting House Press, 2002), 7, 28.

21. Brownell interview; and Maria Koklanaris, "Selling Out, but Not Out of the Family," *WP*, September 21, 1989.

22. 4-H is a youth development and rural education program begun in the early twentieth century and administered at the county level by the USDA and land-grant universities as part of the cooperative extension service. 4-H clubs were ubiquitous across the rural United States by the middle of the twentieth century. See Gabriel N. Rosenberg, *The 4-H Harvest: Sexuality and the State in Rural America* (Philadelphia: University of Pennsylvania Press, 2015).

23. Robert A. Goldberg, "The Western Hero in Politics: Barry Goldwater, Ronald Reagan, and the Rise of the American Conservative Movement," in *The Political Culture of the New West*, ed. Jeff Roche (Lawrence: University Press of Kansas, 2008), 13–50; Stanley Corkin, *Cowboys as Cold Warriors: The Western and U.S. History* (Philadelphia: Temple University Press, 2004); and Michael Coyne, *The Crowded Prairie: American National Identity in the Hollywood Western* (New York: I. B. Tauris Publishers, 1997).

24. The state's western image rests upon a myth rooted in exceptionalist histories and selective forgetting. The classic articulation of the Texas myth is T. R. Fehrenbach, *Lone Star: A History of Texas and the Texans* (New York: Macmillan, 1968). Texas exceptionalism has been generally discredited within academic circles. Walter L. Buenger and Arnoldo De León, eds., *Beyond Texas through Time: Breaking Away from Past Interpretations* (College Station: Texas A&M University Press, 2011); Glen Sample Ely, *Debating Texas Identity: Where*

the West Begins (Lubbock: Texas Tech University, 2011); Gregg Cantrell and Elizabeth Hayes Turner, *Lone Star Pasts: Memory and History* (College Station: Texas A&M University Press, 2006).

25. William Cronon, *Nature's Metropolis: Chicago and the Great West* (New York: W. W. Norton, 1991); and Andrew Needham and Allen Dieterich-Ward, "Beyond the Metropolis: Metropolitan Growth and Regional Transformation in Postwar America," *Journal of Urban History* 35, no. 7 (2009). On the rural influence on southern cities, see David R. Goldfield, *Cotton Fields and Skyscrapers: Southern City and Region, 1607–1980* (Baton Rouge: Louisiana State University Press, 1982).

26. Matthew D. Lassiter, "Big Government and Family Values: Political Culture in the Metropolitan Sunbelt," in *Sunbelt Rising: The Politics of Place, Space, and Region*, ed. Michelle Nickerson and Darren Dochuk (Philadelphia: University of Pennsylvania Press, 2011), 82–109; Lisa McGirr, *Suburban Warriors: The Origins of the New American Right* (Princeton, N.J.: Princeton University Press, 2001); and Roche, *The Political Culture*.

27. Otto Olson, *The Culture of Cigar Leaf Tobacco in Texas*, TAES Bulletin 144 (Austin, Tex.: Austin Printing Company, 1912); George L. Clyburn, "An Agricultural Economic Study of Land Use and Factors Affecting Its Use in Montgomery County, Texas" (M.S. thesis, Texas A&M University, 1940), 36.

28. This number reflects both the depressed crop prices of the Great Depression and the increased labor demands from the local oil boom that began in 1932. Clyburn, "An Agricultural Economic Study," 32, 49; "San Jacinto Soil Conservation District Program," 1944, unmarked folder, Walker County SWCD, 19; Ruth A. Allen, *East Texas Lumber Workers: An Economic and Social Picture, 1870–1950* (Austin: University of Texas Press, 1961), 196.

29. Clyburn, "An Agricultural Economic Study," 48. These statistics are from 1938.

30. Froncell Reece, "A Study of the Economic Status of Fifty Negro Farm Families, Montgomery County, Texas" (M.S. thesis, Prairie View A&M, May 1950), 9, 13, 21. The percentage of rural blacks in the county dependent on off-farm labor was even higher, as Reece's sample included only farm families. See B. T. Price, 1947 annual narrative report, 1, Negro Extension Service, folder 1947, Montgomery County, Texas—Monthly and Annual Reports County Extension Agent, Agricultural Extension Service Records, Special Collections, Prairie View University, Prairie View, Tex.

31. B. T. Prince and Germalean Collins, combined 1955 annual report, Negro Extension Service, folder November 1955, CCR; Prince and Collins, combined 1956 county narrative report, Negro Extension Service, folder November 1956, CCR.

32. Montgomery County Program Building Committee, *Your County Program: Long-Range Program of the Montgomery County Program Building Committee* (Montgomery County: Self-published, 1964), 18, 23–24, Briscoe Center for American History, University of Texas at Austin.

33. D. Clayton Brown, *King Cotton in Modern America: A Cultural, Political, and Economic History since 1945* (Jackson: University Press of Mississippi, 2011), 125–46; and Craig Heinicke and Wayne A. Grove, "'Machinery Has Completely Taken Over': The Diffusion of the Mechanical Cotton Picker, 1949–1964," *Journal of Interdisciplinary History* 39, no. 1 (2008): 65–96.

34. Montgomery County Program Building Committee, *Your County Program*, 29; "San Jacinto Soil Conservation District Program," 1944, 19; Debra A. Reid, "African Americans and Land Loss in Texas: Government Duplicity and Discrimination Based on Race and Class," *Agricultural History* 77, no. 2 (2003): 264 (quotation); and Frederic O. Sargent,

"Economic Adjustments of Negro Farmers in East Texas," *Southwestern Social Science Quarterly* 42, no. 1 (1961): 32–39. See also the oral histories in *African American Experiences in Montgomery County, Texas* (Conroe: Montgomery County Genealogical and Historical Society, 2006); Bernadette Pruitt, *The Other Great Migration: The Movement of Rural African Americans to Houston, 1900–1941* (College Station: Texas A&M University Press, 2013); R. L. Skrabanek and Gladys K. Bowles, *Migration of the Texas Farm Population*, TAES Bulletin 847 (College Station: Texas A&M University, February 1957); U.S. Census of Agriculture, vol. 1, pt. 37, county table 1.1 (1945); Clyburn, "An Agricultural Economic Study," 69; Prince and Collins, combined 1955 annual report, 4.

35. Cattle dipping began in the northern part of the state in 1919 and moved southward. Claire Strom, *Making Catfish Bait out of Government Boys: The Fight against Cattle Ticks and the Transformation of the Yeoman South* (Athens: University of Georgia Press, 2010), 133.

36. *CC*, November 16, 1966 (quotation). The exact cause-and-effect relationship between government programs, declining cotton prices, urban job opportunities, and mechanization in the South's agricultural transformation has been the subject of substantial debate. In Montgomery County the weakness of the cotton economy and the increasing availability of off-farm jobs locally and in Houston meant that out-migration and low prices were likely more significant than dispossession in killing cotton. Jack Temple Kirby, *Rural Worlds Lost: The Rural South, 1920–1960* (Baton Rouge: Louisiana State University Press, 1986), 51–57; and Gilbert C. Fite, *Cotton Fields No More: Southern Agriculture, 1865–1980* (Lexington: University Press of Kentucky, 1984).

37. Betty C. Berry, "An Updated History of the East Texas Chamber of Commerce" (M.A. thesis, Stephen F. Austin State University, May 1976), 50, 90; "Conference to Blueprint for Future Development," *East Texas* 31, no. 4 (1957): 8; and "Accelerated Program for Agriculture Outlined," *East Texas* 37, no. 11 (1963): 8.

38. The Houston Farm and Ranch Club, *Official Handbook and Membership Roster* (self-published, 1965), 6, folder Houston Farm and Ranch Club, box 1456, Harris County Judge William M. Elliot Collection, Harris County Archives, Houston, Tex.

39. Mark Friedberger, "Rural Gentrification and Livestock Raising: Texas as a Test Case, 1940–1995," *Rural History* 7, no. 1 (1996). In spite of intense urbanization, Harris County still had 49,700 head of cattle in 1972, making it fourth in the state. *Big Town, Big Money: The Business of Houston* (Houston: Cordovan Press, 1973), 175–81.

40. Deborah Fitzgerald, *Every Farm a Factory: The Industrial Ideal in American Agriculture* (New Haven, Conn.: Yale University Press, 2003). Because the Farm and Ranch membership rolls only provide members' business addresses, it is difficult to chart the geographic spread of their membership. Lester Goodson, for instance, was a prominent horse breeder and businessman near Magnolia and a member of the Houston Farm and Ranch Club, yet the address listed is that of a car dealership he owned in the city. More than nine out of ten listed a Houston address. *CC*, December 23, 1958; Farm and Ranch, "Official Handbook and Membership Roster"; *CC*, November 3, 1955; and *CC*, July 18, 1956.

41. *CC*, September 24, 1961; Larry Jacobs interview. When the San Jacinto River Authority threatened to inundate prime pastureland along the San Jacinto River in 1959, 25 of the 206 landowners who signed a petition opposing the move listed their address as either Houston or Beaumont. Dick Calfee to Board of Water Engineers, February 9, 1959, Application #002108, Correspondence, 1958–66, box 2002/207-13, TBWE Records, Texas State Library, Austin.

42. "Crimson Clover Successful in East Texas," *East Texas* 24, no. 3 (1950): 7; *CC*, Janu-

ary 12, 1956; *CC,* May 3, 1951; "Crimson Clover: Beauty with a Bonus," *East Texas* 35, no. 9 (1961): 15, 22; *CC,* August 6, 1953; *CC,* March 22, 1957.

43. Varieties of clover, timothy, lespedeza, and alfalfa had been the central building blocks of pasture and hay production outside of the South since the early nineteenth century. The number of acres in these crops, therefore, provides a measure of the productivity of any given livestock or dairy operation along this northern and midwestern model. In 1945 Loudoun farmers harvested 26,582 acres of these crops. Montgomery County, in contrast, harvested only 103 acres. U.S. Census of Agriculture, vol. 1, pt. 24, county table 2.2 (1945), and pt. 37, county table 2.2 (1945); Vanessa Corriher, *Hay Purchases: Grasses Not Adapted to Texas,* Texas A&M AgriLife Extension Bulletin e-614, June 2012, http://foragefax.tamu.edu/files/2013/05/viewpdf_3071_78705.pdf, accessed April 3, 2017.

44. Hybrid Bermuda grass was first developed in Tifton, Georgia, in the 1940s. By 1969 the local soil conservation office recommended Dallis grass, Johnson grass, weeping love grass, carpet grass, and King Ranch bluestem. "District Program and Work Plan, 1969," 16–17; Albert G. Way, "'A Cosmopolitan Weed of the World': Following Bermuda Grass," *Agricultural History* 88, no. 3 (2014): 354–67.

45. The county branch of the Farm Bureau (organized in 1958), the local Soil and Water Conservation District committee, and the local Agricultural Stabilization and Conservation Service all provided social spaces for the exercise of economic and political power by rural white elites. See San Jacinto Soil Conservation District, "Conservation Practices Approved for Montgomery County," 1961, folder Soil Conservation Dist.—Corresp., box 257, sjrar; Dan Waters, "Soil and Water Conservation = Progress," *HC Magazine,* October 1, 1949, 6–7.

46. "Permanent Productive Agriculture Predicted," *East Texas* 25, no. 2 (1950): 7, 14; newsletter, January 1961, and "1969 Annual Report," both in folder Sample Newsletters, Walker County swcd. The Montgomery-Walker swcd only published combined acreage statistics.

47. E. K. Crouch and J. H. Jones, *Pasture Development in the East Texas Timber Country,* taes Bulletin 666 (College Station: Texas A&M University, January 1945); "San Jacinto Soil Conservation District Program," 1944, 15; newsletter, September 1957, folder Newsletters 1955–59, Walker County swcd. For contrast, see Robert R. Rhodes, "The Determination of the Volumes of Forage and Timber Procured in a Pine-Hardwood Stand in Montgomery County, Texas" (M.S. thesis, Texas A&M University, 1951); and Dr. Aaron Baxter, "Coastal Bermuda Offers Money-Making Opportunity," *East Texas* 37, no. 10 (1963): 8.

48. Clyburn, "An Agricultural and Economic Study," 49; Hearing Minutes, 259–60, Application #002108, Reports, 1973–82, folder 2, box 2002/207-14, tbwe Records.

49. *CC,* January 20, 1964; and *CC,* September 9, 1964.

50. As T. H. Breen noted for tobacco planters in eighteenth-century Virginia, the quality of the agricultural good produced "provided a medium within which the planter negotiated a public reputation, a sense of self-worth as an agricultural producer." In this case, the hay defined the man. T. H. Breen, *Tobacco Culture: The Mentality of the Great Tidewater Planters on the Eve of Revolution* (Princeton, N.J.: Princeton University Press, 1985), 58–75, 58 (quotation); Straughn interview; *CC,* May 14, 1956; *CC,* December 3, 1959.

51. *CC,* May 13, 1964.

52. *CC,* October 28, 1964; and History Book Committee, Montgomery County Historical Society, *Montgomery County History* (Winston-Salem, N.C.: Hunter Publishing Company, 1980), 537.

53. *CC*, August 28, 1963; *CC*, June 28, 1956; History Book Committee, *Montgomery County History*, 200–201.

54. Reid, "African Americans"; Pete Daniel, *Dispossession: Discrimination against African American Farmers in the Age of Civil Rights* (Chapel Hill: University of North Carolina Press, 2013); Leo McGee and Robert Boone, eds., *Black Rural Landowner—Endangered Species: Social, Political, and Economic Implications* (Westport, Conn.: Greenwood Press, 1979); and Black Economic Research Center, *Only Six Million Acres: The Decline of Black Owned Land in the Rural South* (New York: Black Economic Research Center, 1973).

55. Reece, "Study of the Economic Status," 13. For an exception, see "Campbell 'Son' Cavil Family" in Montgomery County Genealogical and Historical Society and Lone Star College–Montgomery County, *African American Experiences in Montgomery County, Texas: A Cultural Roots Conference* (Montgomery County Genealogical and Historical Society, 2006).

56. Newsletter, March 1959, folder Newsletters 1955–59, Walker County SWCD.

57. U.S. Census of Agriculture, vol. 1, pt. 37, county tables 1 (1940), 3 (1959), 3 (1969), and pt. 26, county table 2 (1950). Where central Texas saw an increasing number of Latino farmers and laborers during the early twentieth century, Montgomery County remained almost exclusively black and white through the 1980s. In 1950 the county census recorded only five people who were nonwhite and not African American. By 1970 that figure had climbed to 178, a number that likely included the arrival of South and East Asian suburbanites as well. Only by 1980 did this population reach 1 percent, with 2,049 people out of a population of over 128,000. The number of Latino households surpassed that of African Americans in 1990. Yet both remained awash in a sea of white suburbs, and neither accounted for more than 5 percent of households. U.S. Census of Population, 1950, vol. 2, pt. 45, table 42 (1952), 1970, vol. 1, pt. 45, chap. B, table 35 (1972), and 1980, vol. 1, pt. 45, chap. B, table 51 (1982); U.S. Census of Housing, 1990, Texas, sec. 1, table 4.

58. William A. Wilson, "East Texas Now Home of Good Cattle," *East Texas* 27, no. 2 (1952): 8 (quotation). These figures were in spite of the closing of the range in 1956 and the selling off of scrub and range cattle that followed; Montgomery County sold 19,976 cattle for $1,466,000 in 1964. This put the county in the middle of the pack in Texas. Nearby Brazoria County sold 42,834 head for over $3 million. Harris County sold over 47,439 for $4.09 million. U.S. Census of Agriculture, vol. 1, pt. 26, county tables 1, 4.1, and 4.2 (1950), and 1, 10, and 11 (1964).

59. *CC*, December 1, 1965; acreage figure is from Montgomery County Program Building Committee, *Your County Program*, 32.

60. *Visions: Land and Community in Loudoun County* (Purcellville: League of Women Voters of Loudoun County, 1983), 12; and Stephen Turnham, "Loudoun Agriculture Spreading," *WP*, January 24, 1991; Heimlich, "Agriculture and Urban Areas"; Ralph E. Heimlich and Douglas H. Brooks, *Metropolitan Growth and Agriculture: Farming in the City's Shadow*, Agricultural Economic Report 619 (Washington, D.C.: USDA, Economic Research Service, September 1989).

61. Ken Lowery, interview by Allison Weiss, November 5, 2001, Round Hill, Va., LFOHC; Robert R. Lind, Karen T. Richardson, and Donald G. Rypka Jr., *Loudoun Harvest—Faces and Places, Past and Recent, in Loudoun County, Virginia* (Leesburg: Carr Printing and Publishing Company, 1973), 81–83, 117–19; Steve Bates, "New Breed Raising Trees," *WP*, October 16, 1988 (quotation); Harrison interview; Stephen Turnham, "Nurseries Blossom in Va. Countryside," *WP*, September 5, 1991; and "Christmas Trees," *WP*, December 2, 1988;

Eugene M. Scheel, *Loudoun Discovered: Communities, Corners, and Crossroads* (Leesburg: Friends of Thomas Balch Library, 2002), 5:50.

62. James Goode and Peter Penczer, *The History of Loudoun County, Virginia: A Permanent Exhibition* (Bethesda: B. F. Saul Company, 2007), 29, NSLM; Steve Bates, "Virginia's Meredyth Vineyards Up for Sale," *WP*, March 24, 1989; Paul Hodge, "Reaping the Fruits of Their Long Labor," *WP*, November 5, 1992; David L. Robbins, "Grape Nuts," *Virginia Business* 3, no. 10 (1988): 33–39; and Eugene M. Scheel, *The History of Middleburg and Vicinity* (Warrenton: Piedmont Press, 1987), 188. Figure from Virginia Wineries Association, *Virginia Winery Guide 2014, Northern Virginia Region*, www.virginiawine.org/news_releases /region-winery-guides/Northern_Virginia.pdf, accessed February 28, 2014.

63. *Fortune Magazine*, November 1930, reprint Warrenton Antiquarian Society, *Jericho Turnpike: The Storied Route of Foxhunting from New York to Virginia*, ca. 2006, NSLM.

64. Scheel, *The History of Middleburg*, 161; "Morven Park Ground Breaking," *CH*, May 3, 1968; Anne Cocroft, "Hospital for Horses Opening," *WP*, October 11, 1984; Helene Lepkowski, "Report Prepared for the Loudoun County Handbook," December 1986, cited in Raflo, *Within the Iron Gates*, 261; Gerald Strine, "The Pleasure Is Theirs," *WP*, April 28, 1976; and Karl Rhodes, "Betting the Farm," *Virginia Business* 5, no. 9 (1990): 13–20; Virginia Cooperative Extension Office, "Loudoun's Agriculture, 1957–2007," folder 79, Ephemera, TBL.

65. January 14, 1977, August 7, 1970, May 23, 1975, June 22, 1973, July 21, 1961, February 4, 1972, and January 9, 1970, all in *CH*.

66. *CH*, August 5, 1977; and *CH*, February 17, 1978; Vinton Liddell Pickens, interview by Barbara Dutton, July 25, 1990, folder 35, box 2, LCOHP.

67. Virginia Cooperative Extension Office, "Loudoun's Agriculture, 1957–2007."

68. Stan Crawford, "Cowboy," *CC*, September 8, 1965.

69. Lynn Curtis, *Agriculture in the Gulf Coast State Planning Region: Implications for the Future* (Austin: Bureau of Business Research, University of Texas, January 1975), 7.

70. *CC*, April 6, 1966. Out of the hundreds of family histories compiled in History Book Committee, *Montgomery County History*, I found only one example of a nonwhite family participating in exurban ranching or homesteading, a Latino family (457). Evidence of African American participation can be found in Marti Corn, *The Ground on Which I Stand: Tamina, a Freedmen's Town* (College Station: Texas A&M University Press, 2016), 22–27. A small number of rural blacks remained in the countryside and persisted on the margins of the county's booming 4-H equestrian programs. *CC*, October 10, 1979; and Cagle, *History of Montgomery County*, 84–85.

71. Straughn interview; *CC*, January 1, 1964.

72. Tradition, geography, cultural expectation, and Houston's influence placed Montgomery County squarely in the tradition of western riding. Where eastern riding followed the British in focusing on decorum, status, and grace, western riding prized boldness, flexibility, and strength. Eastern riders donned English riding clothes and the trappings of Anglo culture. Western riders embellished the cowboy image and the style that went along with it. In general, eastern riders rode Thoroughbreds; western riders preferred quarter horses. Laura R. Barraclough, *Making the San Fernando Valley: Rural Landscapes, Urban Development, and White Privilege* (Athens: University of Georgia Press, 2011), 119–21; Tex Rodgers, "The All-Around Horse," *Texas Parade* 29, no. 10 (1968): 6–8, 10; and Robert Moorman Denhardt, *The Quarter Running Horse: America's Oldest Breed* (Norman: University of Oklahoma Press, 1979).

73. *CC*, November 18, 1964; and *CC*, February 22, 1970.

74. *CC*, April 10, 1958; *CC*, October 22, 1961; and *CC*, May 2, 1972.

75. *CC*, November 3, 1968.

76. Tracking the number of horses at the county level is difficult. Agricultural census data only cover farms, not subdivisions, and therefore significantly undercount horses. Even so, by the mid-1970s this equestrian resurgence reversed what had been a decades-long decline in both the number of horses and the number of farms with horses in Montgomery county. The former bottomed out at 712 in 1974. By 1978 it was back up to 985. Over the next four years it more than doubled to 1,982. The distribution of the agricultural census also led to undercounting, as it was the responsibility of owners of newly formed farms to opt in to the count. U.S. Agricultural Census, vol. 1, pt. 43, county tables 16 (1974) and 13 (1982); Cory Childs, interview with the author, March 29, 2013, Leesburg, Va.

77. "Leisure Land Supermarket," *Texas Parade* 31, no. 3 (1970): 31–38.

78. "Frontier Hills to Have 'Western City' Display," *HC*, September 15, 1963, special insert; "Conroe: Texas' Most Beautiful City for Family Living," *HC*, April 5, 1964 (first and second quotations); and *CC*, November 22, 1964 (third through sixth quotations). See also Barraclough, *Making the San Fernando Valley*, 1–2, 93–94.

79. *CC*, July 31, 1966 (first quotation); *CC*, November 22, 1964; "Riding, Fishing Enjoyed in Tri-Lake Estates," *HC*, September 15, 1963, special insert; *CC*, November 22, 1964; and "$60 Million Project Set near Lake Conroe," *HC*, November 8, 1984, Lake Conroe Vertical File, HMRC; *CH*, November 17, 1972.

80. William C. Martin and Geoff Winningham, *Going Texan: The Days of the Houston Livestock Show and Rodeo* (Toronto: Herzig-Somerville, Ltd., 1972), 62, 167; *CC*, November 10, 1972; *CC*, February 28, 1975.

81. *CH*, February 16, 1973; *CC*, March 10, 1975 (quotation).

82. Rosenberg, *The 4-H Harvest*; and Thomas Wessel and Marilyn Wessel, *4-H: An American Idea, 1900–1980; A History of 4-H* (Chevy Chase: National 4-H Council, 1982).

83. Population estimate is from *Dallas Morning News, Texas Almanac and State Industrial Guide, 1976–1977* (Dallas: A. H. Belo Corporation, 1975), 336.

84. Straughn interview (first, second, and fourth quotations); Stuart Traylor, interview by the author, November 11, 2010, Montgomery, Tex. (third quotation).

85. *CC*, May 26, 1974. While Loudoun's 4-H focused on training the next generation of progressive dairy farmers, it also expanded show categories that targeted nonagricultural children. Harrison, McComb, and Miller, *Story of Loudoun's Dairy Industry*, 48, 58, 61–62; and Loudoun County 4-H Fair Programs, 1960, 1963, 1966, 1969, TBL.

86. Lynne Chesnar, *February Fever: Historical Highlights of the First 60 Years of the Houston Livestock Show and Rodeo, 1932–1992* (Houston: Houston Livestock Show and Rodeo, 1991), 13–28, 32; Martin and Winningham, *Going Texan*, 58–60; and Jim Saye, "Show and Rodeo: The Houston Livestock Show and Rodeo, a Historical Perspective," *Houston History* 7, no. 1 (2009): 2–11.

87. Chesnar, *February Fever*, 13–28; and Martin and Winningham, *Going Texan*, 58–60. On the role of such events in shaping identity and popular memory, see David M. Guss, *The Festive State: Race, Ethnicity, and Nationalism as Cultural Performance* (Berkeley: University of California Press, 2000); Paul A. Kramer, *The Blood of Government: Race, Empire, the United States, and the Philippines* (Chapel Hill: University of North Carolina Press, 2006), 229–84; and Light Townsend Cumins, "History, Memory, and Rebranding Texas as Western for the 1936 Centennial" in *This Corner of Canaan: Essays on Texas in Honor*

of Randolph B. Campbell, ed. Richard B. McCaslin, Donald E. Chipman, and Andrew J. Torget (Denton: University of North Texas Press, 2013), 36–57.

88. *CC,* January 17, 1963; *CC,* February 13, 1973; *CC,* February 13, 1966 (quotation); and *CC,* February 21, 1965.

89. Roger Galatas and Jim Barlow, *The Woodlands: The Inside Story of Creating a Better Hometown* (Washington, D.C.: Urban Land Institute, 2004), 146.

90. *CC,* February 23, 1966; History Book Committee, *Montgomery County History,* 152.

91. For a fuller treatment of this episode, see Andrew C. Baker, "From Rural South to Metropolitan Sunbelt: Creating a Cowboy Identity in the Shadow of Houston," *Southwestern Historical Quarterly* 118, no. 1 (2014): 1–22.

92. *CC,* February 4, 1968 (first quotation and character names); Martin Dreyer, "The Exodus to Montgomery County," *HC: Texas Sunday Magazine,* June 15, 1969 (second quotation); *CC,* February 18, 1970. On Reaves, see *CC,* May 30, 1976; and History Book Committee, *Montgomery County History,* 449–50.

93. The quotation is a paraphrase from Cynthia Skove Nevels, *Lynching to Belong: Claiming Whiteness through Racial Violence* (College Station: Texas A&M University Press, 2007). On the role of whiteness and historical memory in perpetuating lynching in Texas, see William D. Carrigan, *The Making of a Lynching Culture: Violence and Vigilantism in Central Texas, 1836–1916* (Urbana: University of Illinois Press, 2004). On the significance of the courthouse square as the setting for this event, see Richard H. Schein, "A Methodological Framework for Interpreting Ordinary Landscapes: Lexington, Kentucky's Courthouse Square," *Geographical Review* 99, no. 3 (2009): 377–402.

94. Michael J. Pfeifer, *Rough Justice: Lynching and American Society, 1874–1947* (Urbana: University of Illinois Press, 2004), 2–4. Even a cursory examination of criminal complaints filed in the local district and county courts reveals that death threats, brandishing firearms, beatings, and other examples of rough justice remained common into the 1970s. See, for example, *CC,* March 27, 1968; and *CC,* November 15, 1972.

95. Figures from William Henry Kellar, *Make Haste Slowly: Moderates, Conservatives, and School Desegregation in Houston* (College Station: Texas A&M University Press, 1999), 161, 164. On the Texas Southern University incident, see Kellar, *Make Haste Slowly,* 152–54; and Wesley G. Phelps, *A People's War on Poverty: Urban Politics and Grassroots Activists in Houston* (Athens: University of Georgia Press, 2014), 89–91, 97–105.

96. *CC,* February 24, 1971; and *CC,* February 4, 1968.

97. The trail rides began as a publicity stunt in 1952. Locally, Freeman Dunn used his position as trail boss to help launch his bid for county sheriff in 1976. *CC,* February 24, 1971. The Sam Houston Trail Ride, from Montgomery, began in 1955. The Montgomery County Trail Ride, from Conroe, began a decade later. Martin and Winningham, *Going Texan,* 19–30; Chesnar, *February Fever,* 221; and Ernesto Valdés, "The Trail Rides: The Oldest and Longest," *Houston History* 7, no. 1 (2009): 37–39; *CC,* February 21, 1968; and *CC,* February 22, 1980.

98. *CC,* February 21, 1965.

99. David G. McComb, *Houston: A History,* rev. ed. (Austin: University of Texas Press, 1981), 139–41.

100. The Prairie View Trail Ride, established in 1957 and originating near what is now Prairie View A&M University, brought an African American interpretation of western culture. They rode into town blaring the theme from *Shaft* and the music of James Brown. Dancing girls on the back of the wagon rounded out their performance. This mixture of ur-

ban and western culture drew cheers from African American crowds. The Prairie View Trail Ride carved out space for African Americans within the event, but it did little to destabilize its larger meaning. Such performances drew on a long-standing tradition of black cowboys. Bruce A. Glasrud and Michael N. Searles, eds., *Black Cowboys in the American West: On the Range, on the Stage, behind the Badge* (Norman: University of Oklahoma Press, 2016). The Houston Livestock Show and Rodeo added the Los Vaqueros Trail Ride for Latinos into the celebration in 1974. Martin and Winningham, *Going Texan*, 50; and Ernesto Valdés, "The Trail Rides," 38–39.

101. History Book Committee, *Montgomery County History*, 59; Stagecoach Farms, section 7 plat, June 1963, and election returns, March 1974, both in CCR.

102. Straughn interview.

103. Traylor interview.

104. Barraclough, *Making the San Fernando Valley*, 8; Nickerson and Dochuk, *Sunbelt Rising*, 13–16; and David Delaney, "The Space That Race Makes," *Professional Geographer* 54, no. 1 (2002): 6–14. The presence of the occasional rural black holdout added to the picturesque quality of rural life. In fact, the very rurality of these blacks validated them as "good negroes" in a period that bound black deviance and urbanity together. Bill Bergfeld Jr., interview by the author, July 19, 2012, Conroe, Tex.

105. Michael D. Lassiter, *The Silent Majority: Suburban Politics in the Sunbelt South* (Princeton, N.J.: Princeton University Press, 2006).

106. John Fraser Hart, "Non-farm Farms," *Geographical Review* 82, no. 2 (1992): 166–79; and Frederick H. Buttel, "The Political Economy of Part-Time Farming," *GeoJournal* 6, no. 4 (1982): 296–97.

107. I employ the term "rural gentrification" because it best captures the motivations, process, and impact of the actions of these newcomers. As with urban gentrification, their economic investment combined with new lifestyle- and aesthetic-based property values to transform the economics of agriculture. Mark Friedberger, "Mink and Manure: Rural Gentrification and Cattle Ranching in Southeast Texas," *Southwestern Historical Quarterly* 102, no. 3 (1999): 269–93; Martin Phillips, "Rural Gentrification and the Process of Class Colonisation," *Journal of Rural Studies* 9, no. 2 (1993): 123–40; and J. Dwight Hines, "In Pursuit of Experience: The Postindustrial Gentrification of the Rural American West," *Ethnography* 11, no. 2 (2010): 285–308.

Chapter 3. Damming the Hinterlands

1. Vanesa Castán Broto, Adriana Allen, and Elizabeth Rapoport, "Interdisciplinary Perspectives on Urban Metabolism," *Journal of Industrial Ecology* 16, no. 6 (2012): 853; Joel A. Tarr, "The Metabolism of the Industrial City: The Case of Pittsburgh," *Journal of Urban History* 28, no. 5 (2002): 511–45, 511 (quotation).

2. On urban imperialism, see William L. Kahrl, *Water and Power: The Conflict over Los Angeles' Water Supply in the Owens Valley* (Berkeley: University of California Press, 1982); Gray Brechin, *Imperial San Francisco: Urban Power, Earthly Ruin* (Berkeley: University of California Press, 1999), 71–117; David Stradling, *Making Mountains: New York City and the Catskills* (Seattle: University of Washington Press, 2007), 12–15, 140–76; and David Soll, *Empire of Water: An Environmental and Political History of the New York City Water Supply* (Ithaca, N.Y.: Cornell University Press, 2013).

3. Here I am building on the insights of urban political ecology, which emphasizes the contingent and fundamentally political nature of urban uses of the environment. Alex Loftus, *Everyday Environmentalism: Creating an Urban Political Ecology* (Minneapolis: University of Minnesota Press, 2012); and Erik Swyngedouw, *Social Power and the Urbanization of Water: Flows of Power* (New York: Oxford University Press, 2004).

4. Andrew Needham and Allen Dieterich-Ward, "Beyond the Metropolis: Metropolitan Growth and Regional Transformation in Postwar America," *Journal of Urban History* 35, no. 7 (2009); Martin V. Melosi and Joseph A. Pratt, eds., *Energy Metropolis: An Environmental History of Houston and the Gulf Coast* (Pittsburgh: University of Pittsburgh Press, 2007); and Andrew Needham, *Power Lines: Phoenix and the Making of the Modern Southwest* (Princeton, N.J.: Princeton University Press, 2014).

5. U.S. Senate, Committee on the District of Columbia, *Hearing before the Subcommittee to Investigate the Proposal of Potomac Electric Power Co. to Erect a Steam Plant on the Potomac River in Loudoun County, Va.* (Washington, D.C.: GPO, 1955) (hereafter cited as PEPCO Hearing), 66–70, 74–78; and Frank Raflo, *Within the Iron Gates: Loudoun Stories Remembered* (Dulles: TechniGraphix, 1998), 196–202.

6. "Approval by Loudoun Is First Pepco Hurdle," *WP*, September 16, 1955; and Aubrey Graves, "Power Plant Just Generating Heat Now," *WP*, October 9, 1955.

7. Frederick Gutheim, *Planning for the Future in the Potomac River Basin* (Washington, D.C.: ICPRB, 1950).

8. PEPCO Hearing, 11–13, 33, 63–65, 83. See also Craig E. Colten, *Southern Waters: The Limits to Abundance* (Baton Rouge: Louisiana State University Press, 2014), 163–93.

9. Department of Sanitary Engineering, District of Columbia, *The Potomac Interceptor: Symbol of Metropolitan Cooperation*, September 1968, 5, folder 8, box 17, Noman M. Cole Papers, Special Collections and Archives, George Mason University Libraries, Fairfax, Va.; *A Report on Water Pollution in the Washington Metropolitan Area* (Washington, D.C.: ICPRB, February 1954), 1:3–5; *Drainage Basin Committee Report for the Chesapeake Bay Drainage Basins* (Washington, D.C.: GPO, 1937), 13–23; and U.S. Department of the Interior, *The Nation's River: The Department of the Interior Official Report on the Potomac* (Washington, D.C.: GPO, 1968), sec. III; Abel Wolman, John C. Geyer, and Edwin E. Pyatt, *A Clean Potomac River in the Washington Metropolitan Area* (Washington, D.C.: ICPRB, October 1957), 8; and U.S. Senate, Committee on the District of Columbia, *Water Supply Problems of the National Capital Region* (Washington, D.C.: GPO, 1969), 15.

10. Average flow at Washington, D.C., before withdrawals was around 7,000 MGD. The lowest flow on record would come in September 1966, when the river carried only 388 MGD. The highest was 275,000 MGD. ICPRB, "General Facts and FAQs," www.potomacriver .org/facts-a-faqs/faqs, accessed August 13, 2015; Corps of Engineers, U.S. War Department, . . . *Letter from the . . . Chief of Engineers, United States Army, Dated March 8, 1946, Submitting . . . a Preliminary Examination and Survey of the Potomac River and Tributaries . . .* (Washington, D.C: GPO, 1946), 1–2; *Report on Water Pollution*, 1:1 (quotation); Wolman, Geyer, and Pyatt, *A Clean Potomac River*, 17; U.S. Senate, Committee on the District of Columbia, *Water Supply Problems*, 15–16.

11. Aubrey Graves, "D.C. Engineer Says Area May Face Rationing," *WP*, December 3, 1955 (first quotation); and PEPCO Hearing, 11–13, 83 (second quotation).

12. PEPCO Hearing, 37–38, 66–70, 97, 103, 118–19.

13. Corps of Engineers, U.S. War Department, . . . *Letter from the . . . Chief of Engineers,*

30, 76, 86; and U.S. House, *House Documents, vol. 7-4, Examinations of Rivers and Harbors, III (Potomac River Basin)* (Washington: GPO, 1969) (hereafter cited as Potomac River Basin Report, 1969), vol. 2, app. A.

14. *LTM*, March 29, 1945; and Robert E. Smith, "Potomac Dams Project Meets Strong Reverse," *WP*, April 4, 1945.

15. Loudoun's PEPCO site was 206 feet above sea level. The Riverbend Dam's proposed pool level was 225 feet. PEPCO Hearing, 13, 40, 73, 108–9.

16. PEPCO Hearing, 57 (first quotation); "Potomac Dam Plan Is Labeled 'Pipedream,'" *WP*, November 12, 1955 (second quotation).

17. "Future of the Potomac," *WP*, September 30, 1955 (first and second quotations); "Broad Run Tract Alarms Planners," *WP*, December 14, 1956 (third quotation). On local preservationists, see PEPCO Hearing, 75, 81.

18. PEPCO Hearing, 113–17, 115 (quotation).

19. *Proposed PEPCO Plant, Report Submitted to the Committee on the District of Columbia . . .*, December 16, 1955 (Washington, D.C.: GPO, 1955), 3.

20. Abel Wolman and John C. Geyer, *Report on Sanitary Sewers and Waste Water Disposal in the Washington Metropolitan Region: Summary Report* (Baltimore, Md.: Washington Metropolitan Regional Sanitary Advisory Board, 1962). See also JCWMP, *Water Supply Staff Report* (Washington, D.C.: GPO, 1958); JCWMP, *Water Supply and Sewage Disposal Staff Report* (Washington, D.C.: GPO, 1958); and JCWMP, *Sewage Disposal and Water Pollution Staff Report* (Washington, D.C.: GPO, 1958).

21. Board of Engineers for Rivers and Harbors, Corps of Engineers, U.S. Army, report, December 16, 1963 (hereafter cited as Potomac River Basin Plan, 1963), reprinted in Potomac River Basin Report, 1969, report summary, 50.

22. Wolman, Geyer, and Pyatt, *A Clean Potomac River*, 56.

23. Russ Banham, *The Fight for Fairfax: A Struggle for a Great American County* (Fairfax: George Mason University Press, 2009), 45–48; and Paul E. Ceruzzi, *Internet Alley: High Technology in Tyson's Corner, 1945–2005* (Cambridge, Mass.: MIT Press, 2007), 51–55.

24. Wolman, Geyer, and Pyatt, *A Clean Potomac River*, 31–36; and JCWMP, *Water Supply and Sewage Disposal*, 5.

25. U.S. House, House Committee of the District of Columbia, Subcommittee on Fiscal Affairs, *Relating to Dulles Airport Sewage System*, unpublished hearing, Washington, D.C., May 19, 1960, 5, 19, 37, 43, 49, 52; "Federal Sewer Line Urged in Virginia," *Washington Star*, September 25, 1959, folder 1958, box 6, Northern Virginia History Collection, Special Collections and Archives, George Mason University Libraries, Fairfax, Va.; and Department of Sanitary Engineering, District of Columbia, *The Potomac Interceptor*.

26. Department of Sanitary Engineering, District of Columbia, *The Potomac Interceptor*, 18; U.S. House, House Committee of the District of Columbia, Subcommittee on Fiscal Affairs, *Relating to Dulles Airport Sewage System*, 6. The total federal grant was eventually $15.5 million. Department of Sanitary Engineering, District of Columbia, *The Potomac Interceptor*, 11; Wolman, Geyer, and Pyatt, *A Clean Potomac River*, 32–33.

27. William O. Beck, *A Half Century of Regional Partnership: COG Celebrates 50 Years* (WMCOG, 2007), 15, 90–91; J. Lindsay Almond Jr. to Robertson, April 16, 1959, Robertson to Smith, May 7, 1959, and Fairfax County Water Authority, Resolution, April 16, 1959, all in folder Potomac River Dam, box 141, MSS 8731-c, Howard Smith Papers, ASSSC.

28. Potomac River Basin Plan, 1963, 1:34.

29. Lucas D. Phillips, J. Emory Kirkpatrick, and Stirling M. Harrison to Col. Warren R.

Johnson, November 25, 1961, folder Potomac River Basin, box 171, MSS 8731-c, Smith Papers; *LTM*, June 7, 1962; and Potomac River Basin Report, 1969, vol. 2, app. B, 46–50; J. H. Cunningham to Smith, June 5, 1962, folder Potomac River Basin, box 171, MSS 8731-c, Smith Papers (quotation).

30. Potomac River Basin Plan, 1963, 1:27–31, 42–47, 100–101, 164.

31. Loudoun County Board of Supervisors, "Preliminary Analysis: Impact on Loudoun County of Proposed Potomac Reservoir at Riverbend," November 27, 1961, folder Potomac River Basin, box 171, MSS 8731-c, Smith Papers; *LTM*, June 27, 1963.

32. Elsie Carper, "Loudoun Decries Seneca Dam as Financial Threat to County," *WP*, June 6, 1962.

33. Raflo, *Within the Iron Gates*, 206 (quotation); Loudoun County Board of Supervisors, "Resolution Concerning Proposed Seneca Dam on Potomac River," June 18, 1963, folder Potomac River Basin, box 171, MSS 8731-c, Smith Papers.

34. *LTM*, April 25, 1963.

35. *LTM*, May 31, 1962.

36. "Public Voice Sought on Dam Plans," *WP*, November 26, 1961; Potomac River Basin Plan, 1963, 1:48–49; and "Army's Dam Project Rejected by Planners," *WP*, July 28, 1964. On the suburban roots of environmentalism, see Adam Rome, *The Bulldozer in the Countryside: Suburban Sprawl and the Rise of American Environmentalism* (New York: Cambridge University Press, 2001); and Christopher C. Sellers, *Crabgrass Crucible: Suburban Nature and the Rise of Environmentalism in Twentieth-Century America* (Chapel Hill: University of North Carolina Press, 2012).

37. Timothy John Broedling, "A Study in Program Formulation: Factors Causing Delay in the Development of a Comprehensive Long-Range Plan for the Potomac River Basin" (M.P.A. thesis, George Washington University, June 1967), 53–58; Anthony Wayne Smith, *Analysis of the Potomac River Basin Report of the District and Division Engineers, Corps of Engineers, U.S. Army* (Washington, D.C.: National Parks Association, April 1963).

38. Barry Mackintosh, *C&O Canal: The Making of a Park* (Washington, D.C.: History Division, U.S. Dept. of the Interior, National Park Service, 1991); Mark W. T. Harvey, *A Symbol of Wilderness: Echo Park and the American Conservation Movement* (Seattle: University of Washington Press, 1994, 2000).

39. *LTM*, September 12, 1963.

40. Lyndon B. Johnson, "Special Message to the Congress on Conservation and Restoration of Natural Beauty," February 8, 1965, Lyndon Baines Johnson Library and Museum, www.lbjlibrary.net/collections/selected-speeches/1965/02-08-1965.html, accessed January 27, 2013.

41. Federal Interdepartmental Task Force on the Potomac, *Potomac Interim Report to the President* (Washington, D.C.: Department of the Interior, 1966); and U.S. Department of the Interior, *The Nation's River*, sec. V.

42. National Park Service, Department of the Interior, *Proposed Potomac National River* (Washington, D.C.: GPO, 1977), pt. 13.

43. Mackintosh, *C&O Canal*, 90–100; and Richard L. Stanton, *Potomac Journey: Fairfax Stone to Tidewater* (Washington, D.C.: Smithsonian Institution Press, 1993), 145–61.

44. Thomas W. Lippman, "Army Changes Its Stand on High Dam at Seneca," *WP*, August 25, 1966.

45. Paul Charles Milazzo, *Unlikely Environmentalists: Congress and Clean Water, 1945–1972* (Lawrence: University Press of Kansas, 2006), 163–90.

46. U.S. Department of the Interior, *The Nation's River*, sec. II; WMCOG, "Future Water Supply: Metropolitan Washington Region," report no. 1: requirements and sources, May 1967, reprinted in U.S. Senate, Committee on the District of Columbia, *Water Supply Problems*.

47. *CC*, March 2, 1966. Flow statistics converted from cubic feet per second, Corps of Engineers, Galveston District, *San Jacinto River and Tributaries, Texas Reconnaissance Report on Flood Problem at Whispering Oaks Subdivision, Montgomery County, Texas*, May 1981, 4, folder Flood Control 1979–80, box 392, SJRAR.

48. Dam construction in the South, with the exception of the Tennessee Valley Authority, is only beginning to receive attention. T. Robert Hart, "The Lowcountry Landscape: Politics, Preservation, and the Santee-Cooper Project," *Environmental History* 18, no. 1 (2013); Christopher J. Manganiello, *Southern Water, Southern Power: How the Politics of Cheap Energy and Water Scarcity Shaped a Region* (Chapel Hill: University of North Carolina Press, 2015); and Kenna Lang Archer, *Unruly Waters: A Social and Environmental History of the Brazos River* (Albuquerque: University of New Mexico Press, 2015).

49. "Manufacturing by Counties," in *Texas Almanac, 1958–59* (Dallas: A. H. Belo Corp., 1957), 323; *Texas Almanac, 1966–67* (Dallas: A. H. Belo Corp., 1965), 513; U.S. Census of Population, 1970, vol. 1, *Supp. Report PC(S1)-7*, table 32 (1972); U.S. Census of Population, 1940, vol. 1, *Texas*, table 7-H (1942); Water Supply and Conservation Committee, Houston Chamber of Commerce, *Water for the Houston Area* (Houston, March 1955), 6; and Martin V. Melosi, "Houston's Public Sinks: Sanitary Services from Local Concerns to Regional Challenges," in Melosi and Pratt, *Energy Metropolis*, 130–31.

50. Nationally, the number of water districts tripled between 1945 and 1980. Historian Donald J. Pisani has argued that "the proliferation of special districts and their relationship to county, state, and federal institutions" is "the untold story of the twentieth century" (*Water and American Government: The Reclamation Bureau, National Water Policy, and the West, 1902–1935* [Berkeley: University of California Press, 2002], 292). The legislature renamed the San Jacinto River Conservation and Reclamation District the SJRA in 1951. SJRA, *Master Plan: Report for the Full Scale Development of the San Jacinto River* (Conroe: San Jacinto River Authority, 1951), 5–6, 12, box 398, SJRAR. San Antonio faced similar issues. Heywood Sanders, "Missing Taps, Missing Pipes: Water Policy and Politics," in *On the Border: An Environmental History of San Antonio*, ed. Char Miller (Pittsburgh: University of Pittsburgh Press, 2001), 141–68.

51. SJRA, *Master Plan*, 6 (quotation); Acts 1937, 45th R.S., chap. 426, GSLT; and *CC*, October 31, 1971; Whitson B. Etheridge, *Dad, What Was It Like in Conroe?* (self-published, December 1999), 90–91.

52. SJRA, *Master Plan*, 38; and Walter G. Hall, interview by Connie Simpson, August 17, 1989, 21, folder 6, Hall to C. M. Malone, 2–3, August 25, 1948, folder 13, Hall to Beauford Jester, October 25, 1948, folder 14, and folder 28, all in box 15, Walter Gardner Hall Papers, MS 280, Woodson Research Center, Fondren Library, Rice University, Houston, Tex.; [Hall] to Don Worton, April 19, 1949, folder San Jacinto River C&R—Public Relations, box 536, SJRAR; Brown & Root, *Estimates of Potential Water Supply Development of the San Jacinto River Basin, Texas for the City of Houston, Texas* (Houston: Houston Public Works, August 1959), 14.

53. Five of the six members of the first board were from rural and small-town areas scattered across the watershed. The only exception was one Houstonian who was brought on board through his brother who lived in the county. A similar breakdown held true for

the first permanent board, established in 1941. Between 1941 and 1973 Conroe accounted for fifty-nine years of total service on the board; Walker and Liberty Counties accounted for forty-seven; and Houston, Galveston, and Baytown represented fifty-six total years. Calculated from "Directors of the San Jacinto River Authority," folder SJRA, History of, box 536, SJRAR; Brown & Root, *Estimates of Potential Water Supply*, 13–14.

54. Dickinson is located south of Houston. Walter G. Hall, interview by Chandler Davidson, Walter Buenger, and Louis Marchiafava, July 24, 1979, folder 3, box 16, 12–13 (first quotation), and Hall to C. M. Malone, 2, August 25, 1948, both in Hall Papers; William W. McClendon, "The San Jacinto River Conservation & Reclamation District's Proposed Plan of Full Scale Development of the San Jacinto River," undated, folder San Jacinto River C&R—Public Relations, box 536, SJRAR; Dan Waters, "Soil and Water Conservation = Progress," *HC Magazine*, October 1, 1949, 6–7; Hall, "Agricultural Economy," 1954, 2, folder 6, box 3, Hall Papers; and Hall, interview by Davidson, Buenger, and Marchiafava, 34, November 19, 1979, folder 4, box 16, Hall Papers.

55. *CC*, August 2, 1945; and *CC*, July 26, 1945, folder San Jacinto River C&R—Public Relations, box 536, SJRAR; SJRA, *Master Plan*, 4 (quotation). For a map of the Army Corps plan, see Etheridge, *What Was It Like in Conroe*, 404–5. The number of dams planned fluctuated over the following twenty-five years. An undated engineering report from Hall's tenure put the number at fourteen. The 1951 *Master Plan* would have thirteen.

56. Ike Barrett, "The History of San Jacinto River Authority," ca. May 1972, SJRAR; Hall interview, 12–13, July 24, 1979; and Melosi, "Houston's Public Sinks," 115–16.

57. Water permit no. 1422, February 3, 1947, SJRA, *Master Plan*, 13.

58. Hall to James V. Allred, 2, April 7, 1949, folder 28, Hall to Searcy Bracewell, March 14, 1949, folder 28, and Hall to C. M. Malone, 2, August 25, 1948, all in box 15, Hall Papers.

59. Conroe City Council and County Commissioners Court to Texas Water Development Board, September 1, 1966, CCR.

60. *CC*, November 18, 1954.

61. Unmarked list of resolutions, folder SJRA History, box 536, SJRAR.

62. *CC*, September 30, 1954.

63. History Book Committee, Montgomery County Historical Society, *Montgomery County History* (Winston-Salem, N.C.: Hunter Publishing Company, 1980), 537–38; *CC*, June 20, 1973, and "SJRA Head Weisinger Dies at 66," *HP*, June 16, 1973, both in box 130, SJRAR.

64. A 1943 report predicted the metro area would consume 268 MGD by 1970. It had reached that benchmark by 1954. Water Supply and Conservation Committee, *Water for the Houston Area*, 1; Melosi, "Houston's Public Sinks," 111–16. Statistics on Lake Houston from "The San Jacinto River Authority: A History," second version, first draft (ca. 2006), SJRAR.

65. Total demand for water in the region was expected to rise from 257 MGD in 1953 to 461 MGD by 1960, an 80 percent increase. By 1970 that figure was expected to reach 703 MGD. Water Supply and Conservation Committee, *Water for the Houston Area*, iv (quotation), 10.

66. Robert F. Riggio, George W. Bomar, and Thomas J. Larkin, *Texas Drought: Its Recent History (1931–1985)* (Austin: Texas Water Commission, September 1987); Freese and Nichols, "Estimates of the Potential Yield of the San Jacinto River Basin," 3, February 16, 1959, Application #002108, Reports, 1959–72, folder 1, box 2002/207-13, TBWE Records, Texas State Library, Austin, Tex.

67. "'Houston Has Access to Plentiful Water Supply,' Say Experts," *HP*, April 7, 1957, folder Publicity 1947 thru December 31, 1958, box 130, SJRAR.

68. Freese and Nichols, "Estimates of the Potential Yield," 4.

69. "City Told 2nd San Jacinto Dam Projected," *HC*, August 23, 1952, folder Publicity 1947 thru December 31, 1958, box 130, SJRAR.

70. Water Supply and Conservation Committee, *Water for the Houston Area*, 3; *CC*, January 21, 1954; Barrett, "The History."

71. Max H. Jacobs Agency to W. B. Weisinger, June 25, 1958, folder From W. B. Weisinger Files, box 130, SJRAR.

72. *CC*, November 15, 1957.

73. Walter Mansell, "Water Talks to Be Resumed," *HC*, December 15, 1957, folder From W. B. Weisinger Files, box 130, SJRAR.

74. Charles Hermann Moerbe, "An Analysis of Views on Houston's Quest for Trinity River Authority Water," 19, 22, December 14, 1966, folder 4, box 5, Louise Kennedy Collection, HMRC; Brown & Root, *Estimates of Potential Water Supply*, 24. Lake Livingston would provide 550 MGD for $30 million. The SJRA's first lake would provide only 150 MGD for $25 million. "Water Offer Is Repeated by Authority," *HC*, February 20, 1958, folder From W. B. Weisinger Files, box 130, SJRAR.

75. SJRA, *The San Jacinto River: Logical Source of Houston's Future Water Supply*, 5, April 25, 1958, Houston Public Works Records, Houston, Tex.

76. According to the SJRA's figures, San Jacinto water had 157 PPM dissolved solids and 60 PPM hardness. The Trinity had 296 PPM and 136 PPM, respectively. San Jacinto water required less treatment before use. SJRA, *The San Jacinto River*, 6, 8–9, 17–18; "Proposed Statement of W. B. Weisinger," 1 (third quotation), 2 (first, second, and fourth quotations), November 12, 1957, folder From W. B. Weisinger Files, box 130, SJRAR; *CC*, August 10, 1958 (fifth quotation).

77. SJRA, *The San Jacinto River*, 4 (first through third quotations), 7, 13, 27; and "Water Offer Is Repeated by Authority," *HC*, February 20, 1958, folder From W. B. Weisinger Files, box 130, SJRAR.

78. *CC*, July 2, 1958; Ben C. Belt, "All Possible Speed," *Houston Magazine*, June 1958; Mel Young, "Dam to Be Built near Conroe, City Is Told," July 25, 1958, *HC*, A17; and Max H. Jacobs Agency to W. B. Weisinger, June 25, 1958, all in folder From W. B. Weisinger Files, box 130, SJRAR; June 29, 1958, Minute Record Book, vol. 1991/041-10, TBWE Records. Most of the official records and journalistic coverage at this point spoke in terms of MGD and acre feet, not acreage—in terms of potential water supply rather than potential inundation. The final lake was 21,000 acres and 430,000 acre-feet. A 350,000-acre-feet reservoir would have been somewhere around 17,000 acres.

79. The board application also included a 70,000-acre-feet-per-year dam at the lower Lake Creek site. No one appeared at the hearing to oppose this smaller dam. Minute Record Book, vol. 1991/041-11, 31–32, 39, TBWE Records. On the legal processes involved, see John G. McNeely and Ronald D. Lacewell, *Surface Water Development*, TAES Bulletin 1536 (College Station: Texas A&M University, 1977).

80. "What Do You Know about Montgomery-Walker Soil and Water Conservation District No. 425?," undated, Walker County SWCD; newsletter, August 1955, and supervisors' annual report for 1956, both in folder San Jacinto Soil Conservation District, box 494, SJRAR; "Soil Conservation Meets in Conroe," *Huntsville Item* [Spring 1946], folder San Jacinto River C&R—Public Relations, box 536, SJRAR; Hearing Minutes, 71–74, 144, Application #002108, Reports, 1973–82, folder 2, box 2002/207-14, TBWE Records (hereafter cited as Lake Conroe Hearing); statistics from Waters, "Soil and Water Conservation," 6–7

(quotation); "Soil Conservation Work Completed," May 24, 1960, and "Soil Conservation Report Based on Acreage Percentage," both in folder Soil Conservation Data on Work Done, box 257, SJRAR; Lake Conroe Hearing, 35–38, 144.

81. By 1969 this program had created 2,900 such ponds and lakes in Walker and Montgomery Counties. "District Program and Work Plan, 1969," 26; SJRA, "Stock Tanks and River Development: A Report," box 206, SJRAR. Some of these lakes would later become recreational amenities for rural subdivisions. Elmer Summers, "Land of Lakes," *HC Magazine*, September 7, 1958, folder From W. B. Weisinger, box 130, SJRAR. For the landowners' understanding of this watershed conservation approach, see statement of Wilbourn S. Gibbs, Huntsville, Tex., in front of Texas State Legislature Interim Agricultural Committee, October 11, 1966, folder Misc., Walker County SWCD.

82. Dick Calfee to Board of Water Engineers, February 9, 1959, James Price to TBWE, October 27, 1959, and W. S. Gibbs to Durwood Manford, February 16, 1959, all in Application #002108, Correspondence, 1958–66, box 2002/207-13, TBWE Records.

83. J. H. "Dick" Calfee, Association of Submerged Land Owners and Operators of Montgomery and Walker Counties, to W. B. Weisinger et al., February 10, 1959, in folder From W. B. Weisinger Files, box 130, SJRAR (hereafter cited as Landowners to Board of Directors) (first and second quotations); Lake Conroe Hearing, 51, 53–56, 59, 61–62, 65, 259–60; Acts 1943, 48th R.S., chap. 303, GSLT (third quotation).

84. Lake Conroe Hearing, 32–38, 46 (second quotation), 49, 70, 71 (first quotation), 76 (fourth quotation); James Price to TBWE, October 27, 1959 (third quotation).

85. Lake Conroe Hearing, 47 (quotation). The SJRA would enlarge the reservoir again in April 6, 1965, this time to 430,260 acre-feet. "Permit to Appropriate Public Waters of the State of Texas, No. 1962," and "An Order Amending Permit N. 1962 of San Jacinto River Authority," both in Application #002108, Permit and Amendments, box 2002/207-13, TBWE Records.

86. The Honea dam would cost 1.68 cents per thousand gallons. Costs for the Lake Creek site and Cleveland site were 3.67 cents and 2.1 cents, respectively. Lake Conroe Hearing, 237; Ike Barrett, interview by the author, July 11, 2012, Dobbin, Tex.

87. Landowners to Board of Directors (first quotation); Lake Conroe Hearing, 58 (second quotation), 75.

88. Minute Record Book, vol. 1991/041-11, 68, TBWE Records; "City of Houston $25,000,000 Water System Revenue Bonds Series 1968," 11, folder City of Houston, box 405, SJRAR; Max H. Jacobs to SJRA Board, December 2, 1959, folder From W. B. Weisinger Files, SJRAR; "Trinity Hearing Resumes with a Ruckus," *HP*, January 4, 1960, "S.J.R.A. Attitude Is Inexcusable," *HC*, February 26, 1960 (quotation), and "San Jac Authority Criticizes Editorial," *HC*, March 10, 1960, all in folder From W. B. Weisinger Files, box 130, SJRAR.

89. Contract with City of Houston, box 490, SJRAR; unmarked list of resolutions, folder SJRA History, box 536, SJRAR; *CC*, May 5, 1960.

90. James O. Holley, "Money Settles Muddy Water of River Fuss," *HP*, March 28, 1960.

91. *CC*, May 5, 1960; Minute Record Book, vol. 1991/041-11, 285, TBWE Records.

92. The SJRA had acquired 10,502 acres of the 21,000-acre lake by March 31, 1966. This figure did not include the 5,100 acres of national forest land, which the SJRA would lease for $2.50 per acre per year. "Land Acquisition and Cost Distribution Lake Conroe," folder Miscellaneous Information Lake "C," box 406, SJRAR; "Memo of Understanding Between the San Jacinto River Authority and the U.S. Department of Agriculture, Forest Service,"

March 16, 1970, folder U.S. Forest Service, box 503, SJRAR; *CC*, March 28, 1965; Application #002108, Correspondence, 1958–66, box 2002/207-13, TBWE Records.

93. "Let's Get Going on Lake Conroe," *HC*, December 4, 1967, folder 4, box 5, Louise Kennedy Collection, HMRC; *CC*, April 14, 1968; unmarked list of resolutions, folder SJRA History, box 536, SJRAR; C. W. Curry to Howard B. Boswell, August 28, 1968, folder Lake Conroe Texas Water Dev Board Grant App, box 503, SJRAR.

94. These conclusions are drawn from an analysis of eighty-two property purchases for which I was able to secure complete data. Folder Land Acquisition, Lake Conroe, box 405, SJRAR; confidential memo re meeting with Jack Culp, C. W. Curry, R. A. Scarborough, and H. E. Barrett, February 12, 1971, folder Culp, Jack (supt. Reservoir Proj.), box 405, SJRAR. The courts eventually clarified the extent to which a project could drive up land values for condemnation in Trinity River Authority of Texas v. Barrett, 497 S.W.2d 91, 93 (1973).

95. *CC*, September 21, 1969.

96. James O. Holley, "Relatives of SJRA Head Own Tracts," *HP*, March 18, 1960; Zarko Franks, "SJRA President Buys Up Conroe Reservoir Acreage," *HC*, October 19, 1969 (first and second quotations). On the Weisinger family, see Margaret A. Simpson, *Montgomery County, Texas: Picture of a Dream Coming True* (Virginia Beach: Downing Publishing Company, 1997), 84–86; and History Book Committee, *Montgomery County History*, 532.

97. Holley, "Money Settles Muddy Water"; and Etheridge, *What Was It Like in Conroe*, 404–5.

98. Charles Richardson and Garvin Berry, "Kin of SJRA Head Owns Lake Site Land," *HP*, undated, folder Publicity January 1, 1959, box 130, SJRAR (first and second quotations). Ike Barrett made a similar point in a 2012 interview.

99. Holley, "Money Settles Muddy Water."

100. Holley, "Relatives of SJRA Head Own Tracts"; "Five Lake Tract Owners Granted $960,940," newspaper clipping, October 5, 1969, *CC*, November 2, 1969, and "Land Boom at Lake Conroe," *HP*, January 10, 1971, all in folder Lake Conroe—San Jacinto River Authority, box 130, SJRAR; *CC*, January 7, 1973; *CC*, October 22, 1969; *CC*, October 6, 1971; *CC*, July 25, 1971; and *CC*, December 4, 1972.

101. Richardson and Berry, "Kin of SJRA Head Owns Lake Site Land."

102. W. B. Weisinger was not among this group. As an act of good faith, he had the SJRA condemn his land early on in the process for $250 an acre, before land prices shot up. "Five Lake Tract Owners Granted $960,940." Dick Calfee and Ed Barnes were among the few who refused to sell out or develop. Gary Calfee, interview by the author, October 10, 2010, and July 19, 2012, Willis, Tex.; Blake Kellum, interview by the author, October 2010, Conroe, Tex. For the land acquisitions, see "Lake Conroe Land Parcels: Remaining Tracts to Be Purchased, January, 1969," folder Land Acquisition, Lake Conroe, box 405, SJRAR. At this point there were ninety-seven tracts left, nearly three-quarters of which were fifty acres or less.

103. On the difficulties rural black families had in holding on to their land, see Leo McGee and Robert Boone, "A Study of Rural Landownership, Control Problems, and Attitudes of Blacks toward Rural Land," in *Black Rural Landowner—Endangered Species: Social, Political, and Economic Implications*, ed. Leo McGee and Robert Boone (Westport, Conn.: Greenwood Press, 1979), 64; and Black Economic Research Center, *Only Six Million Acres: The Decline of Black Owned Land in the Rural South* (New York: Black Economic Research Center, 1973), 51–57.

104. I have been unable to find mention of this community in the SJRAR. History Book

Committee, *Montgomery County History*, 549–50, 561–62 (quotation), 373–74; and Dorothy Reece, interview by the author, April 23, 2014, Conroe, Tex.

105. In contrast with the extensive attention they have given to the construction of reservoirs, historians have largely ignored what happens after the dam gates closed. As David Soll's history of the New York water system demonstrates, the ways cities and water authorities have managed their reservoirs reveal just as much as dam building about the relationship between these entities and the rural areas they have inundated. Soll, *Empire of Water*; Courtney W. Curry, "SJR Authority, Its Purposes and Works," *Baytown Sun*, February 21, 1971, folder Lake Conroe—San Jacinto River Authority, box 130, "SB 147," folder Sanitation, box 398, and "Flowage Easement Area, Lake Conroe Reservoir," internal memo, May 14, 1969, folder Cape, E. B. (Director Public Wks.), box 405, all in SJRAR; Board Meeting Minutes, July 7, 1970, folder Directors Meetings (Agendas of), 1964–72, box 39, SJRAR.

106. *CC*, March 29, 1967, folder Lake Conroe—San Jacinto River Authority, box 130, SJRAR; and Montgomery County Chamber of Commerce, *Montgomery County, Texas* (Encino: Windsor Publications Inc., 1971), 15.

107. Keith Elliott, "Doubling a Dreamland," *Texas Parade* 31, no. 8 (1971): 41–48; William B. Alderman, "Lakeway's Way of Life," *Texas Parade* 27, no. 1 (1966): 37–44; and Keith Elliott, "Lakeside Village," *Texas Parade* 32, no. 6 (1971): 35–38; Jorjanna Price, "As Lake Conroe Rises, Development Faster by Dam Site," *HP*, June 28, 1973.

108. Landowners to Board of Directors.

109. "Lake Front Bustling with Developers," *East Texas Outdoors* 2 (May 1973): 4, folder *Houston Post* News Clippings, box 130, SJRAR; "Seven Coves: The Ultimate in Living" and "Come to Walden on Lake Conroe: Discover Life with Nature," both in Lake Conroe Vertical File, HMRC.

110. April Sound advertisement, *CC*, May 26, 1974; *CC*, July 14, 1971.

111. *CC*, November 6, 1968.

112. Folder Recreation, box 406, SJRAR; McClendon, "The San Jacinto River Conservation & Reclamation District's Proposed Plan," 5; SJRA, *Master Plan*, 15.

113. Lynn Coker to Fred Hofheinz and J. Bryan Stratton, February 22, 1974, folder Recreation—FM 830, and J. Bryan Stratton to Lynn Coker, March 28, 1974, folder Recreation, both in box 406, SJRAR; Houston and SJRA Contract, 1969, sec. 1.05, box 260, SJRAR.

114. *CC*, February 27, 1974, folder Newspaper Clippings—*Conroe Courier*, box 130, SJRAR. The SJRA's condemnation power did not extend to parkland until 1967. Acts 1967, 60th R.S., chap. 547, GSLT, box 536, SJRAR; *CC*, March 13, 1975, folder Newspaper Clippings—*Baytown Sun*, box 130, SJRAR (first quotation); C. W. Curry to W. B. Weisinger, March 14, 1972, in folder W. B. Weisinger & W. D. McAdams, box 404, SJRAR; J. Bryan Stratton to Judge Coker, March 28, 1974, folder Recreation, box 409, SJRAR; W. B. Weisinger, speech notes, folder Groundbreaking Ceremony, Lake Conroe, 11-10-69, box 405, SJRAR (second quotation).

115. The SJRA would eventually offer the county a lease on three acres. SJRA Board Meeting Minutes, May 28, 1974, and Jay Bertrand to J. Bryan Stratton, April 25, 1974, folder Directors Meetings—Minutes September 1973–August 1974, box 39, SJRAR; J. Bryan Stratton to Lynn Coker, March 28, 1974, folder Recreation, box 406, SJRAR; Meeting Minutes, SJRA Board of Directors, February 26, 1974, box 39, SJRAR; "J. B. Stratton to Head River Authority," *HP*, June 27, 1973, folder *Houston Post* News Clippings, box 130, SJRAR.

116. *CC*, March 29, 1974, folder Newspaper Clippings—*Conroe Courier*, box 130, SJRAR.

117. The Forest Service had originally planned to develop ten recreational areas on the

lake totaling over a thousand acres. The seventy-three-acre Scott's Run site was all the Forest Service would develop for the first decade. *CC*, August 13, 1974, folder Newspaper Clippings—*Baytown Sun*, box 130, SJRAR; September 1974, CCR.

118. *CC*, May 7, 1974, folder Recreation—FM 830, box 406, SJRAR.

119. There were five publicly accessible boat ramps open by April 1976. At least two of these opened even as the lake was filling. *CC*, October 21, 1976, folder Newspaper Clippings—*Conroe Courier*, box 130, SJRAR; *CC*, April 25, 1976.

120. Monica Reeves, "Confusion Allows Lake Conroe to Be a Spa of Wealthy," *HP*, July 11, 1974, folder Newspaper Clippings, *Houston Post*, box 130, SJRAR.

Chapter 4. Settling the Forest

1. History Book Committee, Montgomery County Historical Society, *Montgomery County History* (Winston-Salem, N.C.: Hunter Publishing Company, 1980), 276.

2. On suburban frontiers, see Joel Garreau, *Edge City: Life on the New Frontier* (New York: Doubleday, 1991); Kenneth J. Jackson, *Crabgrass Frontier: The Suburbanization of the United States* (New York: Oxford University Press, 1985); Dolores Hayden, *Building Suburbia: Green Fields and Urban Growth, 1820–2000* (New York: Vintage Books, 2003); History Book Committee, *Montgomery County History*, 344–45, 360–61, 370–71, 391, 402–3, 460, 469, 476–77, 551–52, 560, 562–63. The most prominent exceptions to this are Herbert J. Gans, *The Levittowners: Ways of Life and Politics in a New Suburban Community* (New York: Pantheon Books, 1967); Jon C. Teaford, *Post-suburbia: Government and Politics in the Edge Cities* (Baltimore, Md.: Johns Hopkins University Press, 1997); and Paul H. Mattingly, *Suburban Landscapes: Culture and Politics in a New York Metropolitan Community* (Baltimore, Md.: Johns Hopkins University Press, 2001).

3. Jackson, *Crabgrass Frontier*; Kevin M. Kruse, *White Flight: Atlanta and the Making of Modern Conservatism* (Princeton, N.J.: Princeton University Press, 2005); Matthew D. Lassiter, *The Silent Majority: Suburban Politics in the Sunbelt South* (Princeton, N.J.: Princeton University Press, 2006); and Thomas J. Sugrue, *The Origins of the Urban Crisis: Race and Inequality in Postwar Detroit* (Princeton, N.J.: Princeton University Press, 1996).

4. Adam Rome, *The Bulldozer in the Countryside: Suburban Sprawl and the Rise of American Environmentalism* (New York: Cambridge University Press, 2001); Christopher C. Sellers, *Crabgrass Crucible: Suburban Nature and the Rise of Environmentalism in Twentieth-Century America* (Chapel Hill: University of North Carolina Press, 2012).

5. *WV*, January 17, 1979.

6. Robert S. Maxwell and Robert D. Baker, *Sawdust Empire: The Texas Lumber Industry, 1830–1940* (College Station: Texas A&M University Press, 1983); Thomas D. Clark, *The Greening of the South: The Recovery of Land and Forest* (Lexington: University Press of Kentucky, 1984); and William T. Chambers, "Pine Woods Region of Southeastern Texas," *Economic Geography* 10, no. 3 (1934): 302–18, 302; Dwight W. Fate, *A Report on Forest Resources and Wood Industries of Montgomery County Texas* (Conroe: Texas Forest Service, October 1961).

7. Gary Haarala, *Changing Land Use* (Conroe: Texas Forest Service, 1964), 3, cited in Leon Charles Hallman, "A Geographic Study of Montgomery County, Texas" (M.A. thesis, Southern Methodist University, 1965), 117. Monetary inflation accounted for only thirty to forty dollars of this increase.

8. *CC*, May 13, 1964; Kay Mayer Dawes and Barbara Lee Hamilton, *The Rise and Fall*

of Fostoria (New Caney: East Montgomery County Historical Society, 2011), 3; and *CC*, February 14, 1968; *CC*, June 27, 1972; *CC*, June 3, 1957. Determining the actual number of subdivisions is difficult. The county did not require developers to submit subdivision plats for approval until January 1961. Even then, many developers chose not to comply. The county's later attempts to enumerate these unrecorded developments suggest that as large a proportion went unrecorded as were recorded during the early 1960s; "Rules, Regulations and Requirements Relating to the Approval and Acceptance of Subdivision Plats for Recording," February 13, 1961, CCR.

9. *CC*, June 9, 1965; Jesse L. Buffington, "A Study of the Economic Impact of Interstate Highway 45 on Conroe, Texas," Research Report No. 4-11, Texas Transportation Institute, Austin, August 1967, HMRC; This figure does not include subdivisions within Conroe's city limits, unfiled subdivisions, or subdivisions whose roads would be owned by the county. Resolution, June 4, 1965, CCR; Carson Earl Watt, "Suburban Recreation Subdivisions in Montgomery County, Texas—a Case Study Analysis" (M.S. thesis, Texas A&M University, May 1969), 84; History Book Committee, *Montgomery County History*, 3; Richard L. Forstall, ed., *Population of States and Counties of the United States: 1790–1990* (Washington, D.C.: GPO, March 1996), 3:166.

10. *CC*, June 11, 1972; Martin Dreyer, "The Exodus to Montgomery County," *HC: Texas Sunday Magazine*, June 15, 1969; and *CC*, August 30, 1964 (quotation).

11. "Conroe: Texas' Most Beautiful City for Family Living," *HC*, April 5, 1964; Virgil W. Cobb to SJRA, [Spring 1964], folder Houston Chronicle (Mr. V. Cobb), box 130, SJRAR (quotations).

12. "Leisure Land Supermarket," *Texas Parade* 31, no. 3 (1970): 31–38 (quotation). A 1967 study found that of the 132 subdivisions with recorded plats in the county up to that point, 53 percent had designated park areas and/or lakes or ponds. An additional 9 percent bordered major recreational areas such as the national forest, the state forest, or the future Lake Conroe. Watt, "Suburban Recreation Subdivisions," 31. The county contained 144 lakes larger than five acres as early as 1969. "District Program and Work Plan, 1969," 26; and Elmer Summers, "Land of Lakes," *HC Magazine*, September 7, 1958, folder City of Ho. from W. B. Weisinger, box 130, SJRAR; *CC*, September 6, 1964.

13. "Conroe: Texas' Most Beautiful City"; "Arrowhead Lakes," *HC*, special insert, April 5, 1964.

14. *CC*, September 9, 1954; Roger Galatas and Jim Barlow, *The Woodlands: The Inside Story of Creating a Better Hometown* (Washington, D.C.: Urban Land Institute, 2004), 146.

15. Grand Jury, Criminal Minutes, Ninth District Court, 7:3, 18–21, 74–75, 117; *CC*, March 13, 1957; *CC*, May 21, 1969; *CC*, April 1, 1970; *CC*, April 10, 1973. On accusations of corruption, see *CC*, February 19, 1957; Texas v. T. J. Peel, October 11, 1958, Criminal Docket No. 9616, Ninth District Court; *CC*, April 26, 1970; Monica Reeves and John Standefer, "County Allegedly Helped Build Marina," *HP*, January 8, 1974; and Cathy Gordon, "FBI Tests Indicate Link in Cut Marks on Tires," *HC*, September 4, 1986.

16. On the powers of county government, see David B. Brooks, *County and Special District Law*, vol. 35, *Texas Practice*, 2nd ed. (St. Paul: Thompson West Law, 2002), secs. 1, 5.

17. On subdivision regulation, see Brooks, *County and Special District Law*, vol. 36a, *Texas Practice*, sec. 43; on roads, see Acts 1957, 55th R.S., chap. 436, GSLT.

18. Only counties with populations over three hundred thousand could purchase landfill sites before 1969. Acts 1955, 54th R.S., chap. 464, GSLT; and Acts 1969, 61st R.S., chap. 405, GSLT. While counties had long possessed the power to address health and sanitation

issues, specific power to clean up litter did not come until 1973. Brooks, *County and Special District Law*, vol. 36, *Texas Practice*, sec. 32; and Acts 1981, 67th R.S., chap. 741, GSLT. On Montgomery County's garbage crisis, see *CC*, April 21, 1965; *CC*, February 25, 1970. On the county's dumps, see *CC*, September 16, 1976; *CC*, September 14, 1976 (quotation).

19. J. C. Davis Jr., "Legal Aspects of the County Commissioners Court," speech before the County Judges and Commissioners Conference, College Station, Tex., February 25, 1959, in folder Speeches by J. C. Davis Jr., box 2004/082-1, AGR; Acts 1957, 55th R.S., chap. 436, GSLT; "Rules, Regulations and Requirements"; Resolution, July 16, 1963, CCR; Resolution, August 1, 1966, CCR; Subdivision Rules and Regulations, April 17, 1967, CCM 18:151–59. Developers could still avoid these regulations by selling their property by metes and bounds rather than subdividing it; April 1, 1971, CCM, 20:155–60.

20. For examples of such complaints, see May 1974, CCM, 22:348; August 6, 1979, CCM, 29:283; May 12, 1980, CCM, 31:198–99; January 4, 1974, CCM, 23:1; letter to County Commissioners, undated [April 1973], CCR (quotation); Melinda Reeves Cagle, ed., *History of Montgomery County, Texas—Volume II* (Baltimore, Md.: Otter Bay Books, 2012), 227–28.

21. *CC*, July 23, 1976. On racketeering, see Audit Report 78-33, Criminal Task Force for Organized Crime, Criminal Justice Division, Office of the Governor, May 15, 1978, box 1991/113-8, AGR. On narcotics, see Gene Reaves to County Commissioners Court, February 8, 1973, CCR. Narcotics crimes dominated the docket of the Ninth District Court during the 1970s. Grand Jury, Criminal Minutes, Ninth District Court, vol. 7, passim; *CC*, March 4, 1980, folder Flood Control 1979–80, box 392, SJRAR. On fire departments, see Jorjanna Price, "Woodlands Planned for 150,000 People in 20 Years," *HP*, December 21, 1972; and *CC*, July 10, 1974.

22. "Montgomery-Walker Soil and Water Conservation District #425: Program and Plan" (1990), Walker County SWCD; and Wendell Daniel, interview by the author, July 31, 2012, Conroe, Tex.; Glen Chervenka and Wendell Daniel, *Supplement to the Soil Survey of Montgomery County, Texas* (Washington, D.C.: GPO, 1983); Marion R. Scalf, Willam J. Dunlap, and James F. Kreissl, *Environmental Effects of Septic Tank Systems* (Ada: Environmental Protection Agency, 1977).

23. *CC*, April 27, 1973, folder News Clippings—*Conroe Courier*, box 130, SJRAR; *CC*, January 14, 1973; CCM, 22:255; *CC*, September 28, 1973, folder News Clippings—*Conroe Courier*, box 130, SJRAR; Rome, *Bulldozer in the Countryside*, 87–118; William R. McClintock, *Soil Survey: Montgomery County, Texas* (Washington, D.C.: Soil Conservation Service, 1972).

24. History Book Committee, *Montgomery County History*, 430–31. For more on the 1940 flood and later flooding data, see Corps of Engineers, Galveston District, *San Jacinto River and Tributaries, Texas Reconnaissance Report on Flood Problem at Whispering Oaks Subdivision Montgomery County, Texas*, May 1981, folder Flood Control, SJRAR, 4. On the county's climate, see *Supplement to the Soil Survey*, table 2; Jonathan Burnett, *Flash Floods in Texas* (College Station: Texas A&M University Press, 2008), 286; Martin V. Melosi, "Houston's Public Sinks: Sanitary Services from Local Concerns to Regional Challenges," in *Energy Metropolis: An Environmental History of Houston and the Gulf Coast*, ed. Martin V. Melosi and Joseph A. Pratt (Pittsburgh: University of Pittsburgh Press, 2007), 118–19, 135–36; and Adine Lundgren, "Developer Promotions under Investigation," *HP*, April 8, 1973, folder Newspaper Clippings—*Baytown Sun*, box 130, SJRA.

25. *CC*, October 3, 1965; *CC*, November 14, 1965; and Texas et al. v. O. J. McCullough, October 25, 1965, Civil Docket No. 22,788, Ninth District Court.

26. Lundgren, "Developer Promotions"; *CC*, February 18, 1973 (quotation); Ike Barrett, interview by the author, July 11, 2012, Dobbin, Tex.; *CC*, January 27, 1965. Montgomery County was not alone in its lack of floodplain regulations. As late as 1970, less than a sixth of local governments across the nation had adopted any such regulation. Rome, *Bulldozer in the Countryside*, 180.

27. *CC*, May 15, 1966; *CC*, May 19, 1968; "River Floods 100 Homes in Conroe," *HC*, June 26, 1968; and *CC*, June 26, 1968, in folder Lake Conroe—San Jacinto River Authority, box 130, SJRAR. The 1973 evacuation figure includes only those from the Peach and Caney Creek watersheds. The damage estimate does not include damage to agricultural and oil and gas properties. "Application for Assistance in Planning and Carrying Out Works of Improvement under the Watershed Protection and Flood Prevention Act," April 29, 1974, CCM, 22:426–36, esp. 430–31; *CC*, June 20, 1973. The June 1973 flood led to most of metropolitan Houston being declared a national disaster area. Texas Department of Water Resources, *Water for Texas: A Comprehensive Plan for the Future* (Austin: Texas Department of Water Resources, November 1984), 2:III-10-5.

28. The state was one of the nine in the nation that had no laws to control such development. Lundgren, "Developer Promotions"; *CC*, January 14, 1973; *CC*, February 18, 1973; *CC*, May 19, 1968 (quotation from *Courier* paraphrase).

29. The SJRA master plan included flood control as one of its primary charges. Acts 1937, 45th R.S., chap. 426, GSLT; Acts 1967, 60th R.S., chap. 547, GSLT; SJRA, *Master Plan: Report for the Full Scale Development of the San Jacinto River* (Conroe: SJRA, 1951), 16–17, box 398, SJRAR. On Houston's lack of interest in flood control, see Freese, Nichols, and Endress Engineers to E. B. Cape, September 18, 1967, in folder Cape, E. B. (Director Public Wks.), box 405, SJRAR; and "Memo Re. City of Houston Letter," August 29, 1967, folder Mayor—City of Houston 1965, box 406, SJRAR; Ike Barrett, interview by the author, November 11, 2010, Dobbin, Tex.; Terry Wilt, "Conroe Dam Didn't Cause Flooding, Says SJRA," *Humble News-Messenger*, May 13, 1979, folder Flooding, Conroe, 1979 (April), box 260, SJRAR; *CC*, May 6, 1980, folder Flood Control 1979–80, box 392, SJRAR; *CC*, March 29, 1973.

30. April 29, 1974, CCM, 22:348; Complaint of Freeway Forest Subdivision Residents, November 8, 1971, CCR (first quotation); HGAC, *Environmental Deficiencies of the Region's Living Areas: A Diagnostic Survey* (Houston: HGAC, 1969), 42 (second quotation); and HGAC, *Subdivision Regulations, Houston-Galveston Area* (Houston: HGAC, 1970).

31. Sellers, *Crabgrass Crucible*, esp. 105–36; and Rome, *Bulldozer in the Countryside*, esp. 87–152, 173–81. On Houston's environmental movement, see Teresa Tomkins-Walsh, "'A Concrete River Had to Be Wrong': Environmental Action on Houston's Bayous, 1935–1980" (Ph.D. diss., University of Houston, 2009); *CC*, April 22, 1970; History Book Committee, *Montgomery County History*, 151–52; February 19, 1974, CCM, 22:88; *CC*, January 24, 1975; "Peach Creek Forest Residents Complain," September 1976, CCR; *CC*, February 3, 1971; *CC*, June 9, 1973; *CC*, April 21, 1971.

32. Resolution, January 12, 1970, CCR (first and second quotations); and Commissioners of Montgomery County, Tex., "Take a Step in the Effort to Control Pollution," *Congressional Record*, January 28, 1970, vol. 116, pt. 2:1597–98; *CC*, special insert, January 25, 1970 (third quotation).

33. "An Order Dividing Montgomery County, Texas, into Four County Commissioners Precincts," August 4, 1969, CCR; George Wood, political ad, *CC*, May 5, 1972; *CC*, May 7, 1974; *CC*, May 10, 1978 (quotations); *CC*, May 5, 1972.

34. *CC*, May 10, 1978.

35. *CC*, November 1, 1970. In 1973, for instance, twenty-three land-use bills were active in the legislature. None made it through. Intergovernmental Affairs Committee, Texas House of Representatives, *Texas Land Resources: Problems and Possibilities*, 64th Texas Legislature, 3, 13, 34, 57, 60, 92–93, box 19, Citizens Environmental Coalition Collection, HMRC; Texas Water Code sec. 16.313, subchap. 1. On federal legislation, see FEMA, *Questions and Answers: On the National Flood Insurance Program*, FIA-2 (Washington, D.C.: GPO, February 1983), 1–2; Resolution, June 29, 1973, CCM, 21:693–96, and Resolution, April 3, 1978, CCM 27:29–30; *CC*, n.d., folder Flood Control 1979–80, box 392, SJRAR; U.S. Senate, Committee on Appropriations, Subcommittee on HUD—Independent Agencies, *Federal Flood Insurance Program* (Washington, D.C.: GPO, 1981), 9–16, 94; Scott Gabriel Knowles and Howard C. Kunreuther, "Troubled Waters: The National Flood Insurance Program in Historical Perspective," *Journal of Policy History* 26, no. 3 (2014): 327–53.

36. Resolution, October 1971, CCM, 20:478–90. An outgoing commissioner would later publicly condemn the health department for failing to enforce these regulations. *CC*, January 2, 1975; *CC*, September 21, 1973.

37. Attorney General John L. Hill was a driving force in the 1973 passage of the Texas Deceptive Trade Practices—Consumer Protection Act (H.B. 417). Joe K. Longley, "Consumer Protection Report"; Longley to John L. Hill, February 7, 1973; and Adelaide C. O'Brien, "The Effects of the Texas Deceptive Trade Practices—Consumer Protection Act," ca. 1974, all in folder Consumer Protection, box 1991/113-4, AGR; *CC*, April 23, 1973; *CC*, April 25, 1974.

38. *CC*, October 13, 1974, and *CC*, [October] 16, 1974, both in folder Newspaper Clippings—*Baytown Sun*, box 130, SJRAR; *Rules and Regulations: Montgomery County Health and Sanitation District*, November 4, 1974, CCR. The board of health fleshed out these regulations in May 1979. Resolution, May 21, 1979, CCM, 28:818–64; *CC*, May 11, 1978.

39. Virginia Marion Perrenod, *Special Districts, Special Purposes: Fringe Governments and Urban Problems in the Houston Area* (College Station: Texas A&M University Press, 1984); *CC*, February 24, 1973; Resolution, January 1974, CCR. On special districts in Harris County, see Melosi, "Houston's Public Sinks," 130, 134–43. The number of these districts nationwide (excluding schools) rose from 17,323 in 1962 to 27,733 in 1982. John Herbers, *The New Heartland: America's Flight beyond the Suburbs and How It Is Changing Our Future* (New York: Times Books, 1986), 171–84; and Joel Garreau, *Edge Cities: Life on the New Frontier* (New York: Doubleday, 1991), 179–208; *CC*, January 22, 1975.

40. Jackson, *Crabgrass Frontier*, 138–56; Acts 1963, 58th R.S., chap. 160, art. 970a, GSLT; Eugene Maier to Mayor Lewis Cutrer, April 27, 1961, folder 4, box 1, Lewis and Catherine Cutrer Collection, HMRC. Houston more than doubled its size through annexation in both 1948 and 1956. It continued to expand into the 1970s. David G. McComb, *Houston: A History*, rev. ed. (Austin: University of Texas Press, 1981), 139–41; and *CC*, August 22, 1965. Oak Ridge North, Whispering Oaks, Shenandoah, Chateau Woods, Woodbranch Village, Panorama Village, Porter Heights, Chapel Lakes, Splendora, Patton Village, and Stagecoach Farms all incorporated during this period. Three other developments had their incorporation attempts voted down. August 1966, December 1966, April 1969, June 1972, May 1973, June 1973, October 1973, March 1974, June 1974, December 1975, August 1977, and February 1979, all in CCR and April 7, 1980, CCM, 30:745; *CC*, February 9, 1973.

41. History Book Committee, *Montgomery County History*, 54; and "Historical Background & Environmental Setting, Oak Ridge North, Texas," folder City History, ORN Records; *CC*, June 16, 1968 (first quotation); *CC*, November 22, 1964; and *CC*, February 18,

1968 (third quotation); Gary Louie, interview by author, November 9, 2012, Spring, Tex.; Jerry Bradford, phone interview by the author, November 5, 2012; and John Planchard, interview by the author, October 29, 2012, Conroe, Tex. (second quotation); *CC*, September 16, 1970; and *CC*, August 25, 1972.

42. *CC*, March 14, 1974; and *CC*, February 13, 1974, both in folder Newspaper Clippings—*Conroe Courier*, box 130, SJRAR; election returns, March 16, 1974, CCR; Gary Louie interview; and Planchard interview.

43. *CC*, April 28, 1974; Mike Bryan, *CC*, May 19, 1974 (quotation); and *CC*, June 30, 1974.

44. Election returns, January 20, 1979, CCR; incorporation map, February 6, 1979; and election return, August 11, 1979, both in folder Incorporation: Town of Oak Ridge North, ORN Records; Ordinance 001-79, Ordinance 014-79, and Ordinance 10-80, in box Ordinances and City Council Minutes, ORN Records; October 25, 1979, folder City Council Minutes, ORN Records; *CC*, January 25, 1980, folder Flood Control 1979–80, box 392, SJRAR.

45. "Whispering Oaks Residents Complain about Flood Waters," December 1976, CCM, 25:116; *CC*, February 27, 1975, folder Lake Conroe—San Jacinto River Authority, box 130, SJRAR; Corps of Engineers, Galveston District, *San Jacinto River and Tributaries*, 5; May 16 and May 26, 1972, CCM, 20:894, 897; *CC*, April 20, 1979, folder Flooding, Conroe, 1979 (April), box 260, SJRAR (first quotation); April 16, 1973, CCM, 21:615; *CC*, April 18, 1973 (second quotation).

46. Jeanne Zuber to K. C. Phillips, September 5, 1972, folder Montgomery County, box 406, SJRAR; *CC*, September 28, 1973; election return, October 1, 1973, CCR; *CC*, October 2, 1973, folder Newspaper Clippings—*Conroe Courier*, box 130, SJRAR; *CC*, April 3, 1974; *CC*, June 27, 1974; December 13, 1976, CCM, 25:116; "Whispering Oaks Gets OK for Waste Treatment Permit," *HP*, July 26, 1974, folder Newspaper Clippings—*Houston Post*, box 130, SJRAR; *CC*, February 16, 1975; April 1976, CCR; *CC*, June 4, 1976; FEMA, *Flood Insurance Study: Montgomery County, Texas, Unincorporated Areas*, vol. 1 (Washington, D.C.: GPO, 1984).

47. The remaining homes were within the one-hundred-year floodplain, which left them vulnerable, but not enough to justify the expense of a buyout. *CC*, [1980], folder Flood Control 1979–80, box 392, SJRAR; *CC*, December 21, 1979; and December 10, 1979, CCM, 30:114–16.

48. Galatas and Barlow, *The Woodlands*, 33–34; George Mitchell, interview; Joseph W. Kutchin, *How Mitchell Energy & Development Corp. Got Its Start and How It Grew: An Oral History and Narrative Overview* (The Woodlands: Mitchell Energy & Development Corp., 1998), 207, 231 (first quotation); and Juren Schmandt, *George Mitchell and the Idea of Sustainability* (College Station: Texas A&M University Press, 2010), 1–10; The Woodlands ad, *HP*, October 13, 1974; *CC*, May 26, 1974 (second quotation).

49. Ian McHarg, *Design with Nature* (Garden City: Natural History Press, 1969; repr., New York: John Wiley & Sons, 1992); McHarg and Frederick R. Steiner, eds., *To Heal the Earth: Selected Writings of Ian L. McHarg* (Washington, D.C.: Island Press, 1998); and McHarg, *A Quest for Life: An Autobiography* (New York: John Wiley & Sons, 1996); WMRT, "Woodlands New Community: An Ecological Plan," 29–30; WMRT, "Woodlands New Community: An Ecological Inventory."

50. Morris Straughn, interview by the author, July 31, 2012, Conroe, Tex.; Kutchin, *How Mitchell Energy*, 61 (first quotation); Constance Holden, "Ian McHarg: Champion for De-

sign with Nature," *Science*, n.s. 195, no. 4,276 (1977): 380; McHarg, Johnson, and Berger, "A Case Study in Ecological Planning," in *To Heal the Earth*, 242–63, 264 (second quotation).

51. WMRT, "Woodlands New Community: An Ecological Plan," 27 (first and second quotations); David Hendricks, email correspondence with the author, November 21, 2012; Kutchin, *How Mitchell Energy*, 17; Ann Forsyth, *Reforming Suburbia: The Planned Communities of Irvine, Columbia, and The Woodlands* (Berkeley: University of California Press, 2005), 186; Dudley Lynch, "The Woodlands Gets Down to Business," *Texas Parade* 37, no. 3 (1976): 44 (third quotation); David Hendricks, lecture at Rice University, November 20, 2012, Houston, Tex. (fourth quotation).

52. Perrenod, *Special Districts*, 35–38. The Woodlands' reputation as an alternative to suburban sprawl has faced criticism for the limits of its ecological approach. Russell Claus, "The Woodlands, Texas: A Retrospective Critique of the Principles and Implementation of an Ecologically Planned Development" (M.S. thesis, Massachusetts Institute of Technology, 1994); and Forsyth, *Reforming Suburbia*; Gary Louie interview.

53. *CC*, June 13, 1980; and *CC*, June 14, 1980.

Chapter 5. Enshrining the Countryside

1. *LTM*, January 30, 1958.

2. Ibid.

3. Adam Rome, *The Bulldozer in the Countryside: Suburban Sprawl and the Rise of American Environmentalism* (New York: Cambridge University Press, 2001); Christopher C. Sellers, *Crabgrass Crucible: Suburban Nature and the Rise of Environmentalism in Twentieth-Century America* (Chapel Hill: University of North Carolina Press, 2012); Hal K. Rothman, *Saving the Planet: The American Response to the Environment in the Twentieth Century* (Chicago: Ivan R. Dee, 2000).

4. Here I join those emphasizing the diversity of environmental activism, yet where others work to expand the term to be more inclusive, I question its usefulness in understanding activism on the gentrified metropolitan fringe. On the breadth of environmental activism, see Adam Rome, *The Genius of Earth Day: How a 1970 Teach-In Unexpectedly Made the First Green Generation* (New York: Hill and Wang, 2013), 9–56; Andrew Hurley, *Environmental Inequalities: Class, Race, and Industrial Pollution in Gary, Indiana, 1945–1980* (Chapel Hill: University of North Carolina Press, 1995); Robert Gottlieb, *Forcing the Spring: The Transformation of the American Environmental Movement*, rev. ed. (Washington, D.C.: Island Press, 2005); Chad Montrie, *A People's History of Environmentalism in the United States* (New York: Continuum, 2011); Brian Allen Drake, *Loving Nature, Fearing the State: Environmentalism and Antigovernment Politics before Reagan* (Seattle: University of Washington Press, 2013); and Chris Wilhelm, "Conservatives in the Everglades: Sun Belt Environmentalism and the Creation of Everglades National Park," *Journal of Southern History* 82, no. 4 (2016): 823–54.

5. This chapter builds on the work of Angela C. Halfacre, who uses the concept of conservation culture to describe a commitment to protecting land, wildlife, and cultural heritage from unregulated development. Where Halfacre uses the term *conservation culture* to emphasize the role played by sportsmen-landowners, I employ *preservation culture* to better capture the role played by Loudoun's historical preservationists and garden clubs. Halfacre, *A Delicate Balance: Constructing a Conservation Culture in the South Carolina Lowcountry* (Columbia: University of South Carolina Press, 2012). See also T. Robert Hart, "The Lowcountry Landscape: Politics, Preservation, and the Santee-Cooper Project," *Environmental*

History 18, no. 1 (2013); and Craig E. Colten, "Contesting Pollution in Dixie: The Case of Corney Creek," *Journal of Southern History* 72, no. 3 (2006): 605–34.

6. This chapter uses the term *Western Loudoun* to demarcate a spatially articulated identity and preservation culture that united those in the county fighting against sprawl and for environmental, historical, and farmland preservation.

7. Michael Kammen, *Mystic Chords of Memory: The Transformation of Tradition in American Culture* (New York: Alfred A. Knopf, 1991), 537–70; David Hamer, *History in Urban Places: The Historic Districts of the United States* (Columbus: Ohio State University Press, 1998), 123–32; and Mitchell Schwarzer, "Myths of Permanence and Transience in the Discourse on Historic Preservation in the United States," *Journal of Architectural Education* 48, no. 1 (1994): 2–11. On the theory of place, see Yi-Fu Tuan, "Community, Society, and the Individual," *Geographical Review* 92, no. 3 (2002): 307–18; and E. Relph, *Place and Placelessness* (London: Pion Limited, 1976), 141 (quotation); Thomas R. Dunlap, *Faith in Nature: Environmentalism as Religious Quest* (Seattle: University of Washington Press, 2004).

8. Joe Goddard, *Being American on the Edge: Penurbia and the Metropolitan Mind, 1945–2010* (New York: Palgrave Macmillan, 2012); and James S. Duncan and Nancy G. Duncan, *Landscapes of Privilege: The Politics of the Aesthetic in an American Suburb* (New York: Routledge, 2004).

9. This elitism was a favorite target of contemporary antienvironmentalism. Aaron Wildavsky, "Aesthetic Power or the Triumph of the Sensitive Minority over the Vulgar Mass," in *America's Changing Environment*, ed. Roger Revelle and Hans H. Landsberg (Boston: Houghton Mifflin Co., 1970); William Tucker, *Progress and Privilege: America in the Age of Environmentalism* (Garden City: Anchor Press / Doubleday, 1982); and Bernard J. Frieden, *The Environmental Protection Hustle* (Cambridge, Mass.: MIT Press, 1979).

10. Kammen, *Mystic Chords of Memory*, 618–54; and Hamer, *History in Urban Places*; Alice M. Bowsher, William T. Frazier, and Jerome R. Saroff, *Virginia Historic Districts Study* (Charlottesville: University of Virginia School of Architecture, August 1975), 43–44.

11. John G. Lewis, *Ladies, Liquor, & Laughter: Mischief of an Architectural Historian, 1930s–70s, Loudoun County, Virginia* (Taylorstown: Friends of Catoctin Creek, 2007), 26; John G. Lewis, "Architectural Survey of the Older and Historic Structure in the Town of Hillsboro, Virginia," ca. 1977, 5 (quotation), in Notebooks of John G. Lewis on Areas of Loudoun County: Aldie, Catoctin & Goose Creek, Hillsboro, Lincoln & Loudoun Settlements, and Middleburg, TBL.

12. Designation as a historic district promised rapid appreciation of property values. In Georgetown, Washington's historic enclave, row houses within the historic district sold for as much as three times the average price of a similar house outside the district. John B. Rackham, "Values of Residential Properties in Urban Historic Districts: Georgetown, Washington D.C. and Other Selected Districts," *Information Sheet* 15 (Washington, D.C.: Preservation Press, 1977), 7; Colonial Leesburg, Inc., Collection, TBL; Agnes Grant and Burr Powell Harrison, interview by Eugene M. Scheel, January 17, 1992, Leesburg, Va., 12–15, in folder 1, box 2, LCOHP; and Frank Raflo, *Within the Iron Gates: Loudoun Stories Remembered* (Dulles: TechniGraphix, 1998), 237–41; Shirley Mastria, "Tourism in Leesburg, Virginia," manuscript, TBL (quotation).

13. PSLC Collection, 1973–2003, TBL; and Loudoun Preservation Society, www.preserveloudoun.org/about/index.html, accessed March 27, 2014 (first and second quotations).

14. Robert and Ruth Boley, interview by Janney Wilson, August 26, 1998, folder 2, box 1,

TBLOHP; and Robert R. Lind, Karen T. Richardson, and Donald G. Rypka Jr., *Loudoun Harvest—Faces and Places, Past and Present, in Loudoun County, Virginia* (Leesburg: Carr Printing and Publishing Company, 1973), 44–46.

15. By 1984 the county had nine districts, fourteen buildings, and three bridges registered as Virginia Historic Landmarks. Calder Loth, ed., *The Virginia Landmarks Register*, 3rd ed. (Charlottesville: University Press of Virginia, 1987), 238–47; and Lewis to Members of the Loudoun County Scenic Rivers Committee and the Goose Creek–Catoctin Creek Task Force, March 4, 1977, in Lewis, "Goose Creek and Catoctin Creek: History and Preservation," March 4, 1977,5, in Notebooks of John G. Lewis.

16. Owners of nearly 98 percent of the land and 182 of the 208 landowners within the historic district supported the move. *LTM,* February 17, 1983; "Goose Creek Gets Historical Designation," *WP,* February 9, 1977; and Wilson Morris, "Old Va. Quaker Settlement Defended," *WP,* October 17, 1976.

17. Lewis, "Goose Creek Historical Preservation Area District: A Brief History," n.d., 8, in Notebooks of John G. Lewis.

18. Becky Nicolaides, "How Hell Moved from the City to the Suburbs," in *The New Suburban History,* ed. Kevin M. Kruse and Thomas J. Sugrue (Chicago: University of Chicago Press, 2006), 80–98.

19. M. T. Broyhill & Sons Corp., *Sterling Park: A Community with Room to Grow* (self-published, n.d.), Sterling Park, Virginia, Collection, TBL; Andrew Wiese, "'The Giddy Rise of the Environmentalists': Corporate Real Estate Development and Environmental Politics in San Diego, California, 1968–73," *Environmental History* 19, no. 1 (2014): 31–34.

20. Helen Dewar, "Levitt Plans Development near Dulles," *WP,* January 23, 1969; and Raflo, *Iron Gates,* 222–24 (quotations).

21. This per-capita debt figure does not include the cost of roads or water and sewer extensions. B. Powell Harrison to the Virginia Advisory Legislative Council Committee for the Study of Land Use Policies, December 2, 1972, ASSSC.

22. *LTM,* January 6, 1972.

23. Raflo, *Iron Gates,* 222–25 (quotations); *LTM,* January 6, 1972. Loudoun modeled its zoning moratorium after similar efforts in neighboring Fairfax County. Russ Banham, *The Fight for Fairfax: A Struggle for a Great American County* (Fairfax: George Mason University Press, 2009), 71–77, 103–22. In contrast with Levitt, the Sugarland development, a project of the Boise Cascade company, gained county approval because it preserved a fifth of the land in open space and did not share the Levitt name. The first homes there opened in January 1971. *LTM,* September 24, 1970.

24. Colonial Leesburg, Inc., *Opportunity, Leesburg, and You* (self-published, May 1949), in folder 1, Colonial Leesburg, Inc. Records, TBL; A. G. and B. P. Harrison interview, 19 (first quotation); B. Powell Harrison, *Protecting Virginia's Piedmont* (Leesburg: Piedmont Press & Graphics, 1994), 3 (second quotation); Philip Ehrenkrantz, interview by the author, March 14, 2013, Taylorstown, Va.; and John F. Harris, "The Harrisons of Loudoun: 40 Years of Activism, and Still Fighting," *WP,* August 16, 1987.

25. William H. Whyte Jr., "A Plan to Save Vanishing U.S. Countryside," *Life,* August 17, 1959, 88; and Margo Tupper, *No Place to Play* (Philadelphia: Chilton Books, 1966); *Beauty for America: Proceedings* (Washington, D.C.: GPO, 1965). The first interpretation is Rome, *Bulldozer in the Countryside,* 119–52. The second is Sellers, *Crabgrass Crucible,* 243–84. For an example, compare the conservation-oriented *Virginia's Common Wealth* (Virginia Outdoor Recreation Study Commission, 1965) with the environmentalist language of *The Vir-*

ginia Outdoors Plan, 1970, vol. 4 (Commission of Outdoor Recreation, Commonwealth of Virginia, May 1970).

26. Margaret T. Peters, *Conserving the Commonwealth: The Early Years of the Environmental Movement in Virginia* (Charlottesville: University of Virginia Press, 2008), 9–59; and *Virginia's Common Wealth.*

27. Harrison, *Protecting Virginia's Piedmont,* 4–6; A. G. and B. P. Harrison interview, 19; Raflo, *Iron Gates,* 242; and *LTM,* January 13, 1972.

28. Jeremy Burchardt, *Paradise Lost: Rural Idyll and Social Change in England since 1800* (New York: I. B. Tauris Publishers, 2002), 156–67, 162 (quotation). See also David Matless, *Landscape and Englishness* (London: Reaktion Books, 1998), 215–24.

29. The Dillon Rule remained in force because state business interests preferred to focus their lobbying efforts in Richmond rather than having to invest resources in shaping policy decisions at the county and municipal levels. Dennis Montgomery, "The Dillon Dilemma," *Virginia Business,* December 1992, 53–58; and Stanley K. Schultz, *Constructing Urban Culture: American Cities and City Planning, 1800–1920* (Philadelphia: Temple University Press, 1989), 66–75.

30. "A Brief Summary of the History of Land Use Planning in Loudoun County," October 14, 1983, TBL; and Raflo, *Iron Gates,* 229–33, 233 (quotation).

31. The county sorely needed this money, as it had a projected deficit of $3.2 million for 1972. Ken Ringle, "Loudoun Veto of New Town Points Up Growth Pressure," *WP,* February 12, 1971.

32. Jay Mathews, "Loudoun Planners Reject Big Project," *WP,* February 14, 1973; Kenneth Bredemeier, "New Levitt Loudoun Plan Heard," *WP,* May 11, 1973; and Ken Ringle, "Loudoun Rejects New Town," *WP,* July 3, 1974. Levitt would eventually sell its land to another developer, who constructed the Countryside development in the 1980s. Raflo, *Iron Gates,* 227–35, 236 (quotation); Megan Rosenfeld, "Fairfax Is Dealt Two Zoning Blows by Va. High Court," *WP,* June 17, 1975; Board of Supervisors of Fairfax County v. Roy G. Allman, Trustee, et al., 211 S.E.2d 48 (1975); Board of Supervisors of Fairfax County v. Thomas R. Williams, et al., 216 S.E.2d 33 (1975); and Banham, *Fight for Fairfax,* 103–23.

33. T. Rees Shapiro, "Arthur W. 'Nick' Arundel, Newspaper Publisher and Philanthropist, Dies at 83," *WP,* February 8, 2011, www.washingtonpost.com/wp-dyn/content/article /2011/02/08/AR2011020806127.html, accessed March 27, 2014; McGhee to Mellon, February 24, 1970, in "Early History of the Piedmont Environmental Council, May 23, 1969 to Dec. 22, 1972," by George C. McGhee, folder PEC, Vertical Files, NSLM.

34. McGhee to Arundel, May 13, 1970; McGhee to Arundel, June 2, 1970; and McGhee to Mellon, August 22, 1972, all in McGhee, "Early History."

35. McGhee to Mellon, August 22, 1972, in McGhee, "Early History"; Piedmont Environmental Council Papers, ASSSC.

36. McGhee to Arundel, June 2, 1970, and McGhee to Mellon, August 22, 1972, both in McGhee, "Early History."

37. *Piedmont Environmental Council Newsreporter,* May 1982, 1–2 (first through third quotations); George C. McGhee, "Conservation of the Virginia Piedmont: A Proposal," 5; McGhee to Mellon, August 22, 1972; and [Harrison] to Graham W. Ashworth, December 21, 1972, all in McGhee, "Early History"; A. G. and B. P. Harrison interview, 24, 25 (fourth quotation).

38. Eugene Scheel, "Loudoun County's Anti-billboard and Sign-Control Ordinance: It's Forty Years Old," Eugene Scheel Research Collection, TBL.

39. Harrison to the Virginia Advisory Legislative Council Committee (first through sixth quotations); Harrison, *Protecting Virginia's Piedmont*, 4 (seventh quotation).

40. Harrison to the Virginia Advisory Legislative Council Committee and *LTM*, September 28, 1972; *LTM*, June 16, 1977 (quotation). A 1984 study found that for every dollar of tax revenue collected in Loudoun, suburban areas required $1.28 in services. Agricultural areas, in contrast, required only $.11. American Farmland Trust figures are slightly higher for agricultural land but follow the same pattern. "American Farmland Trust, Farmland Information Center Fact Sheet: Cost of Community Services Studies," American Farmland Trust, Northampton, 2006.

41. Northern Virginia Regional Planning and Economic Development Commission, *Open Space Easements in the National Capital Region* (September 1965); Open-Space Land Act, 1966 sess., chap. 461, Acts of the Virginia Legislature; Gerald P. McCarthy, "Protecting Virginia for Virginians: Council on the Environment, Commonwealth of Virginia," *Virginia Record*, October 1974, 6–15; *Piedmont Environmental Council Newsreporter*, October 1981, and May/June, 1981.

42. Heimlich, "Agriculture and Urban Areas," 141–47; Tim Lehman, *Public Values, Private Lands: Farmland Preservation Policy, 1933–1985* (Chapel Hill: University of North Carolina Press, 1995), 55, 73, 98. On farmland loss, see Robert C. Otte, *Farming in the City's Shadow: Urbanization of Land and Changes in Farm Output in Standard Metropolitan Statistical Areas, 1960–1970*, Agricultural Economics Report No. 250 (Washington, D.C.: USDA, Economic Research Service, 1974).

43. *LTM*, April 29, 1965; and *LTM*, October 20, 1966; Dave Lamie and Gordon Groover, *A Citizens Guide to the Use Value Taxation Program in Virginia*, Publication 444–037 (Blacksburg: Virginia Cooperative Extension, November 2000); Monica Licher and Gordon Groover, "Use-Value Taxation in Virginia: A Brief Description," *Horizons* 18, no. 1 (2006); *Virginia Code* (1971), sec. 58.1, 3229–44.

44. *LTM*, April 15, 1971 (first through third quotations); *LTM*, September 28, 1972; *LTM*, November 1, 1973 (fourth quotation); Raflo, *Iron Gates*, 212 (fifth quotation).

45. Eleanor Adams, "Working Farmers: Survey Reveals They Want to Stay That Way" (ca. 1973), TBL; *LTM*, October 5, 1972; *LTM*, October 26, 1972; *LTM*, August 16, 1973; *LTM*, June 7, 1973; *LTM*, March 22, 1973. These figures are for the number of landowners signed up with the local soil conservation office, a prerequisite for the LUT. The actual number of LUT participants was slightly smaller. Loudoun SWCD Annual Report 1976, 2; and Loudoun SWCD 1980 Annual Report, both in Loudoun SWCD District Offices, Leesburg, Va.

46. Potts interview.

47. A. G. and B. P. Harrison interview, 30.

48. Mark Friedberger, "The Rural-Urban Fringe in the Late Twentieth Century," *Agricultural History* 74, no. 2 (2000): 502–14; Tom Daniels, *When City and Country Collide: Managing Growth in the Metropolitan Fringe* (Washington, D.C.: Island Press, 1999); and Dan Carey and Pradyumna P. Karan, "From Horse Farms to Wal-Mart: The Citizens' Movement to Protect Farmland in the Central Bluegrass Region of Kentucky," in *Local Environmental Movements: A Comparative Study of the United States and Japan*, ed. Karan and Unryu Suganuma (Lexington: University Press of Kentucky, 2008), 145–64; Kathleen A. Brosnan and Adam Rome, in turn, concede the costs and limits of open space preservation even as they celebrate its successes. Brosnan, "Crabgrass or Grapes: Urban Sprawl, Agricultural Persistence, and the Fight for Napa Valley," in *Cities and Nature in the American West*, ed.

Char Miller (Reno: University of Nevada Press, 2010), 34–56; and Rome, *Bulldozer in the Countryside*, 119–52.

49. Burchardt, *Paradise Lost*, 158 (first quotation), 163 (second quotation). On cultural imaginations of the countryside, see Raymond Williams, *The Country and the City* (New York: Oxford University Press, 1973); and David B. Danbom, "Romantic Agrarianism in Twentieth-Century America," *Agricultural History* 65, no. 4 (1991): 1–12; *Visions: Land and Community in Loudoun County* (Purcellville: League of Women Voters of Loudoun County, 1983), 8; David J. Walbert, *Garden Spot: Lancaster County, the Old Order Amish, and the Selling of Rural America* (New York: Oxford University Press, 2002); and Kathleen A. Brosnan, "Urbanity and Pastoralism in Napa Tourism," in *City Dreams, Country Schemes: Community and Identity in the American West*, ed. Brosnan and Amy L. Scott (Reno: University of Nevada Press, 2011), 133–55. On myth in agricultural history, see James C. Giesen, *Boll Weevil Blues: Cotton, Myth, and Power in the American South* (Chicago: University of Chicago Press, 2011).

50. Catherine Gudis, *Buyways: Billboards, Automobiles, and the American Landscape* (New York: Routledge, 2004); John A. Jakle and Keith A. Sculle, *Signs in America's Auto Age: Signatures of Landscape and Place* (Iowa City: University of Iowa Press, 2004), 135–56; Daniel M. Bluestone, "Roadside Blight and the Reform of Commercial Architecture," in *Roadside America: The Automobile in Design and Culture*, ed. Jan Jennings (Ames: Iowa State University Press, 1990), 170–84; and Lewis L. Gould, *Lady Byrd Johnson: Our Environmental First Lady* (Lawrence: University Press of Kansas, 1999), 90–108.

51. Eugene M. Scheel, *The History of Middleburg and Vicinity* (Warrenton: Piedmont Press, 1987), 141–43 (quotation on 141); Lewis, *Ladies, Liquor, & Laughter*, 69–70; and Scheel, "Loudoun County's Anti-billboard." On rural planning and zoning, see Raflo, *Iron Gates*, 188–95; Terry Hirst and Vinton Liddell Pickens, interview by Eugene Scheel, June 21, 1977, and Vinton Liddell Pickens, interview by Eugene Scheel, June 20, 1977, both in folder 1, box 1, TBLOHP; and Vinton Liddell Pickens, interview by Barbara Dutton, July 25, 1990, folder 35, box 2, LCOHP. As late as 1951, only 173 counties nationwide had rural zoning in place. Erling D. Solberg, *Rural Zoning in the United States*, Agricultural Information Bulletin 54 (Washington, D.C.: USDA, January 1952), 8–9.

52. Harrison, *Protecting Virginia's Piedmont*, 3.

53. Jakle and Sculle, *Signs in America's Auto Age*, 135.

54. Matless, *Landscape and Englishness*, 26.

55. Lizabeth Cohen, *A Consumers' Republic: The Politics of Mass Consumption in Postwar America* (New York: Vintage, 2003); and Vance Packard, *The Waste Makers* (New York: David McKay Co., 1960); Martin V. Melosi, *The Sanitary City: Urban Infrastructure in America from Colonial Times to the Present* (Baltimore, Md.: Johns Hopkins University Press, 2000), 190–94, 206. On the "garbage crisis" in post–World War II America, see Melosi, *Garbage in the Cities: Refuse, Reform, and the Environment*, rev. ed. (1981; Pittsburgh: Pittsburgh University Press, 2005), 190–226, 338–54; Louis Blumberg and Robert Gottlieb, *War on Waste: Can America Win Its Battle with Garbage?* (Washington, D.C.: Island Press, 1989), 10–15; and Heather Rogers, *Gone Tomorrow: The Hidden Life of Garbage* (New York: New Press, 2005), 102–27.

56. Thomas W. Fenner and Randee J. Gorin, *Local Beverage Container Laws: A Legal and Tactical Analysis* (Stanford, Calif.: Stanford Environmental Law Society, July 1976), 3–4. On the beverage industry, see Blumberg and Gottlieb, *War on Waste*, 237–40; Rogers,

Gone Tomorrow, 134–41; and Robert Friedel, "American Bottles: The Road to No Return," *Environmental History* 19, no. 3 (2014): 505–27.

57. Kenneth Bredemier, "Loudoun Votes Landfill Dump 4 Miles South of Leesburg," *WP*, December 2, 1970; *LTM*, December 17, 1970; KLB to Loudoun County Board of Supervisors, December 3, 1970, folder 12, box 3, KLBC.

58. Solid waste issues receive marginal attention in accounts of environmentalism, accounting for only two pages in Samuel P. Hays, *Beauty, Health, and Permanence: Environmental Politics in the United States, 1955–1985* (New York: Cambridge University Press, 1987), 80–81; a passing mention in Rothman, *Saving the Planet*, 125–26, 129; and no mention in either Rome, *Bulldozer in the Countryside*, or Sellers, *Crabgrass Crucible*.

59. Such movements have generally been examined as part of the national beautification movement. Gould, *Lady Byrd Johnson*; Earl Hale Jr., "Presidential Proposal and Congressional Disposal: The Highway Beautification Act," in *Congress and the Environment*, ed. Richard A. Cooley and Geoffrey Wandesforde-Smith (Seattle: University of Washington Press, 1970), 32–46; and *Beauty for America*, 17–22.

60. *LTM*, April 30, 1970, and *LTM*, April 23, 1970, both in KLB scrapbook, folder 6, box 5, KLBC.

61. Rogers, *Gone Tomorrow*, 142 (quotation). See also Bartow J. Elmore, "The American Beverage Industry and the Development of Curbside Recycling Programs, 1950–2000," *Business History Review* 86, no. 3 (2012): 477–501.

62. Mrs. J. Earle Weatherly, memo, November 1965, folder 8, box 3, KLBC; *LTM*, August 27, 1970, folder 2, box 5, KLBC; Berta Mikesell, *LTM*, undated, folder 2, box 5, KLBC; Mills E. Godwin Jr., "Spruce Up Virginia," October 7, 1975, in *Leadership in Crisis: Selected Statements and Speech Excerpts of the Hon. Mills E. Godwin, Jr.* (n.p., 1978), 144–46; *LTM*, April 23, 1970, in KLB Scrapbook, 2.

63. A. G. Harrison to the farmers of Loudoun County, July 5, 1977, folder 4, box 3, KLBC; A. G. and B. P. Harrison interview; *LTM*, May 6, 1971, folder 2, box 5, KLBC; and *LTM*, April 1, 1982, A17. By 1987 KLB membership had climbed to seven hundred. Newsletter, January 1987, folder 1, box 5, KLBC. For a summary of KLB activities, see *LTM*, August 27, 1970, folder 2, box 5, KLBC.

64. *LTM*, April 15, 1971, folder 2, box 5, KLBC (first quotation); A. G. and B. P. Harrison interview, 8–9; *LTM*, April 23, 1970 (third quotation); A. G. Harrison to Board of Supervisors, April 27, 1970, folder 4, box 3, KLBC (fourth quotation). The air pollution mentioned here is in reference to trash-burning dumps.

65. "Summary of Spring Clean Up, 1972," folder 12, box 5, KLBC. Including Loudoun, four of these counties (Fairfax, Va., Montgomery, Md., and Howard, Md.) were in the D.C. metro area. Fenner and Gorin, *Local Beverage Container Laws*, 11–13. On Loudoun's passage of the law, see *LTM*, January 21, 1971, folder 2, box 5, KLBC; and *LTM*, May 20, 1971.

66. Loudoun County Board of Supervisors Minutes, July 11, 1977, folder 4, box 4, KLBC; *LTM*, January 3, 1980; McClain v. Board of Supervisors of Loudoun County, Virginia, Circuit Court of Loudoun County, in Chancery No. 4156 (1976), cited in Fenner and Gorin, *Local Beverage Container Laws*, 14, 40–41, 44–45.

67. KLB newsletter, Spring 1983, folder 1, box 5, KLBC.

68. *Citizens Guide to Historical, Cultural, and Environmental Organizations in Loudoun County* (Round Hill: PSLC, 2007).

69. Eleanor Adams, interview by the author, March 15, 2013, Waterford, Va.

70. *LTM*, January 30, 1958.

71. *Loudoun County, Virginia: Welcome to Virginia's Garden County* (n.p., ca. 1969), Ephemera, TBL (first and second quotations); and Raflo, *Iron Gates*, 237–42; Scheel, *Loudoun Discovered*, 4:106–8; Evelyn Porterfield Johnson, "About 'Our Town,' Bluemont and the First Fair," 1994, Ephemera 150, TBL; and Carol Krucoff, "Muskets, Mimes, Dunking Vats: 'Court Days' Recreate History," *WP*, August 17, 1978; Loudoun County Chamber of Commerce, *Loudoun County Information and Buyer's Guide, 1977–1978*, 46–47, folder Tourism, Ephemera, TBL.

72. Loudoun County Marketing Council, *Loudoun County*, ca. 1975, Ephemera 196, TBL (quotations); Joel Garreau, *Edge Cities: Life on the New Frontier* (New York: Doubleday, 1991), 92–94; Chamber of Commerce, *Virginia's Garden County*, 61, Ephemera, TBL.

73. *Virginia's Loudoun County: Recreation, History, Beauty*, ca. 1971–80, Ephemera 73, TBL.

74. *Sterling Park: A New Level of Leisure Living in the Rolling Hills of Virginia* (Arlington: M. T. Broyhill, 1965); program, Loudoun County 4-H Fair, 74, August 8–12, 1989, TBL.

75. Bili Layton, "A History of Countryside," May 12, 1992, TBL.

76. Barbara M. Haller, "The History of Countryside," 1993, TBL.

Conclusion. A Tale of Two Villages

1. Works Progress Administration, *Virginia: A Guide to the Old Dominion* (New York: Oxford University Press, 1940), 524–29.

2. Historic American Buildings Survey, Va., 54-WATFO, Prints and Photographs Division, Library of Congress.

3. "A Blind Man, an Heiress, and a Builder: The Remarkable Origins of Waterford's Resurrection," in *Waterford Homes Tour & Crafts Exhibit* (Waterford Foundation, 2013), 52–55.

4. Polly Rogers, "On the Early Days of the Waterford Foundation," July 31, 1975, 1, transcribed by John Souders, May 18, 2004, WFLHC.

5. "A Blind Man," 55.

6. Marian Marsh Sale, "Waterford: Quaker Charm, Virginia Hospitality Make a Very Special Blend," *Commonwealth: The Magazine of Virginia*, October 1972, 37–41, 38 (quotation); Edward L. Crook, "An Informal Review of the Contributions of the Waterford Foundation toward the Restoration and Preservation of Waterford during Its First 27 Years," ed. Bronwen C. Souders, 1970, 2003, WFLHC; and Edward Chamberlin to Mr. and Mrs. De Forest Anthony, October 8, 1949, WFLHC.

7. Rogers, "Early Days," 3; Raymond Williams, *The Country and the City* (New York: Oxford University Press, 1973), 68–86, 165–81.

8. Grace Brooks, "Quaint Waterford Prepares for Handicraft Exhibit," *WP*, September 28, 1946, 3.

9. Solange Strong, "In Virginia: Waterford Wakens," *Magazine Antiques* 56 (October 1949): 280–83.

10. Rogers, "Early Days," 5; McDaniel to Members of Waterford Foundation, April 19, 1951; and Paul V. Rogers, memo, 1951, WFLHC.

11. McDaniel to Board of Directors, Waterford Foundation, March 19, 1945, WFLHC.

12. Katharine Best and Katharine Hillyer, "Town of the Month: Waterford, Virginia," *Good Housekeeping* 131, no. 4 (1950): 4, 374–75.

13. McDaniel, memo, November 22, 1948, WFLHC.

14. By 1954 an estimated quarter of the town's two hundred year-round residents made

the ninety-mile round trip to D.C. each workday. Ruth Shumaker, "Waterford Spruces Up for Exhibit," *WP*, September 30, 1954, 48.

15. David Walbert, *Garden Spot: Lancaster County, the Old Order Amish, and the Selling of Rural America* (New York: Oxford University Press, 2002).

16. John F. Harris, "Loudoun's 'Different' Village," *WP*, August 31, 1986.

17. Elizabeth A. Brabec and Mary Ann Naber, *Linking the Past to the Future: A Landscape Conservation Strategy for Waterford, Virginia* (Waterford Foundation and Preservation Assistance Division, National Park Service, 1992), WFLHC.

18. Sale, "Waterford," 38.

19. Crook, "An Informal Review."

20. Rogers, "Early Days," 1.

21. John A. Jakle and Keith A. Sculle, *Signs in America's Auto Age: Signatures of Landscape and Place* (Iowa City: University of Iowa Press, 2004).

22. Harris, "Loudoun's 'Different' Village."

23. Marti Corn, *The Ground on Which I Stand: Tamina, a Freedmen's Town* (College Station: Texas A&M University Press, 2016); *CC*, May 26, 1974; *CC*, September 5, 1971.

24. *CC*, January 10, 1971; April 16, 1971, CCM, 20:181; *CC*, October 3, 1971.

25. Renee C. Lee, "Tamina Residents Suffer amid Political Squabbles," *HC*, June 5, 2005, www.chron.com/news/houston-texas/article/Tamina-residents-suffer-amid-political -squabbles-1498499.php, accessed March 1, 2016; "Tamina Group Will Dissolve," *HC*, November 25, 2004, www.chron.com/news/article/Tamina-group-will-dissolve-1978678 .php, accessed March 1, 2016; Jerry Bradford, interview by the author, December 11, 2012, Conroe, Tex.

26. Renee C. Lee, "Tamina Residents Balk at Water Fight Truce," *HC*, July 7, 2007, www .chron.com/neighborhood/woodlands-news/article/Tamina-residents-balk-at-water-fight -truce-1786532.php, accessed March 1, 2016 (quotation); Beth Kuhles, "Tamina Wants Help from Commissioners Court," *HC*, June 3, 2004, www.chron.com/news/article/Tamina -wants-help-from-Commissioners-Court-1478457.php, accessed March 1, 2016. On looming development, see Shirley Grimes, interview by the author, April 17, 2014, Tamina, Tex.; Corn, *The Ground*, 93, 97.

27. Corn, *The Ground*, 22–27, 117–18.

28. Tupper, *No Place to Play*, 18–19; Adam Rome, *The Bulldozer in the Countryside: Suburban Sprawl and the Rise of American Environmentalism* (New York: Cambridge University Press, 2001), 119–52; Francesca Russello Ammon, *Bulldozer: Demolition and Clearance of the Postwar Landscape* (New Haven, Conn.: Yale University Press, 2016); C. Vann Woodward, "The Search for Southern Identity," in *The Burden of Southern History* (Baton Rouge: Louisiana State University Press, 1968), 6–10; Joshua Blu Buhs, *The Fire Ant Wars: Nature, Science, and Policy in Twentieth-Century America* (Chicago: University of Chicago Press, 2004), 25–34; Thomas D. Clark, *The Greening of the South: The Recovery of Land and Forest* (Lexington: University Press of Kentucky, 1984), 134; Mason C. Carer, Robert C. Kellison, and R. Scott Wallinger, *Forestry in the U.S. South: A History* (Baton Rouge: Louisiana State University Press, 2015), 225–28; David Beatie, "Dozer Spare That Tree," *TGF* 22, no. 10 (1964): 4–6; and Kari A. Frederickson, *Cold War Dixie: Militarization and Modernization in the Modern South* (Athens: University of Georgia Press, 2013).

INDEX

Northern Virginia Development Company, 159

not in my backyard (NIMBY), 90, 101

Oak Ridge North, Tex. (development), 130, 139, 140; incorporation of, 133–35; Tamina and, 176

Oatlands Plantation, 148, 154

oil, 38, 118; industry, 17, 103, 115

open range, 16–18; cattle industry, 56; closing of, 24–25; defense of, 22; development and, 24, 51; fences, 22, 24, 28, 32; foxhunting and, 13–14; 1952 election, 19–20; 1953 election, 20–21; 1956 election, 21–24; weakening of, 18–19

open space, 7, 91–93, 142–43, 150–51, 177; governmental protections of, 153; horses and, 65, 67; land-use taxation to preserve farmland and, 156–60; limits of, 159–60; river development and, 85–86, 91, 99–100; western myths and, 77–78. *See also* preservation

Open Space Land Act, 157

orchards, 45, 63

Panorama, Tex. (development), 36, 72

Peel, T. J., 14, 107

Penn, Carleton, 152

Pickens, Vinton, 155, 161–62

Piedmont Environmental Council (PEC), 143, 167; charges of elitism against, 155; farmland preservation, 156–60; origins of, 154–55; purpose, 155–56

place, 142–44

Planchard, John, 133

poaching. *See* hunting

police, 37, 123–24. *See also* law enforcement officials

pollution, 129, 140, 142

Porter Heights, Tex. (development), 126

Potomac Electric Power Company (PEPCO): dam construction, 85, 88; decision on, 86; land purchases, 81–82, 84–85; pollution, 82, 84, 86; suburban development, 92

Potomac Estuary, 82–83, 87–88

Potomac Interceptor Sewer, 87, 89, 92, 141

Potomac River: development summary, 112; Nation's River, 81, 91–92; opposition to

damming of, 85–86, 88–90, 104; sewage cleanup plans, 87; source of drinking water, 82–83

Potomac Watershed, 81–82; industrial development, 84–86; recreational development, 85–86, 91–92; suburban development, 82–83, 86–87, 93

Powell, R. A., 95

preservation, 7–8, 90, 104; agrarianism and, 141, 160; class refinement and, 143, 147, 151, 155; contrasted with environmentalism, 141–42, 150–51, 156, 162, 165–66; as development, 160; in England, 151–52, 154, 160; of farmland, 156–60; paternalism and, 149–50; religious language of, 143; suburban development strategy, 138, 168–69; visual landscape and, 142, 146–47, 155–56, 161–62; Waterford Foundation and, 171–74. *See also* historic preservation

preservation culture, 115, 142–43, 220n5

preservation Society of Loudoun County (PSLC), 145–46

Public Health Service, U.S., 87

Quakers, 43–44, 170

quarries, 123

Raflo, Frank, 145

railroads, 44, 46, 81

ranching, 51, 53, 56; improved pastures, 45, 57–58. *See also* open range

reapportionment, 21, 130

Reaves, Gene, 72

recreation, 27; parks, 92, 110; subdivision sales, 117–18, 138

Reece, Dorothy, 108

Richmond, Va., 45, 145

Riverbend Dam. *See* Potomac River; U.S. Army Corps of Engineers

River Plantation, Tex. (development), 125, 130

roads and highways, 9, 46, 117, 153; maintenance of, 122–23, 136; opposition to, 144, 146–47; safety of, 19–22, 24, 33; scenic highway program, 151

Rodgers, Polly, 170–71, 173

Royal Town Planning Institute (England), 151

ENVIRONMENTAL HISTORY
AND THE AMERICAN SOUTH